SILICON
STATES

SILICON STATES

THE POWER AND POLITICS
OF BIG TECH AND WHAT
IT MEANS FOR OUR FUTURE

LUCIE GREENE

COUNTERPOINT
Berkeley, California

Silicon States

Library of Congress Cataloging-in-Publication Data
Names: Greene, Lucie, author.
Title: Silicon states : the power and politics of big tech and what it means for our
    future / Lucie Greene.
Description: Berkeley, California : Counterpoint, 2018.
Identifiers: LCCN 2018010153 | ISBN 9781640090712
Subjects: LCSH: High technology industries—Social aspects—United States. |
    Technology—Political aspects. | Social responsibility of business.
Classification: LCC HC79.H53 G74 2018 | DDC 338.4/760973—dc23
LC record available at https://lccn.loc.gov/2018010153

Jacket designed by Darren Haggar
Book designed by Jordan Koluch

COUNTERPOINT
2560 Ninth Street, Suite 318
Berkeley, CA 94710
www.counterpointpress.com

Printed in the United States of America
Distributed by Publishers Group West

10 9 8 7 6 5 4 3 2 1

Dedicated to my friends and family, my constant supporters

With special thanks to J. Walter Thompson

CONTENTS

SILICON
STATES

Introduction

A Changing Landscape

The year is 2014. Crowds have gathered for one of the final talks of the day at the Web Summit, the annual tech hurrah. Every year since 2009, European startups, marketers, social media managers, and hangers-on convene for this affair, flocking to Dublin during perhaps the city's soggiest, purple-skied month. At the conference, attendees walk through the acres of stands collecting flyers, watching motivational talks, and gawking at the great and the good of Silicon Valley who are flown in to spout their entrepreneurial wisdom onstage. At night, everyone swigs pints of Guinness. (It's since migrated to Lisbon, but the format remains the same.)

Each year I attend about twenty of these conferences, with their interchangeable executives in lapel microphones reciting carefully crafted soundbites and bombastic statements about what's to come in technology, retail, marketing, and beyond. "Data is the new oil!" "Content is king!" "Disrupt yourself to survive!" I and a migratory pack of journalists and tech executives attend them in hotspots around the world to gain access to these self-proclaimed visionaries and speak on behalf of our companies about what we believe the future holds. The schedule has become ever more crowded over the past few years, each new gathering competing for a share of corporate travel budgets and Buzzfeed column inches. They have become well-oiled, navel-gazing marketing events, albeit with a lot of shouting. I've been to so many that they have started to blend into one long, undifferentiated TED talk.

This one, though, was different.

Caroline Daniel, then editor at *FT Weekend,* was gleefully ribbing billionaire Peter Thiel about Silicon Valley's hubristic "Change the World" sloganeering (that and his recent statement that Europeans have no work ethic). She was also teasing him about what he had next on the agenda, alluding to his obsession with longevity research. Thiel is famed for his efforts to become immortal, in wilder reports even exploring having transfusions of young people's blood to stay youthful—an act so quintessentially far-out Silicon Valley that it had been parodied on the HBO TV series of the same name. With one eyebrow arched and a flicker of a smile, she asked: "So, do you really think you can live forever?"

I stopped scribbling notes and looked up. There had been rumblings of Thiel and other Silicon Valley luminaries' interest in immortality, but until this moment it had seemed a slightly crackpot endeavor, an idle pursuit for billionaire playboys, not a tangible business pursuit and potential reality. But Thiel's unabashed certainty was disarming. He was serious, and, I'd soon discover, there were others working in this vein. All of this was a long way from restaurant recommendations or online marketplaces. Silicon Valley's ambitions, it seemed, had spiraled to new levels in breathtaking if unnerving ways.

People today, Thiel said, have been trained not to be enthusiastic about the future and about the promises of technology. We'd come to see space travel and scientific progress in dystopian lights. Who'd want to leave the planet after watching a movie like *Gravity,* he asked, when space exploration was shown in such a way? (This has since become a refrain for Thiel.) We should be more ambitious about solving world problems, he continued. Where had our ambition gone?

Technologists, he argued, were a "counterculture" in today's society simply for championing the future. Sitting before a crowd of 22,000 prosperous tech nerds, gawking in admiration, this seemed like a stretch to me. But Thiel doubled down on his vision of Valley techies as twenty-first-century punk rockers. Not only were they underrepresented in government, he argued, the government was actually trying to curtail progress, regulating technologies it doesn't understand. Politics, and the ignorance of politicians, was holding us back.

Then Daniel asked, "Do you really have the right as the technologist to determine and say we're going to change the world?"

"These questions of rights are always very tricky," Thiel answered, head tilted to one side in thought. "You can always flip it around and say what gives the people in [Washington] DC the right to stop medical inventions that could save many people's lives? What gives people the right to stop technology in one form or another?"

I squirmed. Daniel seemed to squirm, too. Thiel continued: "It's not as though we're living in a perfect world. We're living in a world in which there are enormous problems, where there are many things that are incredibly screwed up. And so I think it is imperative on us to try to fix these problems as quickly as possible. And sometimes that means not asking for permission—but really asking for forgiveness later."

As I considered Thiel's statement in the frenetic years since, it has come to epitomize a distinct attitude developing in the Valley about its role in the world, one characterized by an increasingly nonchalant regard for effecting seismic, irreversible change with an air of distant sociopathic paternalism, especially for those left behind by this relentless drive for progress.

Amid the high-flying urban millennials using on-demand driverless flying cars, after all, countless workers will lose jobs from automation. Fast-food workers will be replaced by machines. Airlines have already replaced ticket stewards and suitcase labelers with machines. In singular, distinct entities, these are all logical efficiencies. But taken together, they represent enormous, painful change for a huge swath of the population; and that change is casually being rationalized by Silicon Valley billionaires as "progress."

But is this the progress we want? And do we even realize how fast it is happening? And how irreversibly? Are we comfortable with Silicon Valley defining the future?

I should be clear that when I refer to Silicon Valley, I'm talking specifically about the group of businesses that have come to embody the culture and industry of digital technology. In other words, Facebook, Amazon, Uber, Google, Apple, Snapchat, and Tesla—the most ambitious and powerful tech companies the world has seen that are attempting to shape our future. Some of them have even been given their own acronym, GAFA (Google, Apple, Facebook, and Amazon). Not all of them are from Silicon Valley geographically, but collectively, this group of businesses has come to embody similar power, influence, and values. Since the resurgence of Apple, tech companies have not only become mass market, they have become globally monumental, region-transcending brands in sync with a powerful new generation of millennial consumers who have incorporated digital socializing, mobile use, and the internet into every facet of their lives.

In the past twenty years, the power and influence of Silicon Valley's giants has increased rapidly, supplanting many traditional industries like automobiles and energy, not to mention retail, entertainment, communication, and tourism. Walmart launched in 1962. Unilever launched in 1929. Nestlé launched in 1905. My employer, J. Walter Thompson, a multinational advertising agency, launched in 1864 and took decades to become global. These traditional companies are now grappling with Amazon (1994) and other tech companies launched long after—but which are already bigger, or taking away significant market share.

Similarly, in an incredibly short timespan there has been a fundamental power shift in society from the middle class to the uber-wealthy and a fundamental intellectual shift in our ideological culture from revering astronauts and Hollywood actors to putting the CEOs of tech corporations up on pedestals. This has coincided with a fundamental economic shift from manufacturers and traditional businesses to algorithms and data—and these tectonic shifts stem from these technologists' work and ideas.

Now, as they mature and start to take themselves more seriously, these companies and leaders are moving into key civic areas and co-opting new power centers. Their cultural influence surpasses government, academic institutions, and even Hollywood. Having taken over our lifestyles, they are vying for our health care, infrastructure, energy, space travel, education, and postal systems. And they are applying the tools that won them success—platforms, AI, big data, and consumer-centric on-demand models—to disrupt them. How these approaches fare when it comes to these stickier, more complex sectors will be interesting to watch. But it's telling that alongside this, Silicon Valley leaders are starting to think bigger, growing beyond scaling to considering new societal models, systems, town planning, and visions of future worlds. With characteristic hubris, they're also looking at the world around them—they've changed our social life, our commercial life, why not our political and biological life as well?

They're already memorializing themselves with vast, lavish headquarters in every city, each serving as de facto Silicon neighborhoods. What happens when we all live inside the Silicon State?

Some would say we already do.

There have been signs of cultural pushback, at least in 2018. Early in the year, consumer packaged goods (CPG) giants like Unilever, and its CMO Keith Weed, started referring to the digital "swamp" when referencing Google's and Facebook's lack of transparency when it comes to selling digital advertising. Many brands have publicly withdrawn ads on YouTube, among other similar sites, when their logos have appeared next to extremist content or fake news. Reports have emerged questioning audience size estimations of Facebook in the UK and Australia.

Then there was the explosive scandal in March surrounding Facebook's data breach of 87 million accounts (harvested by political consultancy Cambridge Analytica for commercial use in attempting to shape political campaigns in the U.S., UK, and other countries). The scandal, exposed by Britain's *Guardian*, *Observer*, and Channel 4 news on TV, and by *The New York Times* in the U.S., hit Facebook's stock price by 13 percent and knocked off as much as $75 billion in market cap from the social media giant in the week that followed. Authorities in both countries launched investigations and demanded appearances from Zuckerberg and Facebook (and in the UK, the associated whistleblower from Cambridge Analytica, Christopher Wylie). The immediate aftermath of the scandal was outrage and furious media debate, along with widely shared social media hashtag #DeleteFacebook. Pundits quickly went to town critiquing Facebook's slow response, the leadership skills of its executives Sheryl Sandberg and Mark Zuckerberg, and their tone-deaf TV interviews in the aftermath. Rival tech baron Elon Musk famously deleted his company's Facebook pages (ooh, burn!!). Apple CEO Tim Cook used the occasion to trumpet Apple's strict privacy policies and said he thought it was too late for the social network giant because they did not proactively self-regulate (double burn!). The scandal also prompted a wave of other investigations and allegations on both sides of the pond, not least Zuckerberg's sensational appearance before Congress to answer questions about Facebook's behavior. It brought to the surface Cambridge Analytica's reported association with other tech companies and figures including Peter Thiel–backed Palantir, the data analysis company that is contracted by the Pentagon and police services in the U.S. to aid in work such as surveillance, which was also alleged to have used Facebook data. (It did not look good that Thiel is also a Facebook board member.)

Taken together, the Facebook/Cambridge Analytica scandal marked a collective loss of innocence for the public about tech's role in the way we live. And yet, it's difficult to tell what real impact it has made. Facebook's audience, and its neighboring services WhatsApp and Instagram, seem undented. Zuckerberg refused to appear personally for the British authorities' investigation in a stunning display of Big Tech bravado (or more frightening, Zuckerberg's untouchability). Despite European Union fines and the beginnings of a crackdown in the UK, from banning Uber in London (temporarily) to promising more gig economy worker rights, tech companies are still thriving in these regions. In the U.S. Amazon continues to evade antitrust investigations as it becomes grocer, clothing retailer, shipping company, and more.

The toughest check on this group seems to be the stock market, where even the hint of withering popularity is directly hitting share prices for Silicon Valley brands. Added to Facebook's dive, Snapchat, after its wildly misjudged post making light of Rihanna's experience of domestic violence by singer Chris Brown, saw its stock price tumble, and was also hit recently by a $1 billion loss when Kylie Jenner declared it unhip. Facebook's stock rebounded after Zuckerberg's Congress appearance. It's an example of the massive volatility of these companies' value. But it usually seems to be fleeting. Rightly or wrongly, there's still a tension between privacy fears and popular discourse, and how deeply embedded these companies are in consumer behaviors and habits. Their success continues to be driven by frequent, daily, minute-to-minute consumer buy-in and de facto apathy. Opt outs en masse, at an unprecedented scale, might be the only thing that stops them. But will that happen anytime soon? It's unlikely. Because we don't click as we preach.

Silicon Temples

From the back of a taxi on a clear day, it's possible to see the skeletal, withered New York Pavilion Towers, once a glittering, illuminated centerpiece of the 1964 New York World's Fair. It is strange to look at these decaying monuments of the future, decades after they were imagined and erected, especially sitting in bumper-to-bumper traffic, crawling on pot-holed roads toward Manhattan from JFK Airport.

The '64 World's Fair was one of a series of expositions celebrating science, culture, national achievements, and the future. New York's was an unbridled festival of midcentury consumerism in jet-set architecture with grand domed pavilions. Ford, Pepsi, IBM, and General Motors all took part. On London's Southbank, there are remnants of the 1951 Festival of Britain, designed to showcase the "genius of British scientists and technologists." It featured the largest dome ever constructed and a floating tower dubbed the "Skylon." Some aspects, such as the concrete blackened by pollution, are viewed less affectionately. Only etchings and a ruined foundation remain of the Crystal Palace, centerpiece of the 1851 Great Exhibition—the first of such fairs celebrating the feats of the Industrial Revolution. These eras were times of unbridled enthusiasm for the future and the power of private industry to build things for our collective benefit.

The old headquarters of mighty industries past can be revealing, particularly those built from scratch in company heydays. These often served as the ultimate expression not only of that company at its peak, but also that company's industry at its peak. Today they are cultural landmarks. The Express newspaper building, built on London's Fleet Street in 1932, is a glittering memorial of a time when two-thirds of the British newspaper-buying population read the paper every day. Everything about the sleek black façade communicates power, opulence, and futurism, with art deco lines, rounded corners, and gilded details. IBM's 1950s Minnesota headquarters even had a brochure tagline, "Where today meets tomorrow," and was lavish in its countryside stateliness and minimalism. The Victorian industrialists in the UK even built model villages around their factories, bringing the world-tour aesthetic to buildings in eclectic combinations, with soaring ceilings and elaborate columns. They hoped to inspire workers with refined designs in rural settings, while adding modern techniques to improve welfare through ventilation and heating. (Trips to the pub were often banned by the owners, and churchgoing was encouraged in these paternalistic idylls.) Today many of these buildings remain, but in altered forms. The pubs of Fleet Street, once crowded with reporters sipping ale and trading stories, are now largely empty.

It's emblematic that pretty much every significant Silicon Valley company has recently completed, or is in the throes of constructing, its own original headquarters. All are designed by superstar international architects with superhuman efficiencies, new features, and capabilities. And obsequious architectural magazine articles to venerate them.

These brand temples are built with no expense spared and are an expression of their owners' maturity and might. They're conceived as elegant statements of corporate identity, but they are also symbols of the future—and therefore are revealing in their execution, but also in the fact that they exist at all. They symbolize tech's enlarged ambition.

Each building uses the latest in techniques and sustainable technology as they give body to a new philosophy for work and innovation. In their size and scope, many of these also serve as mini-townships—Amazon's new geodesic domes are being aligned with Seattle's Space Needle as a potential tourist attraction. Others get pitched as new model communities.

"There's this rising understanding that the built environment is like hardware. Led by Apple, it coincides with other Silicon Valley companies starting to build hardware," observes Ryan Mullenix, partner at architecture firm NBBJ, which designed new headquarters for both Samsung and Amazon. "Architecture is becoming product design on a grand scale. The space and experience in there is inherently tied to who that company is."

All these projects are a departure from the philosophy of Silicon Valley, in which companies historically—and intentionally—inhabited bland office parks, where they could expand and contract, flexible according to company fortunes. To do anything so visible and indelible goes against everything Silicon Valley companies have stood for. Adaptability, shrinking, growing has been key to Silicon Valley's successful ecosystem. But, like Thiel's quest for immortality, Silicon Valley's ambitions are now bigger than its unremarkable office blocks.

"Silicon Valley companies have thrived on extremely flexible space, so that's why the office park dominates here," says Louise A. Mozingo, professor of architecture and environmental planning and urban design at the University of California, Berkeley. "You grow, you shrink. You retreat, retract, and regroup, or retreat and disappear. That suited the Silicon Valley economic cycle extremely well. Investing in large, custom-made buildings that can't be easily repurposed is unprecedented."

Mozingo's office is situated in a 1960s Brutalist Wurster building on the Berkeley campus. She has spent years observing the Valley's evolution. A petite, bobbed, and bespectacled character, she's the antithesis of a Silicon Valley jock, but her words are sharply delivered. "One of the huge issues with these massive investments is that nobody's ever going to move into that building. How do you repurpose such a building?" she says. "The Facebook building is always going to be identified with Facebook and Mark Zuckerberg, as opposed to these much more anonymous buildings elsewhere in the Valley. These new designs are very costly to maintain. You need a fleet of people and continuing investment in the building. It's interesting when you relate it to companies on the East Coast, old industrial and insurance companies: Connecticut General, the Bell Labs building, American Can, Union Carbide, of the 1950s to 1970s. They built these huge white elephants that nobody now knows what to do with. I think this is Silicon Valley's Versailles moment."

This trend sits amid a wider move by Silicon Valley companies to elevate their design cues, shedding the thrown-together logos of their formative years with more sophisticated, grown-up design aesthetics, defining their brands for the long haul with more rounded personas.

What's clear is they are now trying to leave their mark.

Silicon Versailles

Drive up to the Googleplex in Mountain View and crowds are taking photographs against the lime-green Android statue. The grasses. The primary colors. The glistening corporate box buildings. There's a sculpture park with giant toys, where each plastic statue represents code names for versions of Google's Android mobile operating system, all of which are named after desserts and sweet treats, and are giant, indistinguishable, cartoonish. There's a gift shop selling merchandise, T-shirts, pens. It's overrun with eager tourists.

A major addition is Google's forthcoming Charleston East headquarters designed by Danish architect Bjarke Ingels from the Bjarke Ingels Group (BIG) and London-based designer Thomas Heatherwick of Heatherwick Studio. There will be pavilions. The roof will be made of curved metal squares, including "photovoltaic solar panels" and "smile-shaped clerestories" to bring spaces direct, indirect, and diffused natural light. All the language is like that of a resort.

The designs serve as a mood board for Google's template of utopia, blurring the lines between nature and buildings—bike paths, lush gardens, wood-and-rope bridges across streams, owl habitats, cafés, and, no doubt, workers enjoying yoga sessions beneath the planned sun-drenched, soaring, transparent canopy.

Facebook's recently expanded headquarters in Menlo Park is a bit like a Disney village—similarly vast and tourist-frequented. The 430,000-square-foot office was designed by Frank Gehry, who said his design facilitates collaboration and "did not impose itself on their open and transparent culture." In just three years the building was designed and constructed from metal, concrete, and glass. About 2,800 employees inhabit the space, essentially one large room, known as MPK20. A 3.5-hectare rooftop park features a walking trail, a coffee stand, and over 400 trees. Mark Zuckerberg, in intended egalitarian style, has placed his glass-box office in the middle of the building.

"The building itself is pretty simple and isn't fancy. That's on purpose," Zuckerberg has said. "We want our space to feel like a work in progress. When you enter our buildings, we want you to feel how much left there is to be done in our mission to connect the world."

Amazon's Seattle campus, less famous, is fully integrated into the urban landscape. The company's headquarters buildings are set across a few blocks in the South Lake Union area and retain the feeling of being in a normal urban center, with retail, roads, cafés, and farmers' markets, leased to curated tenants, on the road below. But everything from the first floor up is office space. It's effectively an Amazon neighborhood. Visit the farmers market. The local store. Brewhouse. Bike park. It all simulates the feeling of a town, but it's not. It's Amazon.

Amazon recently commissioned tech architecture favorite NBBJ to extend its headquarters in Seattle to include giant glass biodomes filled with plants. A new 3.3-million-square-foot complex has three connected biospheres attached to a 500-foot office tower. The domes feature 40,000 plants from 300 species from 30 countries, including carnivorous pitcher plants, exotic philodendrons, and orchids from Ecuador. Suspension bridges inside the domes allow employees to enjoy the greenery, and there are meeting spaces resembling bird nests perched among the trees. Amazon has employed a full-time horticulturalist. The belief is that the connection to nature will boost productivity and innovation, and because some species are rare, there is also a conservation aspect to the project.

More recently, Amazon has invited cities to launch competing bids to play host its second U.S. headquarters. The $5 billion project will add 50,000 jobs to the city that lands it. The bids, as cities are pitted against each other, came with offers of substantial tax breaks. In fact, Chicago offered to redirect 50 to 100 percent of Amazon employees' income taxes back to Amazon. Newark reportedly offered Amazon up to $7 billion in tax breaks. Many pundits question the real benefits of offering such deals to corporations like Amazon, arguing that it takes much-needed tax income away from local resources such as infrastructure, housing, and education. It also creates more demand for these services as workers and other sought-after talent flock to a new employment hub.

Perhaps the most ambitious of all Silicon Valley temples is Apple's new ring-shaped headquarters. The Infinite Loop, a gigantic circular "spaceship" made with continuous curved glass at a cost of $5 billion, is the most expensive headquarters ever. Designed by Norman Foster, it incorporates meadows and forests. It covers 176 acres and features a 100,000-square-foot fitness center and a giant subterranean auditorium, entered via a glass pavilion topped by a futuristic saucer. It's described by many as the swan song of the late Steve Jobs, his final project to be approved by the Cupertino City Council.

Silicon Valley is also remaking the landscape by dipping its toe into the altogether more ambitious area of city planning and urban development. After all, if it can design a smart campus, why not a city?

In 2016, Y Combinator, the Silicon Valley startup accelerator (which helped launch Airbnb and Dropbox), announced a "new cities" initiative to build cities from scratch, using China's Shenzhen and other new mega-cities as its inspiration.

Facebook, in the style of company towns from the Victorian era, is building Willow Village on a fifty-nine-acre site near its Menlo Park headquarters, with worker houses and low-income housing, drug and grocery stores and a cultural center. It's being lauded as Facebook's first step into town planning. Facebook will build bike paths and has the ambition to refresh the railway line running alongside the site.

Google's smart-city spinoff company, Sidewalk Labs, focused on technology to rethink how cities could work and be designed better. Sidewalk Labs announced in October 2016 that it was partnering with Transportation for America to help sixteen cities better prepare themselves for inventions like self-driving cars and ride sharing. Sidewalk Labs also announced its most large-scale project to date, a futuristic vision for a twelve-acre chunk of the lakefront in Toronto, Canada. The plan, envisioned for Quayside in the city's east end, is a data-oriented high-tech neighborhood that will collect data on air quality and water use.

Though this too can be read as ghoulish. Already in London and New York concerns have arisen about Link hubs appearing in place of phone booths, supported by Alphabet-backed Sidewalk Labs. They offer charging and wi-fi but also carry cameras and sensors, creating privacy concerns.

All of these initiatives will be indicative of how Silicon Valley might progress in a civic role. The campuses—their attributes, successes, their failings and claims—reflect the vision and ambition Silicon Valley companies hold for their products and services in the future. When carefully examined, these edifices, and the visions they embody, house both magnificence and imperfection. Within their elegance are significant holes and demons. Within the claims and headlines, there are also falsehoods. Beyond the idyll, there is also creepiness. After all, sensors around cities might be great for recording real-time weather and creating traffic alerts, but they are another form of surveillance. A building itself might run sustainably, but it's still brand-new, built from scratch using new materials. A campus may technically be porous and open to the community, but when it's set outside of an urban center, with no clear thoroughfares or communal spaces, it isn't really.

Like the hipster coffee joints rapidly being placed inside suburban headquarters to simulate urban life, in many cases it's a veneer.

The Rise and Rise and Rise

I've had a front-row seat to Silicon Valley's expansion, first as a journalist and later as a futurist for London-based consultancy The Future Laboratory and more recently J. Walter Thompson. My role for the past decade has been to present a vision of what's to come. Futurism is part social science, part journalism, and part scenario planning. It's done by cross-referencing various types of research, like connecting dots on a board, looking for patterns of change as they emerge.

My team looks at data. We interview people (asking teens what they think of soda, pop stars, and the world). We conduct surveys. We analyze trends. We look at subcultures, design, and packaging. We monitor social media and consult heads of industry and academics.

I'm in the business of forecasting mindset and desire. My focus is on understanding consumers and how the world around them is changing and how that might affect the way they live, what they buy, and what their aspirations are. As the Silicon Valley companies radically alter our lives, I have been examining how we, the consumers of their wares, view the companies and the changes they are igniting and implementing at exponentially faster rates. (What brands used to plan for in ten years happens in five. In fact, even planning for five years is now a stretch. The world is changing, fast.)

For most of my career, my forecasts have largely involved this group of tech companies. For several years I have stood in the boardrooms at Fortune 500 brands explaining why they should worry about companies like Amazon, Facebook, and Google—these gigantic beasts, these new models of companies seemingly sprung from the ether to huge scale in no time at all, without the staff or infrastructure of traditional business. And using counterintuitive models—such as scaling, and being free—ahead of turning a profit. I was either laughed at or ignored when I told luxury brands in 2012 that—yes—even high-net-worth consumers, particularly ones in emerging markets where they are statistically younger than age thirty and tech savvy, will shop for luxury items not just online but on their iPhones and social networks. Why millennials, not just backpackers, are starting to favor Airbnb over traditional hotels. And why Amazon is becoming not just a retailer but a shopping search engine. And I've watched as some of these boardrooms have seen not just their company but their entire economy sector unseated at an unprecedented speed.

The change brought on by Silicon Valley is swift and sweeping, and it is essential that we understand exactly what is at stake.

Thiel's comments about tech solving "aging" and striding forth unfettered by government no doubt resonated with many in the audience at the Tech Summit, who in London, New York, or farther afield encounter creaking infrastructure, bureaucratic inefficiency, and a ponderous slowness in addressing issues at odds with a culture used to getting what it wants quickly. People don't see their futures represented in the parade of white-haired politicians and outdated government websites. While brands are tripping over themselves to seem "transparent" and have "purpose" to win trust from consumers, politicians aren't in any hurry to do the same. They don't need to. Consumers can leave a brand at any second. Elections only happen every couple of years, and that's assuming you even vote.

So, it is no wonder that Silicon Valley's promise to fix everything is so compelling. But that doesn't mean Silicon Valley is the right replacement for the state. While it is true that governments are flawed, at least they are composed of people who are elected, who occupy positions with the understanding that they serve the whole of society and not just shareholders.

If Silicon Valley takes on a wider civic role, we must examine what moral framework its leaders would erect. Until recently, Uber's philosophy was that a sexist and hostile workplace was just fine, so long as the company was successful. And while the headquarters of Amazon are glamorous, and populated by educated professionals, the drudgeries of working in its fulfillment plants are well-storied. As is its unscrupulous treatment of suppliers.

Silicon Valley's agendas are set by groups of largely affluent, educated, male individuals; advised by white, affluent, male, baby boomer futurists and white, affluent, male, baby boomer professors. (And reported on in the media—largely—by white, educated, male tech reporters.) The denizens of

Silicon Valley are the new inhabitants of the ivory tower. They are shaping culture and yet they do not interact on a regular basis with people outside of their socioeconomic group—the luxurious transit buses that ferry employees between tech campuses and San Francisco are among the most potent and widely reported examples. These companies are dominated by Ivy League–educated male staffers with access to limitless abundance of food, drink, and services on a day-to-day basis. These are not people who walk among us, so it's unclear if they can represent the wider population at large.

Silicon Valley companies have done a good job presenting themselves as friendly, egalitarian democratizers. The projected value system of this group is largely positive. They're pro-LGBT, pro-sustainability, pro–social good. But it's on their own terms, and self-regulated. (Evidenced by their famously hostile work environments, gender inequality, and seeming disinterest in the very real homeless problem in their hometown of San Francisco.)

All of this is significant as Big Tech's reach extends. It is one thing if a company monopolizes a service—don't subscribe to it. Or a product—don't buy it. But what happens when that company is providing everything? And all those things are interconnected and controlling the way you live, the loans you get, the insurance you can buy, and the prices you pay for them. When your health data defines whether you get access to credit. When your productivity declines and is connected directly to your salary. The veneer of control quickly vanishes, and you're left with monopoly not just of what you buy, but how you live. It's a consumerist police state.

Right now, Silicon Valley companies' most outrageous activities have been regulated by public shaming and newspaper headlines. As consumer brands who need to maintain a good reputation, they cease and desist certain behaviors if there's enough public outcry. But as Silicon Valley eats all consumerism, not to mention media—which reports on these scandals—control quickly vanishes.

The steady creep of their expanded societal role is being facilitated by a power vacuum. According to a J. Walter Thompson consumer poll, a majority of Americans feel that government and democracy are broken. Trust is gone. Among millennials, staggeringly, there is also a unilateral enthusiasm for Silicon Valley to take more of a governmental role.

Rightly or wrongly, there is also a loss of faith in government to build our future. Like traditional travel agents surpassed by internet services offering peer-to-peer reviews and cheaper prices, government is at risk of being surpassed by cooler, more efficient tech-savvy companies.

President Barack Obama and former U.S. Chief Technology Officer Megan J. Smith recognized government's image problem and embarked on a campaign in Obama's second term to connect his administration with the glamour of the tech world. But the president could also see the Valley's limitations in fulfilling all its bold promises. At the White House Frontiers Conference in Pittsburgh in 2016, Obama poured scorn on Silicon Valley's hubris in blowing up all existing, outdated systems. "Government will never run the way Silicon Valley runs because, by definition, democracy is messy. This is a big, diverse country with a lot of interests and a lot of disparate points of view. And part of government's job, by the way, is dealing with problems that nobody else wants to deal with."

In bringing up these problems, Obama was reminding the audience of our era's recent significant turn inward—its insatiable self-regard and dying communitarian spirit. Silicon Valley, after all, has been exceptionally good at catering to our individual needs (selfies and overnight doorstep delivery). It has also been exceptionally good at making services and products affordable, accessible, and easy to get on a day-to-day basis. Hotels, taxis, all can be cheaper. Or even free, if you consider Google Maps free, and not something you are paying for when access to your personal data and online behavior is leveraged to sell highly targeted advertising. But these applications have been driven by scale, profit, and market forces, often without accountability. Or self-mediating accountability in the form of reviews. And while they're affordable to many, they're not affordable to all.

So, what happens if they become a replacement for the state? What happens if Silicon Valley powers our hospitals, provides our education, builds our cities?

These questions sent me on a journey to explore the tension between Silicon Valley's wild ambition and limitless resources, and the reality of what a Silicon world built in their image (free from the irritation of government constraint) might look like. I wanted to make sense of the changes happening now and to understand what they might mean. Before it's too late.

1

The New Power Map

In San Francisco, clapboard Victorian homes dot tree-lined streets. Tourists eat ice cream by the docks. Ride the trolley cars. Buy overpriced chowder, hooded sweatshirts, and pose with men dressed as sea captains at the Argonaut Hotel overlooking Alcatraz and the Golden Gate Bridge. Save for a smattering of tired tower blocks, or the isolated plinth of Salesforce's newly added soaring 1,070-foot tower, it's largely a low-rise town, not a city. On the best days, its rolling hills are bathed in bright Pacific light. On the worst, they are shrouded in damp mist.

Drive south into Silicon Valley along a winding highway and you'll reach the bland confines of Palo Alto. It's aggressively suburban. Low-rise boxy campuses are surrounded by lawns and serviced by cookie-cutter terracotta-hued Spanish revival retail developments, featuring Starbucks, nail salons, and dry cleaners in replicate arrangements. Nothing about this city by the bay, or the towns surrounding Silicon Valley's headquarters, signals proximity to wealth, or that you're frequenting what is now perhaps one of the world's biggest global power centers.

Historically, when it comes to wealthy cities, power has been about display—about monumental opulence and vision, like Paris's grand avenues, or concentrations of vertiginous pointy buildings with shiny, masculine surfaces like Chicago or New York, their soaring skylines built around history, communicating wonder and might. And these monuments have become intertwined with the central urban fabric and architecture. Not Silicon Valley, which, in the Bay Area at least, still seems to keep the full magnitude of its iceberg beneath the surface, or obscured at a distance by green pastures and campus-like optimism, and in fortress pastures like Apple's new ring, which you can only take stock of from above and which are outside town centers. This is a sprawling but low-rise power. Or it was, until recently.

How did Silicon Valley go from a microchips hub to a global power-house? The Valley's ascent was at first stealthy but is now truly bold-faced. Silicon Valley has mastered soft power. Its economic and cultural influences have become magnetic forces. Luminaries of industries all flock there. Where once Washington, DC; Wall Street; Hollywood; Detroit; hell even Dallas led their respective sectors of politics, finance, movies, cars, and energy, Silicon Valley now owns a piece of all these industries and more.

"Silicon Valley has evolved from a wonky backwater to a major power center that kind of snuck up on other power centers," says Margit Wenn-machers, perched on a stool in the Battery, one of San Francisco's new wave of hip, Soho House–style members' clubs serving its new-tech royalty. German-born, Wennmachers speaks with a slight European lilt. "If you look at the U.S., it used to be Washington, DC; then New York; then L.A. [that dominated in their fields]. Now, all of a sudden, Silicon Valley has become a major power center with a lot of companies that are growing very fast, that are interesting, and are potentially replacing existing industries."

Wennmachers, a venture capitalist and partner at Andreessen Horo-witz, is slim, dark-haired, with clear eyes and pale skin. She was a cofounder of OutCast Communications, one of the tech world's top public relations firms, and has been dubbed "the real queen of Silicon Valley" by CNN for her role in the rapid rise of its most iconic companies.

Wennmachers is known for identifying and evaluating new startups for investment potential, to date including Twitter, Jawbone, Foursquare, Face-book, Groupon, and Zynga. She's a key connector in the Valley, hosting salon-style dinners at her home. Beyond her strategic investment advice, she's often credited with being the chief architect of the very magic, and the narrative, that has made these companies so successful. (At Andreessen Horowitz, her use of PR to amplify the venture company's reputation, as well those of the startups it invests in, is a competitive advantage.)

When I ask Wennmachers about the magnitude of all the changes wrought by Silicon Valley and how centralized its power seems, she acts as if to even raise the question is to voice a conspiracy theory. "There's no central authority in Silicon Valley and there's no plan that says 'Let's take over all of these existing industries.'"

Massive centralization is, however, happening.

"Education and health care are very hot right now," she says. "There's a huge boom in FinTech," referring to financial technology, a new segment of online-banking, money-transfer, payment, and currency startups emerging in recent years to disrupt the traditional finance industry. "And that is not the databases that sit in the guts of the bank, but actual innovation on how consumers and business customers interact with financial services."

In fact, finance, like every sector, is being disrupted by new upstarts, thanks to smartphones and relaxed regulations. Millennials are fleeing the big banks in part because of mistrust after the 2007/8 global economic crisis. The top four U.S. banks ranked among the ten brands least loved by millennials in 2015, according to a three-year study from Viacom Media. Expectations of banks are changing. Millennials want to be able to make international transfers free of charge and are happy banking purely through their phones. One in three respondents in the same Viacom study believed they won't need a bank at all in the all-digital future.

Payments are also being transformed with contactless mobile transfers and apps, making Silicon Valley the gatekeepers to swaths of new behavioral data. The Apple Pay system, which allows consumers to keep several credit cards stored on their iPhone or Apple Watch, saw its payment volume rise 450 percent in 2017. Facial and thumbprint are increasingly forms of financial ID. (Alibaba recently unveiled its "Smile to Pay" system, which uses facial recognition to process payments.) At both Amazon and Alibaba's much-vaunted "cashierless" supermarkets and fashion pop-ups, customers must download the brand's respective app in order to pay before they can emerge with any products.

Silicon Valley is expanding into almost every sector. Powerful industries that used to be closely associated with region, and dotted across the country or world, now eye encroaching Silicon activity. Hollywood has been scooped up with burgeoning entertainment and streaming ventures. Medicine, health care, and pharmaceuticals are next. Detroit is on the block.

Tesla is producing highly successful cars too—and is now more valuable than Ford. Then there's the emerging focus on reinventing food itself, with products like Soylent and Impossible Foods—which has re-created the molecular structure of beef from vegetables, an eco-friendly burger that cuts down the carbon footprint of cattle.

"There's a lot of movement and who knows what will happen? Tesla and Google have a project, Apple is working on something and Uber is working on something," Wennmachers says. "Detroit, and companies such as Volvo and Toyota, might be moving into driverless cars, but they're now competing with Northern California."

Indeed. As technology, data, and science become central to all aspects of how we live, Silicon Valley (and San Francisco) is an ambidextrous center for influence. Brands, from food to beauty and luxury, flock here to launch experimental "labs," stage workshops, and meet with executives, as if proximity to the tech world will breed the future by osmosis.

The Valley has taken on incredible symbolic significance. Where creativity, concepts, and culture could be innovative before, technology and data are now the primary things associated with the future. And Silicon Valley has the tech experts—which gives this stretch of land on the U.S. West Coast massive ideological and economical influence.

The Rise of "Silicon Valley"—the Brand

It's helpful to think of Silicon Valley as not a single entity but a tribal community, suggests Danah Boyd, principal researcher at Microsoft Research and scholar of social media, from her office in the Flatiron District of New York.

It's a summer morning, the cool air-conditioning is streaming, befitting of sweaty summer months in Manhattan where blistering heat and sunshine are shielded from office incumbents by grey, pollution-freckled glass.

One of the biggest challenges when looking at Silicon Valley, says Boyd, is the common assumption we're dealing with a homogenous infrastructure, a Big Tech monolith that somehow happened all at once. In fact, Silicon Valley is quite tribal, and evolved into its current state in multiple layers. "There are really interesting and unique stages," she says.

But Silicon Valley as a concept is important to examine because it has evolved to represent so much more than a sector or industry, and does represent something holistic. It's a culture, a state of mind, an ethos, a language, and an aesthetic. There are common Silicon Valley tropes and values, meaning that Amazon is based in Seattle but still feels intuitively like a "Silicon Valley Brand." Ditto Snapchat in Los Angeles. There is now a legion of would-be imitators in the shape of Silicon Roundabout, Silicon Beach, you name it. All trying to associate themselves with that same mystique.

The term Silicon Valley was coined in 1971 and referred to a clutch of silicon-chip manufacturers based in Santa Clara Valley in the southern part of the San Francisco Bay Area. Geographically, the original Silicon Valley has spread to areas such as San Francisco and Oakland (Uber announced it was relocating there in 2015).

Fifty-three businesses in the Fortune 1000 are based in the Golden State. California's economy is the sixth largest in the world, bigger than France's, with a GDP of $2.46 trillion. The only countries with higher GDP output are the U.S. as a whole, China, Japan, Germany, and the UK.

Examining Silicon Valley's rise from the 1970s to the post-2000s, with the revival of Apple to the landscape of global tech megabrands we have now, is pivotal to understanding its cultural influence and the state of play we exist with today, and perhaps the reason we scrutinize it less than other industries.

Today this group of companies has come to represent something collective and symbolic. They are not only economic powerhouses, but they established the notion that technology and platforms are more than just products—they were world builders, ways of life, aspirational tools, and their outlook was at one with the "future." This group of companies has created communication strategies specifically to this end. And as they have grown, their point of view, messaging, and slogans have pervaded.

Innovation has been integral to Silicon Valley's identity. But until recently it wasn't ingrained in the public's consciousness the way it is now, in part because its clientele were businesses and the government. Its products were not marketed aggressively and sold to the general public.

The Valley's early life was as a hub for STEM research (science, technology, engineering, and mathematics) with a military and Navy focus, driven by Stanford University (founded in 1885) and its affiliates from 1939 onward. Innovation at this time was applied to helping the war effort, created and funded by the federal government. As the Valley shifted, or rather, expanded, from being a supplier of government and industry to provider of everyone's pocket shopping and music devices, so too has its psychological role in society grown. As well as its promise. Like with any major brand sold to us, from Coke to Nike, the process of selling it has necessitated attaching more significance to its products and their powers. If Coke united different nations and Nike empowered athletes, Silicon Valley companies were way more than just phones, communication platforms, and computers.

With Silicon Valley's rise, so too the notion of "startup" culture has taken on great influence. Every traditional industry (including mine) has redesigned its space to look, feel, talk, and operate like a startup. We don't change, we "hack." The jargon is embedded in our vernacular. "Disrupt," "innovate," and "unicorn" are all now in our cultural lexicon, thanks to Silicon Valley.

Stanford University is credited with a major role in creating the Valley's original startup culture. Frederick Terman, dean of engineering during the 1950s, is famous for encouraging graduates to take their education and use it to start their own companies—examples include Hewlett-Packard and Varian Associates. Varian built the research and development lab on the edge of Stanford's campus that later became the Stanford Research Park.

The 1970s saw a number of shifts in Silicon Valley, but chief among them was the switch from providing business systems to making products and ideas geared directly toward the consumer, though with none of the hyperbole attached to today's raft of brands. Technology, even consumer-facing, was about business and work. This was the era of microchips and blue-chip tech businesses, such as Intel, which launched its first microprocessor in 1971, and "Big Blue"—IBM's nickname. Both have since tried to refashion themselves in groovier reiterations, following new-wave Silicon Valley's lead. (See Watson, IBM's cognitive learning computer. And Intel's recent Creators Project with Vice Media, connecting it to digital cool kids.)

The association of technology with freedom starts around this time, but from a different place. Besides the giants, another group of San Francisco enthusiasts saw technology as a counterculture tool, and a weapon to sidestep governmental systems for liberation. This was when the legendary Homebrew Computer Club—a garage-based, grassroots endeavor that brought together tech geeks and computer hobbyists—was formed. Steve Wozniak was inspired to dream up the Apple 1 at the club, passing around the schematics and even helping other members to build their own. Steve Jobs and Wozniak formed a partnership to sell the computers they built in their garage at night.

In contrast to the corporate nature of the microchip business, at Homebrew the personal computer was positioned as a force for democracy and freedom. The group was influenced by the *Whole Earth Catalog*, a counterculture magazine published by Stewart Brand starting in 1968 that featured detailed product reviews and essays. The magazine's countercultural spirit had a major influence on Steve Jobs, who quoted its final issue's goodbye message, "Stay hungry, stay foolish," in his 2005 Stanford University commencement address. Kevin Kelly, founding executive editor of *Wired*, says Brand "invented the blogosphere" long before the arrival of the internet, as it was a "great example of user-generated content."

An emblematic marker of this mindset is "A Declaration of the Independence of Cyberspace," John Perry Barlow's piece, now more than twenty years old, written in response to the first time that the World Economic Forum, at Davos, Switzerland, decided to pay attention to technology.

Barlow's piece now seems positively romantic, in view of 2018's reality that the rollback of net neutrality rules in the U.S. is likely to transform internet use to a series of sprawling but mutually restrictive internet empires, and make access to information and websites closely dictated by commercial interests.

When John Perry Barlow wrote his piece, the internet represented the antithesis of the commercial internet we now have that's dominated by internet service providers or Silicon Valley giants. It starts: "Governments of the Industrial World, you weary giants of flesh and steel, I come from Cyberspace, the new home of Mind. On behalf of the future, I ask you of the past to leave us alone. You are not welcome among us. You have no sovereignty where we gather . . . Cyberspace does not lie within your borders . . . We are creating a world that all may enter without privilege or prejudice accorded by race, economic power, military force, or station of birth . . . We are creating a world where anyone, anywhere may express his or her beliefs, no matter how singular, without fear of being coerced into silence or conformity . . . Your increasingly obsolete information industries would perpetuate themselves by proposing laws, in America and elsewhere, that claim to own speech itself throughout the world . . . In our world, whatever the human mind may create can be reproduced and distributed infinitely at no cost."

Parts of this remain, of course, though the freedom of speech part is presenting its own challenges and debate when it comes to extremist user-generated content. And it assumes that a lot of consumer information can exist online in the public space, even if you didn't put it there (as the landmark Right to be Forgotten case explored). But our internet interactions have become product, in the form of data, in many instances for advertisers to better target us. Visibility for a small company or platform in searches is now something that must be paid for. Our behavioral data is the commodity, not the hardware sold to us. It's a commercial engine unrecognizable from the innocent days when the internet was a gateway to any universe of your choosing. But that early association with the internet as special, freeing, and decentralized has remained—and has been used as a tool by tech brands and internet providers to dodge criticism, especially concerns about privacy and/or anticompetitive behavior. We regulate water, power, roads, and television. But the internet is still defended as somehow "special." We view it very differently from other services and commodities.

Tech leaders have historically spoken out in favor of net neutrality, but in the wake of recent debates, they have gone markedly quiet. In part, because many Silicon Valley giants are now too big to need it—after all, net neutrality is the principle of enabling equal access to sources, pages, and websites regardless of commercial bias. It's about free speech, and websites, and small companies being as easy to find and use as big ones. Facebook, Google, Amazon, and Netflix are the biggest fish of all. And they are shaping the way we use the internet in ways similar to the internet providers.

The ideological battle continues between the original "free" internet and the capitalist machine it's become. The European Union's decision to fine Google €2.4 billion for anticompetitive behavior in its shopping and listing services was as much about fair trade as about the kind of internet it wanted—one that is free, liberating (to small businesses), and fair. Much like the net's original champions had in mind.

The 1980s were significant for turning technology into a mass consumer product with the advent of personal computing. NASA and military funding fueled software development that was subsequently applied commercially. PARC, the Xerox research center founded in 1970, is credited with developing laser printers, graphical user interfaces, screens, the personal computer, and Ethernet, among other examples. PARC is indirectly connected to the launch of Apple, Cisco, and Microsoft. In 1981, IBM took on Apple with its own personal computer (with an operating system supplied by Microsoft), paving the way for an explosion in the PC market. Microsoft launched Windows in 1985 and became the dominant operating system on personal computers with Windows 3.1 in 1992.

Leslie Berlin, a Silicon Valley historian and academic at Stanford University, tells me over breakfast in Palo Alto that the rise of venture capital was the spark that moved computing from being a specialist pursuit to something found in most people's living rooms. Our surroundings feel apt when we chat. We meet at a slightly frayed but popular hotel restaurant; several baby boomer businessmen, clad in slacks and golfing sweaters, conduct breakfast meetings. Outside, a small army of neatly groomed millennials, sporting T-shirts, jeans, North Face vests, and branded merchandise of their respective tech employer, pound the streets, park bicycles, and sip lattes. Collectively Palo Alto is spookily, and literally, similar to the stereotype painted in Mike Judge's hit show *Silicon Valley*. We are now in the heartland of this major transition of tech as specialist equipment to ubiquitous consumer segment.

Following the rise of consumer tech, the next stage in Silicon Valley's influence ascent was the introduction of the internet. The first World Wide Web page was launched at CERN, the European particle physics research facility, by Tim Berners-Lee in 1991, leading, says Danah Boyd of Microsoft, to a two-part Silicon Valley. One: classic business mindsets, the chip manufacturer ecosystem and hardware innovation labs synonymous with Silicon Valley's origins, meet with Two: a new world of consumer-facing, culturally connected businesses centered on lifestyle, retail, and culture.

"You have this new movement of upstarts and troublemakers that become part of what we understand as Silicon Valley lore. This gets born here," Boyd says. "That group starts to shape a whole set of things that would move forward."

With Netscape's Navigator, the first widely used web browser, Marc Andreessen—cofounder and a venture capitalist whose eponymous firm Andreessen Horowitz would become legendary for funding Facebook, Foursquare, Pinterest, and Twitter—arrives on the scene. "He plays an important role through to the present," says Boyd. His firm Andreessen Horowitz, founded in 2009, spearheaded the celebritization of venture capitalists. (Venture capitalism used to be seen as a very unsexy business. Thanks to Andreessen—a figurehead for technology as a thought leader of the future—being a VC is almost as glamorous as being a startup founder.)

The new consumer internet made for a melting pot of creativity, business, and innovation in Silicon Valley. It attracted an influx of new talent, money, and interest.

A host of dot-coms rose up during this time, from Amazon and Napster to Google and eBay, fueled by intense speculation and increased internet access. Between 1990 and 1997, the number of American households with access to the internet rose from 15 to 35 percent. The boom gained pace after 1995 with a slew of new companies launching.

"By 1999, we have a flood of MBAs coming in on a get-rich-quick scheme," says Boyd. But it could only last so long. Company valuations were rising exponentially by the end of the 1990s, regardless of their inherent value or earnings or due diligence or proven business models. Dot-coms were able to launch and achieve stock market floatations without ever having turned a profit, or revenue. By 2001 the fever spiked. The ill-fated merger of America Online (AOL) and Time Warner is regarded as the tipping point in confidence, and the path to the dot-com bubble bursting. Dell and Cisco also created panic by launching large sell orders on their stocks. Investment capital dwindled fast, prompting rapid decline in startups. Companies valued at millions were worthless within months. Market value of $1.755 trillion was lost, and many of the boom-era startups folded.

While the bubble bursting was disastrous economically, the 1990s and the dot-com boom led to important shifts in consumer behavior, which have only fueled Silicon Valley's current ascent. During this time, internet use for a number of tasks became naturalized. We learned to use the web for shopping and seeking information; consuming content and media became commonplace. All this would prove a precursor to subsequent additions and business models. It would also create a trust in using online tools to bank, pay taxes, and share personal information.

We also see the rise of the "PayPal mafia," the term jokingly given to the former PayPal staffers and executives who sold it in 2002 and have since gone on to found many of Silicon Valley's leading companies. They invested in most of the rest and, in many ways, define Silicon Valley culture today. PayPal founder Peter Thiel, X.com founder Elon Musk, PayPal CTO Max Levchin, Dave McClure, Chad Hurley, and LinkedIn cofounder and former PayPal EVP Reid Hoffman, among others. (There's a long list.) Palantir, SpaceX, Tesla, LinkedIn, Yelp, and YouTube all sprung up in the wake of PayPal from this famously close network. The founders (many of whom are now billionaires) were propelled to celebrity status. A 2007 profile in *Fortune* magazine described their growing importance.

"This group of serial entrepreneurs and investors represents a new generation of wealth and power," the article said, adding: "In some ways they're classic characters of Silicon Valley, where success and easy access to capital breed ambition and further success. It's the reason people come to the area from all over the world. But even by that standard, PayPal was a petri dish for entrepreneurs."

In this group we see Peter Thiel, a die-hard Libertarian, champion the notion of government as interfering and slow. We also see the rising theme of going against the mainstream and being counterintuitive to innovate. (This extends to Thiel's famed support for shunning university degrees in favor of creating companies that change society or other pursuits that are more meaningful.)

"The PayPal mafia is a really important set of characters because they start to bring in the first wave of a finance mindset," says Boyd. "They're not coming in with any of the cultural history, and while they have technical jobs, they're seeing tech as a tool to restructure an existing system through the fetishization of destruction."

This is a key point in the rise of Silicon Valley: the birth of "disruption" and change not as something scary, or sinister, but as something cool, desirable, and progressive—and for that terminology to be adopted en masse. It's the birth of disrupting other businesses, and models, to make money. It's the birth of tech determinism, a Darwinistic theme that continues to be propagated by Silicon Valley leaders: innovation should rightfully progress, evolve, and shape the world unthwarted by constraints, government, or anything else. Even if, like Uber, you're disrupting a profitable industry, you're predicated on cheap non-unionized labor, and you have yet to make a profit. In fact, you're making losses, but as long as confidence in your growth is high, you can continue to attract funding.

The opportunity to dismantle existing outmoded industries became a cult pursuit at this point. Companies framed their mission statements with it, helped by the continued influence of *The Innovator's Dilemma*, Harvard professor Clayton M. Christensen's pivotal 1997 book that disseminated the idea of disruptive innovation. (It identified how innovations could displace market leaders by creating new markets and value networks using cheaper versions.) It's now a mantra in Silicon Valley.

After the 2001 devastation of the dot-com bubble, the Valley's rebound gathered steam in the 2000s and is often attributed to the PayPal mafia described above. With the rise of these brands, and the security they provided to a shaky national economy, came the worship of technology for all, driven by the marketing of these companies. It was further propelled by the rise of smartphones as mass consumer products and the explosion of apps.

Important launches include: Google, 1998; Apple's comeback under Steve Jobs, 2000; SpaceX, 2002; LinkedIn, 2002; Facebook, 2004; Palantir, 2004; YouTube, 2005. Then the second wave: Twitter, 2006; Airbnb, 2008; Uber, 2009; WhatsApp, 2009; Instagram, 2010; Snapchat, 2011. This resurgence was affected, but not thwarted, by the 2008 global economic crisis. Another important date: the iPhone launched in 2007.

This later wave was propelled by a new narrative, espoused in part by innovative communications figures like Margit Wennmachers. A new type of storytelling about Silicon Valley companies rendered them much more special than tech. The internet was more than just a way to connect and search for information. Beyond Thiel's beloved disruption was the idealistic notion that technology could shape and change the world for the better. As these companies started to catch up with Coca-Cola, Nike, Adidas, and McDonald's as the most powerful consumer brands of all time, they also began to believe their own hype.

"Everything explodes in 2000–2001 [with the bubble], and what that means is that the MBAs leave, but the people who still believe that technology can actually be transformative stay," says Boyd.

Having cofounded the Bill & Melinda Gates Foundation in 2000, Bill Gates moved into philanthropy full-time in 2006, taking on extreme poverty and disease globally, often propelled by new technologies. Musk launched SpaceX in 2002, a commercial venture with space travel in its sights. Founders Fund was opened in 2005 for companies building "revolutionary technologies." In 2008, the Singularity University incubator was founded by Peter Diamandis and Ray Kurzweil at the NASA Research Park in California. "We believe our world has the people, technology, and resources to solve any problem, even humanity's most urgent, persistent challenges," Singularity proclaims. In 2009 Google Ventures began investing in companies that "push the edge of what's possible" in life science, health care, artificial intelligence, robotics, transportation, cybersecurity, and agriculture. "Our companies aim to improve lives and change industries."

"Change the world" becomes a marketing mantra, as well as a business philosophy. It leads to the next significant transition in the history of Silicon Valley. In tackling big problems while also adopting sweeping altruistic rhetoric, the Valley starts to encroach on the state's role as world-builder, moral compass, and thought-leader.

Gates doesn't mark tech's first move into philanthropy. But he does perhaps start the trend for highly visible, high-profile philanthropical work that will only continue as Silicon Valley's luminaries make their billions and want to use their power and influence to solve the world's problems. Gates also began Silicon Valley's trend for combining philanthropy with commerce.

"That's where you start to see an interesting shift," says Boyd. Capitalists started to view not philanthropy, she says, but market structures as the route to solving the world's challenges. "That's where you get that very intense, neoliberal-libertarian-capitalism combination that becomes templated as Silicon Valley." This was also the time when social networking and blogging sites began to grow. "The cultural geeks come back and start to reimagine things, and a lot of those early social network sites, blogging and social media, were reimagined by those cultural geeks. The money wasn't at all relevant." They often started, she says, with an idealistic mission, but when these businesses could scale and get funding, money of course does become relevant.

Wennmachers sees the move from military to consumer products as the biggest factor in how Silicon Valley reached its current influential status. "In the initial phase, nuclear technology was primarily built for other technologies, and it was built for the military, then it was built for the financial services, but it was always built for professionals and for sectors that were using technology in the guts of the organization." She reflects, "It wasn't really outward-facing. A lot of really important stuff was created that then formed the foundation for what's happening today. Increasingly, software solutions were being applied to nontraditional sectors."

There's another important change too—Silicon Valley companies became the stars, not just the facilitators. They made their own brands, not the channel or the mechanism.

"There was a phase where software companies tried to create software to sell to traditional industries. For example, there was a whole wave of applications that would optimize the logistics for the taxi industry," says Wennmachers. "It turned out that the taxi industry is not necessarily a sophisticated software buyer and nothing ever came from it, and then Silicon Valley companies start to go, 'I'll provide the entire solution, rather than relying on the traditional industry to adopt what I think might be the future.' That's where you get Uber and Lyft. So, as a result, a lot of the iconic new brands are coming from California."

The fame of these new consumer brands quickly reached an international scale too, she says. California was making America known for technology that appealed directly to the consumer. It was at this point that Silicon Valley became intertwined generally with America.

The first result was the iPhone, which switched the balance of power from Asian countries like Japan and Taiwan to the U.S. because of the core importance of the software. "People spend a lot of time talking about the way the hardware looks, but it's about how the hardware is integrated with beautiful software. That is the competency of Silicon Valley and, as it turns out, not of Japan," says Wennmachers. All of a sudden, iconic companies in California burgeoned, and the Valley elevated the country economically and—perhaps more important—culturally.

This happened in sync with technology becoming not just a daily interaction, but something even more intense: a habit, a lifestyle, a compulsion. Suddenly there was a new relationship between consumers and their tech brands.

"The word I would use is intimacy," says Stanford's Leslie Berlin, who has studied Silicon Valley for twenty years. "We have an intimate relationship with these technologies that colors our sense of who we are, and that is new. That is the way that Silicon Valley has gotten under everybody's skin."

Some of Silicon Valley's famed, altruistic vision is real, some of it is whipped into a frenzy for headlines, and some of it has changed over time as these companies have moved from being the inventions of clever techies to money-making machines.

"The fact that I now have Google on my phone and I can look up anything that's in the Library of Congress and Wikipedia is genuinely life-changing," says Wennmachers. The bold ambitions of some Silicon Valley companies should be encouraged, she believes. "We want it to work, because if it does, it will make for a lot of positive change."

This kind of genuinely innovative thinking is perhaps one of Silicon Valley's greatest strengths. "Silicon Valley is a giant experimentation lab," says Wennmachers. "There is a set of Silicon Valley entrepreneurs, just like there is a set of people who make movies and a set of people who pass laws, who make very lofty claims that it will change people's lives for the better," she says pragmatically. "Sometimes that's true and sometimes it isn't."

Silicon Valley companies continue to rely on soaring rhetoric, but in recent years the media has grown more critical of tech leaders and tech company behavior. Reportage now shows Silicon Valley leadership as rampant imperialists, or the architects of our automated doom. In snarkier columns, its arrogance, ambition, and tone-deafness are lampooned. But the picture is more nuanced, says Puneet Kaur Ahira, a special advisor to Megan J. Smith, America's CTO during the Obama administration. (Ahira and Smith are both former Googlers.) Seated in a bustling Le Pain Quotidien in Manhattan in late December, beset by holiday shoppers and workers grabbing coffee, she talks about her experiences on both sides of the fence. Many of these companies were started with bold, genuine, optimistic idealism, she points out.

"If you look at where the flow of logic started, when Larry [Page] and Sergey [Brin] founded Google, their ambition was to organize the world's information in a useful and universally accessible way. That's no easy task, and what they developed was magnificent in terms of a solution that's elegant as well as intuitive. I think there's something powerful in setting a mission of that magnitude and then actually achieving it," Ahira says. "The fact that they satisfied the initial vision for the company meant that the bar got raised even higher. Across the tech community there is this prevailing discourse where you hear people asking each other, 'How can we use our talent, our knowledge, our resources to turn the impossible into the possible? What pursuits are truly worthy of our time, our energy, and effort?' The sentiment is absolutely genuine. There's a belief that if you go after the biggest problems, the money will follow. But alongside these visions of grandeur also comes a dangerous level of arrogance and hubris."

Silicon Valley's public and economic strength has created cultural changes inside their companies. Talk to many staffers at any of these giants, and you hear a genuine, sometimes bordering on cultish, belief in the founders and their noble intentions, even if those intentions evolved when they went public.

Boyd, musing on the same topic, had firsthand experience of Silicon Valley's evolving persona working at several of its leading companies. "I've lived through all of these buildings. They're weirdly open and yet not, that's how they all play out," she says, adding that an initial public offering (IPO) is often a turning point. "Google was actually extremely porous until its IPO [in 2004], which was the breaking point for it. I was inside at the time. Larry and Sergey do something called TGIFs, Thank God It's Fridays, where they would get up and share whatever's relevant for the week, and also answer questions—I remember when they came onstage on the Friday before the IPO was to happen."

Boyd recalls this was a key moment in Google's transition from a "Don't Be Evil" company of idealists to a closed, profit-driven corporation: "They came onstage and they're like, 'We need you to know that we're not able to tell you anything in advance of stockholders anymore. We're not allowed to, so we're not going to be able to answer most of your questions.' It was a really radical change because the culture was such that employees always knew what was going on. But because of how the Wall Street structures work, you're no longer allowed to do that with a public company. That changes the dynamics, and they were very upfront about it. I remember that meeting, because they made it very clear that their hands were tied. This has been the challenge. That was when they started locking down the lunch rooms, because the company was so scared of leaks."

They have continued, though, to host labs and support innovation in far-reaching and ambitious feats—called "moonshots"—from space travel to solving world problems. This, Boyd says, continues because it's a key draw for talented and idealistic engineers. "They're about talent acquisition," says Boyd. "They're saying 'Hey, you're a young computer scientist and you're building neural nets because you love it and you dream of being able to have autonomous cars. We're the company that you should work for.' The moonshots aren't about profitability at all."

Although, she adds, founders are often attached to them: "Larry was always there for the moonshots. That's all he cared about. He didn't give a shit about sustaining a company, that was Eric [Schmidt's] job . . . What Larry cares about is the most interesting, the hardest technical problems. He's trying to pull in the interesting talent, and in order to get good talent, you need to give people dreams that they can work on."

Technical feats are one thing, but Silicon Valley is not stopping there. Increasingly its ambition covers the unknown, and the very traditional mundane areas of our lives, from pavements to schoolrooms, with promises to reinvent both. Silicon Valley leaders are looking at governance and politics as another cable network or suburban mall to be disrupted, and building on the soft civic influence they already have, which transcends border regulations, elections, and state controls. What happens when Silicon Valley sets its sights on government?

2

Government and Silicon Valley

As political scenes go, it's picture-book. Planting gardens honoring Dr. Martin Luther King Jr. at community centers in Dallas, arm in arm with residents; sitting down with DACA Dreamers and U.S. Army veterans; manfully shaking hands with Dale Earnhardt Jr. at the Charlotte Motor Speedway in North Carolina; speaking about the importance of diversity to an audience packed with young African American students at North Carolina State University. Place a square-jawed, slacks-wearing, button-downed (with sleeves rolled up) guy in there and you'd have a cookie-cutter candidate for public office. Except this time, he's pale, curly-haired, slightly nerdy, sporting a dark grey T-shirt with blue jeans.

Speculation continues to mount about Mark Zuckerberg's potential presidential ambitions, which, despite explosive revelations about Russia-backed content influencing the U.S. election and Facebook links to Russian state investors, seems to continually resurface. Though whether they will cease in the face of Facebook's data breach will be interesting to watch.

It first hit fever pitch after Zuckerberg announced his famous 2017 goal to get to know America's real people. In the wake of the controversial presidential election, his posturing on the "tumultuous year," ambition to "talk to people about how they're living," hear their personal stories, and examine how technology could "change the game so it works for everyone," news outlets were abuzz that Zuckerberg might be planning (at least eventually) to run for office. And Facebook's board admitted it had granted the CEO up to two years leave for public service, while still retaining control of the company, if he wishes.

Zuckerberg's public statements continue to take on a more stately rhetoric. His 2017 Harvard commencement speech was filled with civic overtures, calling on millennials to recognize the challenges facing the world, embrace a sense of collective purpose and community, and forge ahead to solve the biggest problems facing humanity via innovation, entrepreneurialism, and bravery. He called for a "new social contract" that enables equal access to opportunity for all, through concepts like universal basic income and constant education throughout adulthood to adapt to ongoing technological changes.

"The challenge for our generation is creating a world where everyone has a sense of purpose," he said to a crowd of rain-soaked graduates, parents, and academics at the Ivy League institution, harking back to the Space Race and invoking figures like JFK and Herbert Hoover as evidence of times when America came together to take great steps forward and build great things.

Referring to those exact challenges, Zuckerberg said: "When our parents graduated, purpose reliably came from your job, your church, your community. But today, technology and automation are eliminating many jobs. Membership in communities is declining. Many people feel disconnected and depressed, and are trying to fill a void. As I've traveled around, I've sat with children in juvenile detention and opioid addicts, who told me their lives could have turned out differently if they just had something to do . . .

"Every generation has its defining works . . . Millions of volunteers immunized children around the world against polio. Millions of more people built the Hoover Dam and other great projects.

"These projects didn't just provide purpose for the people doing those jobs, they gave our whole country a sense of pride that we could do great things. Now it's our turn to do great things . . ."

In many ways, Zuckerberg's political awakening is in sync with a wider shift among millennials at large toward political engagement, as growing numbers of them reach candidate age. More are likely to follow Zuckerberg. Already, entrepreneur and talent manager Scooter Braun, thirty-six, has diversified from managing Justin Bieber to politics, reportedly considering running for California governor—his company, SB Projects, describes itself as a "diversified entertainment and media company with ventures integrating music, film, television, technology, and philanthropy."

Historically, millennials have been defined by political apathy. They will use social media "likes" in support of causes such as marriage equality and ALS (with the Ice Bucket Challenge). They will buy ethical goods. But until recently, there has been markedly low tangible action at the polling booth. Which is ironic given the enormous economic challenges they've been handed due to student debt, rising costs of living, and climate change. Now, in the wake of the U.S. presidential election and Brexit, both of which saw large generational splits (the young at the losing end), they are starting to engage proactively. This could create dramatic change in the coming decade. In the 2016 presidential election, millennial and Gen X voters outnumbered boomers for the first time, according to the Pew Research Center. In the United Kingdom, Labour's surprising 2017 gain in the share of seats was credited mostly to younger voters. An *Evening Standard* poll revealed significant shifts to Labour, the left-leaning party, among thirty-five- to fifty-four-year-olds. And in general, millennials are showing a more liberal bent in their attitudes and values.

Will Zuckerberg be the one of the next presidential candidates? The last year marked a particular escalation in his political overtures, but it follows a distinctive longer-term campaign to reposition him as a likeable, well-rounded public figure.

Skim back through the Instagram posts of Mark Zuckerberg, or "Zuck" as he likes to be known in digital social circles, and you'll notice a subtle change that goes back as far as 2014. That's when you see the foundations being laid for strategically cultivating brand "Mark" as an approachable, smart, family man. There are pictures of dogs. And his daughter Max. Though, like a lot of Silicon Valley attempts to sync with culture, it is a touch tone-deaf and lacking in self-awareness. Zuckerberg's attempts to round out his public persona as a fun guy include ill-advised awkward comedy skits with Bill Gates and Morgan Freeman, the voice of Facebook's AI assistant. There was the famously misjudged live virtual reality tour of Puerto Rico in the aftermath of Hurricane Maria. The objective was to bring to life Facebook's donation of $1.5 million to the rescue cause. That fell flat, as Zuckerberg in animated avatar form was shown exploring the very real destruction, before quickly visiting the moon and then his living room to see his dog.

Many of his "candid" social snaps are palpably effortful—the staged saccharine family shots of Zuckerberg attending a New Orleans Mardi Gras, or going on date night (how did the cameras know to shoot him and his wife, artfully silhouetted against the lights, from behind?), or the earnest picture of him and his three sisters when he announces he's having a second baby girl. His tone-deaf or vague responses when grilled by U.S. Congress in 2018 were also a source of social media mockery.

In some ways, Zuckerberg is the model template for the next generation of politician. If previously politicians have been lawyers and bankers in suits and power ties, then the thirty-two-year-old, Chinese-speaking, sneaker-wearing Mark Zuckerberg—technology magnate, philanthropist, globalist, and icon of social media—is the embodiment of millennial values.

The idea of Zuckerberg as politician raises some uncomfortable questions. If the election and Brexit were lessons in the raw power of social media to shape political discourse (and the outcome of elections), what if the mountains of data Facebook has collected were used with strategic intent? The most startling example of this is still unfolding in the wake of the Cambridge Analytica scandal, which showed the myriad ways in which Facebook content could be tailored to push highly personalized hot-button subjects and potentially sway perception and sentiment with regards to elections. The full extent to which Russian-backed Facebook pages and posts impacted the U.S. election is still unknown, but the impact of fake news, social media avatars and bots, and their ability to shape and distort the digital sphere are increasingly apparent. Not least following Robert Mueller's indictment of four former Trump advisers, thirteen Russian nationals, three Russian companies, one California man, one London-based lawyer, and counting. Social media avatars, posts, groups, and stolen identities across Facebook, Twitter, Instagram, and YouTube were identified as key tools in exacerbating divides among Americans. Facebook came out particularly prominently, mentioned thirty-five times in the thirty-seven-page indictment. Facebook has been publicly positive about the indictment and welcoming to its findings, save for a rogue Twitter tirade by VP of Ads Rob Goldman that appeared to repudiate the work of Robert Mueller; this stance was quickly rebuked by the company. What's clear from the indictments is that Russia-backed ads are just a fraction of the tools used within Facebook to effect change and distortion. According to a *Wired* report, roughly 11 million people saw Russian ads, compared to 150 million who saw content by Russia-controlled posts. A multi-pronged, targeted, immersive social media experience to effect change. This was, of course, beyond Facebook's knowledge at the time. But imagine if that were wielded cynically.

Mark Zuckerberg, in this scenario, could be a kingmaker. Could he make himself king?

At the moment, his image outside Facebook is harder to control, as exemplified in the widespread criticism of his leadership following Facebook's Cambridge Analytica breach. Zuckerberg's stilted TV interviews, and continued nonsensical referrals to Facebook as a "community," like the social network is some kind of church hall, displayed a stunning lack of self-awareness. As did COO Sheryl Sandberg's theatrically earnest tropes about trust in the same week. But tellingly, it didn't matter. Both were near unilaterally unchallenged by interviewers in staged, heavily managed engagements (with the exception of Recode's interview by Kara Swisher and Kurt Wagner). No interviews were given to the British media outlets Channel 4, *The Guardian*, or *Observer*, which broke the story, and would therefore likely have given Zuckerberg a bumpier ride. Channel 4 news anchor Jon Snow even published an open letter calling for Facebook to respond. But what happens once Facebook *is* the media? The game could completely change.

Subtle manipulation isn't only possible on Facebook. And it could become even more pervasive as new consumer technologies such as facial recognition, voice activation, and interactive home hubs become the norm. At J. Walter Thompson (JWT), the Internet of Eyes and Ears was one of our biggest consumer tech trends for 2018. The trend explored how new consumer technologies are able to listen to us, and watch us, and then respond rapidly, at a remarkable rate. Everyday objects are outfitted with smart cameras and the latest in visual recognition technology, then combined with machine learning to analyze images, emotions, and facial expressions—and identify people (and even pets). Meanwhile, developments in speech recognition and natural language processing (NLP) now allow people to talk to computers in a way that might recently have seemed like a sci-fi movie. The technology helps people to activate products with their voice, converse with virtual butlers, and ask for information they might otherwise have typed into a Google search. Fifty percent of mobile internet searches are now being done verbally, according to industry analyst Gartner. Twenty-two million Amazon Echos were sold in 2017. The combination of these new technologies gives new, intimate layers of insight into people's lives that could easily have political application.

Facial recognition is moving beyond the passport gate to be a form of financial ID. In China, in 2018, users visiting KFC branches just have to smile to pay for their chicken, with Alibaba's Smile-to-Pay app. The iPhone X debuted Apple's facial recognition system for unlocking the phone. Google-owned Nest has the $299 Nest Cam IQ with built-in facial recognition technology to differentiate between family members and strangers.

"The Internet of Eyes enables all inanimate objects to see by leveraging computer vision analysis," Evan Nisselson, general partner at visual technology venture fund LDV Capital, told us recently at JWT. "Inanimate objects with cameras enable companies to own the first step in gathering the data for computer vision and artificial-intelligence algorithms to analyze. Analysis may include object recognition, sentiment analysis, gesture recognition, and many more human actions which will impact all business sectors and humanity." LDV Capital predicts at least 220 percent more embedded cameras in the next five years.

Pretty soon, if Amazon Echo (and its ilk from Google Assistant to Apple's Siri) is the ear to our homes, Big Tech companies will be able to analyze our reading habits, conversations, and political discourse—a new layer in what has been screen-led interactions. Already Amazon is a shopping search engine that 89 percent of millennials visit when shopping for any item online, according to JWT data. Amazon's new AI-powered photo recognition shopping aid Amazon Echo Look is a cognitive consumer census on steroids—it will snap photos of customers, crowd-source opinions on their outfits, keep and analyze visual content, and make tailored recommendations. Could the information gathered by these applications go beyond consumerism and encroach upon our civic engagement to eventually shape an electoral campaign? Could Thanksgiving dining-table political conversations be used to create even more hyper-tailored and targeted advertising and messaging? Could photo recognition on connected TVs read emotional sentiment during political advertising? It's not that much of a step—assuming it's not happening already.

Consumers, and in particular young people, seem to look favorably on the concept of Silicon Valley as political leaders. In a poll conducted by J. Walter Thompson in 2017 for this book, 84 percent of American consumers stated they would vote for a Silicon Valley leader in a government position ranging from city mayor to president. Democrats (91 percent), city dwellers (89 percent), and minorities (Black/African American: 89 percent, Hispanic: 89 percent) were more likely than average to vote tech figures into government positions. Younger respondents, unsurprisingly, would also be more likely to vote tech leaders into governmental positions: 90 percent of those age fifteen to twenty, 88 percent of twenty-one- to thiry-four-year-olds, 85 percent of thirty-five- to fifty-four-year-olds, and 79 percent of over-fifty-fives. That means 88 percent of millennials would vote someone from Silicon Valley into public office.

Even if Zuckerberg does not try to make himself president, Facebook could be a powerful force in defining a successful candidate and affecting the outcome of an election. Consider the combination of swaths of personal data with artificial intelligence in learning and preempting people's emotions. Or even the scope in creating (as Google, Twitter, and Facebook do) millions of personalized, targeted experiences. Designing a unique candidate who suited everybody in their individual digital setting is not too far in the distance. Netflix's homepage is already personalized, after all. It's interesting to consider this leaping off the page, too, as future Facebook technology moves into 3-D avatars, augmented reality, virtual reality, and beyond. If Hillary Clinton was criticized for not being in key states, Zuckerberg might soon be able to appear, virtually, everywhere. All of this goes hand-in-hand with the greater role that digital platforms, social media, and technology play in politics and elections in general.

If Zuckerberg or one of his peers were to run and be elected, there could be big changes ahead. Some would say Facebook and Amazon are near nation-states already (almost a third of the world's population is on Facebook, after all), but their platforms and services are still participatory, limited to certain behaviors such as socializing and shopping, and malleable around each of our own universes. They are, to an extent, monitored by at least a veneer of consumer power. Meanwhile, the biases and skewed beliefs of their founders are confined to their philanthropic and investment ventures. Elon Musk's belief that universal basic income might solve the unemployment crisis looming at the hands of automation is a soapbox talking point, not a policy. A new tech-driven, hyper-personalized approach to education is seen as a way to fix the broken schools, create equal opportunity for lower-income citizens, and future-proof society. It ignores education's intangible variances affected by socioeconomic structure, systemic multi-generational unemployment, and cultural disenfranchisement—but is, for now, limited to new test private schools supported by tech billionaires. Silicon Valley–backed scientific prize funds dramatically and disproportionately support white men; that does not stop women scientists, and is not their only source of funding. Until it is.

When these are writ large on society, and start to replace the state, their distorting power will be magnified. More than social networks, products, or internet supermarkets we can step in and out of, we'll be forced to actually live inside these constructs.

Everything starts innocently, and positively. Why wouldn't you want data to be freely shared? Why wouldn't you want seamless service? Many government systems would be made more efficient, automated, and digitized in a Silicon Valley regime. Although, that could easily extend to TaskRabbit-style platforms replacing emergency services, or on-demand fire services powered by contractors, or social media regulating services such as water and roads. (What happens when there's surge pricing, not enough Uber firefighters, or no background checks?) When working at Facebook itself, work, life, and socializing are already blurred into one. In a not-too-distant world, the lines between citizenship, employment, and a consumerism could similarly blur in a continuous ecosystem that combines consumer voting, personal government documents all stored on Facebook, and people's résumés up for public scrutiny.

As companies such as Amazon move into financial services and identity verification, higher-income consumers could be treated more favorably. As Amazon becomes a social network with devices like Echo Look, financial clout and social influence could be combined and assessed to inform election campaigning or policies. Sustainability and LGBT rights seem high on Facebook's public agenda, as well as a broadly neoliberal belief system—again all part of Facebook being a major consumer brand, but that could create its own alienating dictum. Could Millennial Neoliberalism replace the far-right leadership we have in the U.S. now? And be as divisive? Trump may be alienating to coastal liberals, but the belief systems of privileged, Ivy League–educated men living and working in rarified confines of Northern California do not represent everyone either. After all, progressivism itself is a somewhat elite concept. Or maybe government becomes the ultimate, algorithmically driven, constantly updating consumer brand, affected by reading consumer sentiment continuously. Blockchain (the decentralized, instantly updating database technology) could power our voting on a multitude of issues instantaneously. Or we could simply vote like we're taking a BuzzFeed survey.

Robert Moses, the legendary mid-twentieth-century urban developer, is in many ways a prophetic warning of the consequences of Silicon Valley's civic influence. Moses imposed his vision on postwar America, stripping cities of undesirable neighborhoods, building new modern developments, parks, and swimming pools—and making way for the automobile, which he saw as central to America's economic future. He cut superhighways over and through existing historic cities. He built new housing projects, social experiments to accommodate the poor, under the banner of "urban renewal," many of which alienated and damaged those same communities. He was immune to the existing and largely successful complex ecosystems housed within cities, which were observed, championed, and highlighted in Jane Jacobs's famous 1961 book *The Death and Life of Great American Cities*. Silicon Valley is selling us an updated, data-driven, tech-obsessed future with similar vision, prejudices, and blind spots. And it's getting increasingly close to realizing similar ambitions. Do we really want a sky full of drones delivering everything for us? Should public transport be on-demand? Is the driverless car really the future? Efficiencies, increased sustainability, and technological advances are great, but as more of the city becomes connected, more of our interactions are commercialized, too.

After all, Amazon Echo and Google Home hubs are given away at knock-down $30 prices, because the gadgets aren't the product, we are. Our interactions, behaviors, and purchases generate valuable data for targeted offers and advertising. When the city becomes connected, all urban life is another product.

Silicon Valley is now better positioned than most industries to wield political influence. And in ways we have not seen before. It is at once government vendor, collaborator, sponsor, advisor, communicator, rival, and enemy on any given day. Its platforms are now integral to democracy, elections, and governments. Its companies and venture-capital funds have had access to more money than ever before. Apple's cash reserves in 2017 were more than $250 billion; total Federal Reserves in November 2016 were just over $118 billion. The Valley's strength as an economic powerhouse is coupled with a gigantic boom in consumer technologies, which is shifting all innovation focus toward commercial products; government is no longer spurring innovation as it did in the 1930s–1980s. The global consumer technology market is estimated to be worth $3 trillion by 2020, up from an estimated $1.45 trillion in 2015, according to Future Marketing Insights. India and China are driving new demand, while the U.S. is expected to continue to invest in upgrading established technologies.

Silicon Valley companies today know consumers, citizens, better than perhaps anyone else. Collectively they know each individual better, in some ways, than friends or family ever could. And certainly better than other industries do. Pharma doesn't know how often you check your horoscopes. Exxon doesn't know when you last took Plan B, or if you were traveling in Mexico City, Jaipur, and Shanghai last week, and what information you searched for while there. Silicon Valley's wealth of rich data on consumers transcends geographic borders and governance. The type of data being accessed is becoming more intimate and comprehensive. Electronic records capture our health and biological data, our bank account information, the data taken from voice recognition commands. This kind of technology can read facial expressions to analyze emotion in real time.

Silicon Valley also operates in the traditional spheres of influence. It is multinational, as many oil and pharma companies are, and as such has scaled up investment in Washington, DC in step with its rapid growth. It lobbies, it has policy heads, and it has a presence there. But Silicon Valley companies also have a wealth of cultural influence and consumer intimacy to exploit, which creates interesting new tensions. It lobbies like big oil and pharma, but also uses its citizen base of workers and consumers (who are often the same thing) to effect change, even if that means rebelling against traditional government.

The power dynamic between government and Silicon Valley companies, particularly the bigger brands, continues to shift gears. The large tech companies, compared to other corporations, have shown a greater interest in making political statements, a necessary outgrowth of their self-conscious branding as forces for good (not just for profit). Apple and Google are ranked among Disney and Coca-Cola as the most influential brands in the world. Unlike previous waves of industry, wonder, more than just power, is attached to what they do. And now they are using politics as a marketing tactic. Several of the ten most powerful global brands have taken political stances on issues such as Brexit, personal privacy, and the 2016 presidential election, marking a powerful move toward publicly challenging governments after historically being mostly neutral. It's a paradigm shift when a commercial brand feels sufficiently confident to speak out openly on a political issue against a government. Leaders from Apple, Facebook, Google, and Microsoft actively criticized President Trump for withdrawing from the Paris climate accord. Patagonia, the outdoor clothing brand, is suing the U.S. government over shrinking protections for national parks. Zuckerberg, not the president of the United States, is meeting with DACA Dreamers. But this activism is linked to their role as consumer brands—they need to show connection to the zeitgeist and opinion en masse, even if a president does not. And on this basis they are being scrutinized in a way that pharma and other corporate categories might not be. Many brands made overtly political campaigns in sync with the 2017 Super Bowl. Airbnb's #WeAccept, for example, launched after President Trump's immigration ban against Muslim countries to highlight its own policy of inclusivity. (Though, as a testament of their limits, not one person in the campaign wore a hijab. It's unclear whether this was a tactical omission—or just stupid.)

Silicon Valley's relationship with the government grows more complex when they seek to mobilize their audiences with rallying cries when something goes against their interests, or may stop their members earning income. "You don't want this! Write to your governor!" Uber has used this tactic to help overturn restrictions and bans on its activities. Airbnb has created a whole platform out of mobilizing its users, or in Airbnb language "community," to lobby governments on its behalf about renting out apartments and properties, raising awareness and advising customers on whom to write to. Describing Airbnb-ers as a new sharing economy "guild," it has made a comprehensive strategy out of rallying consumers to campaign for short-term property rentals. It may have heads of policy, it may lobby, but here it also occupies the curiously counter position as "revolution rouser," except for its own commercial gain. The symbolism is important. Airbnb, a corporation, becomes the champion of the People, not the State.

This sea change arises from the fact that Silicon Valley wields more financial clout than the U.S. and many other governments; it leads innovation in key sectors the government used to; and it is increasingly taking on key tasks of governance. It's not just Musk building spaceships. More NASA contracts, and more government contracts in general, are going to Silicon Valley because Silicon Valley commercial companies have more money and are leading more innovation. Which has prompted federal programs to actively court Silicon Valley robotics startups, and acquire stakes in new technologies that could be relevant for military and government use. The driving force of problem-solving and innovation has now flipped. The British Government is turning to Google's Deep Mind for machine learning for the UK's health services, and to Palantir for analytics (New Orleans has already reportedly been experimenting with Palantir's predictive policing techniques). Silicon Valley is becoming the Expert friend—and that power shift is very visible to all of us as citizens. Where once government took us to space, our government scientists built the internet, and our prime ministers strategized war—we now look to tech companies to lead us into the future.

The tech group is increasingly dominating not only political discourse, but also amplification of that discourse, as an engine of social media marketing for both government and political channels. Campaigns are run on social media, and won. Political news is read, and then distorted, on social media. Facebook, Twitter, YouTube, and Instagram are used for political campaigning now, and have official government pages. Here is another instance where, as data analysts and mobile targets, Silicon Valley minds have become key advisors to government.

Societies, and many aspects of government, are becoming digitalized, often requiring input from private industries. And as economic growth is being driven by businesses from these sectors, many governments want to cultivate Silicon Valley as a business partner. Barack Obama joked at SXSW Interactive that he wanted to hire every member of the audience. Governments are trying to align visibly with technology because it has become synonymous in the people's minds with the future.

On the other end of the spectrum is the wider view. The one where Silicon Valley technologies are ultimately exacerbating all the pressures on governments and eroding their revenues—thus undermining their strength. Automation, robotics, AI are all driving up unemployment. Driverless cars, sensors, and automation will dramatically reduce parking tickets and speeding fines, much-needed channels of income. Platforms like Airbnb are distorting home and rental prices, forcing out lower-income consumers. New technologies are creating a multitude of ethical dilemmas to research, understand, and forecast—but also regulate, putting further pressure on government resources. Widespread drone use alone will need monitoring for privacy reasons. Taken together, it's death by a thousand cuts, a slow (or not so slow) battle of attrition by "efficiencies" against the slowness and bureaucracy of government. And its slowness, even when deliberate and considered, is being positioned openly by tech rivals as a halt on progress. Who will win?

Silicon Swamp: The Changing Scene in Washington, DC

It's a cold, frosty morning in late December 2016. Many are already in holiday mode, shopping, traveling to families, playing hooky from work to meet with friends. Not Sheila Krumholz, the executive director of the Center for Responsive Politics (CRP), a Washington, DC–based nonprofit, nonpartisan research group that tracks the effects of money and lobbying on elections and public policy, looking for conflicts of interest. Krumholz is tired. After months of relentless activity building up to the presidential election, another maelstrom—the election aftermath of President Donald Trump—is creating a raft of new things for her company to track.

"Our role is to promote the notion that, whatever your position is, you need to have access to information in order to be able to do the basic due diligence, hold government accountable. To make sure policy is based on the merits and not on the money," says Krumholz, referring to the Trump administration. "Money is flooding into our system. The degree to which billionaires and immensely wealthy businesspeople—who are inexperienced in politics, I might add—are being appointed to the most powerful positions in government is unprecedented."

Before Trump's election, a lot of her focus was on Silicon Valley's rising influence in Washington. There were headlines about its growing lobbying, the revolving door between the Obama administration and tech giants, and the presence of Silicon Valley generally in the city. And it's taken something of the magnitude of Trump, the multitude of his potential conflicts of business interests, perhaps, to deflect that.

"Technology's presence in our daily lives is so pervasive that we're surrounded by it 24/7, unlike almost any other interest. We're not surrounded by insurance, or even so much by fashion or Hollywood. You can barely pass five minutes without using technology, so it's hard to compare it to anything else. In Washington, DC specifically," she says.

But even as the months unfolded in the wake of the election, Silicon Valley leaders became a key part of the new presidency—critiquing Trump, or being criticized for aligning with him. The fact that Silicon Valley's stances, in either direction, gained bigger headlines than any industrial heads in auto, energy, and finance is telling of Silicon Valley's cultural influence.

Private interests and industry lobbying have always been in politics—top spenders in 2016 were the U.S. Chamber of Commerce, the National Association of Realtors, pharmaceutical and medical organizations, Boeing, and AT&T. But there's now another player at the table: Silicon Valley, in record-breaking time, has contributed an amount comparable to these well-established industries. "We've seen their presence grow and we've also seen gleaming towers to technology spring up and house Google and all the rest," says Krumholz, referring to new Silicon Valley offices in the nation's capital, hubs for their lobbying.

Alphabet, the holding company that owns YouTube, Google, and other Google properties in its restructured new form, spent just over $18 million on lobbying in 2017, according to the CRP. Amazon spent $12.8 million.

Facebook spent $11.5 million. Collectively with Apple, spending amounted to around $50 million in 2017. In the 2016 presidential race, Hillary Clinton was their top recipient with $4 million.

Even with Donald Trump elected, Silicon Valley's influence looks set to continue to grow. Peter Thiel as Trump delegate, campaign donor, and early member of his White House transition team is perhaps the most obvious example of how these ties continue.

What's unique about Silicon Valley's influence in Washington?

"It's complicated," says Krumholz. "They are, in one way, just another industry. They represent jobs, and to the degree they represent jobs, constituents are going to care about them. And of course, they care about the amazing products they produce. But they also have popular appeal. They have wealth, and they have the expertise that the government needs. They *are* the communications industry. It's not like agriculture or defense." Silicon Valley players combine hard and soft power and everything in between.

Partly, there's a lack of understanding of what this means in Washington, says Krumholz: "There are going to be members of Congress who are hostile to Silicon Valley, perhaps because they don't understand it, perhaps even more because its perceived to be allied with the Democratic Party, and Republicans [as of 2017] are in the majority now. And of course there are those in Silicon Valley who still feel superior to Washington and don't really want to have to play this game because they think they can do a better job and wish that they could automate Washington—as opposed to leaving it to the legacy system that has grown up here."

She adds: "But there's still talk of revolutionizing politics and I think many of us are still waiting for technology to, if not revolutionize Washington, then to revolutionize the way Americans participate in politics."

"Government" and "politics," of course, mean a lot of different things to a lot of different people. And it varies by country. In the U.S., "government" is part civil, part military, part federal, part state, part local, and part law enforcement. It is also NASA and health care, Medicare. It's national parks. It's everything from your driver's license to your taxes to assistance when your boat sinks out in the ocean. There are so many different interactions, and people feel differently about each one. But the overall concept of "government" seems to be coming up for scrutiny.

"Politics" has different but equally discouraging perception issues. If Brexit and the U.S. election were votes against state dominance, young people (who voted to remain in the EU and for Hillary Clinton) were "pro" state. Nevertheless, this same group is disengaged in politics and voting systems and is suspicious of politicians.

Voter turnout in 2016 dipped to nearly its lowest point in two decades, with approximately 55 percent of voting-age citizens casting ballots in the presidential election—the lowest turnout since 1996, when 53.5 percent of eligible citizens voted. "Most Americans are checked out," Krumholz says. "Many of them are still enduring economic hardship from the economic crisis, and more importantly from forty years of wage stagnation. There is such a small percentage of Americans who are active in politics at any level.

"You would think there would be a price to pay for producing nothing but gridlock, but a do-nothing Congress and a diminishment of government power and authority is what some people want," she observes. "There has not been a price to pay thus far. Maybe that is where we're headed: rather than some kind of technological solution to wider participation and democracy, a withering of the democratic process. I don't know. But at some point, it ceases to become a democracy, it begins to be a different form of government."

"People are cynical, they don't believe that the people in charge have their best interests [at heart]," agrees Macon Phillips, former coordinator at the U.S. Bureau of International Information Programs and former White House director of new media. Phillips, who in person is tall and preppy, is musing on this topic from a café in Dupont Circle. Phillips was also a digital strategist on the Obama election campaign, and has spent his career trying to transform legacy organizations for the digital era, but with a sense of conscience. "There is a widely held view that it's inefficient and out of date . . . A generation has grown up having seen the record industry fall apart and die, be disrupted, the newspaper industry fall apart and die, be disrupted. I think that one of the big questions that we have to grapple with, as people who care about institutions, is what part of the government needs to fall apart and what part of the government is worth saving? And that's a very difficult challenge."

It helps that, as consumer brands, Silicon Valley companies seem more accountable to the populace than politicians, and elections are daily, not every four years. This change is coupled with a rising sense of citizen consumerism, one where consumers are more politicized and using their buying power to effect change—they can withdraw from a service or wage social media outrage when they dislike a brand's behavior, prompting those brands to respond, which creates the perception of control.

Even in the wake of tumultuous political events, it is not the polling stations but these new media platforms—Twitter, Instagram, Facebook—that millennials are using to express their newly energized political views. So far with limited focus or effectiveness. Facebook live videos are being shared. Memes are being uploaded. Protests on a scale rarely seen are being held, and yet, in March 2017's Los Angeles mayoral election, only 12 percent of voters cast a ballot. Less than two months earlier, 500,000 to 750,000 people, 20 percent of the city's entire population, took part in the Women's March, an event largely organized on social media.

These problems are not unique to the U.S., though. The breakdown of trust between governments and citizens is happening globally. Some blame social media for propelling divisive political discourse and say governments haven't been quick enough to respond and have thereby made themselves irrelevant. Elsewhere, it's argued that globalization itself has made it impossible for regional governments to retain power because they can't guarantee security and jobs in the face of such a potent, ubiquitous force. There have been examples of increased nationalism and retrenchment, but are those the ultimate answer? As trans-border, consumer-centric entities, Silicon Valley companies are in a prime position to trump regional governance and are already mobilizing memberships and citizens to push forward their agenda.

And it's an agenda that, in the U.S., is at odds with President Donald Trump's. Silicon Valley favors scientific research, believes renewable energy is the future, and wants automation. Trump, during his 2016 campaign, promised to return jobs to the U.S. and appeared to believe that global-warming fears were overblown. (Former White House chief of staff Reince Priebus told Fox News at the end of 2016 that Trump thought climate change was "a bunch of bunk," but that he'd "have an open mind and listen to people.") Where Silicon Valley sees the world as borderless and globalized, Trump wants to build a wall. Yet in some ways their missions are aligned, too. After all, few industries will benefit more than Silicon Valley if more aspects of government are privatized.

From Platforms to Politics

It's fair to say that Silicon Valley has historically regarded government, and governance, with a degree of snobbery—as an interference and a slow-moving beast. But this view has evolved as tech companies have matured and grown, coming up against many different areas of regulation, requiring the hiring of policy heads to navigate political systems. Entrepreneurs have recognized the opportunity in government contracts and influence. As these companies' success has grown, so too has their expanded mission and self-belief in rethinking all systems, including government.

"When I first arrived in Silicon Valley, there were zero political interests by Silicon Valley people," comments Shervin Pishevar, the former executive chairman of Hyperloop One and managing director of Sherpa Capital. "There was also a snobby view of L.A. and media and Hollywood. And all of those forms of hubris were obviously wrong. There's a codependence and a symbiosis between all three."

The main interaction between the latest wave of Silicon Valley brands and government has been tracked back to 2011, when venture capitalist John Doerr hosted a now-storied dinner at his home attended by Barack Obama, Steve Jobs, and Mark Zuckerberg. Jobs, according to his biographer Walter Isaacson, had to be persuaded to attend and came away frustrated, complaining: "The President is very smart [but] he kept explaining to us reasons why things can't get done. It infuriates me." Could this be one of the patronizing CEO conversations Obama was referring to in his Pittsburgh address about Silicon Valley execs thinking they can run government?

Since then, the relationship between Silicon Valley and the government has grown with each company's scope and complexity. Silicon Valley has an official body, FWD.us, a lobbying organization to advance key policies that serve its interests. It was cofounded in 2013 by Mark Zuckerberg (among others) as an advocacy group for Silicon Valley, with a focus on immigration reform. It raised $50 million in funding and was backed by Bill Gates.

On the lobbying front, Silicon Valley's first spike of presence was linked to big-policy debates such as Obamacare and the financial crisis of 2008, along with important technology battles. Much of this is par for the course. In the life of any corporation, when it reaches a certain size it needs to fit with current policy and understand legislation.

The influx of tech has led to something of a cultural change in Washington, DC, though. "I really felt it more in the last five or six years," Edward Alden said in 2016. Alden is the Bernard L. Schwartz senior fellow at the Council on Foreign Relations, specializing in U.S. economic competitiveness. "You see representatives of these companies at a lot more events. You really saw it with the effort in the second term of the Obama administration to get immigration reform. They enlisted the tech companies at a far deeper level than I've ever seen before."

Yet it was through two acts of legislation that Silicon Valley's approach started to change tack. Here Silicon Valley realized its power and switched from schmoozing to defiance, mobilizing its mass consumer reach to squash the proposed controls in new legislation. The Stop Online Piracy Act (SOPA) 2012 and the PROTECT IP Act (Preventing Real Online Threats to Economic Creativity and Theft of Intellectual Property Act, or PIPA) 2011 focused on enforcing sanctions for cybersecurity and against copyright infringement and piracy; they saw the first coordinated action by Silicon Valley against the government.

In response to attempts to control these companies' platforms and make them accountable for copyright infringement, Google and English Wikipedia, along with a few thousand smaller sites, coordinated an all-out internet blackout and elsewhere encouraged petitions to protest the bills. The legislation was positioned as censorship, anti–free speech, and against the freedom of the web. In response, the Recording Industry Association of America (RIAA) said: "It's a dangerous and troubling development when the platforms that serve as gateways to information intentionally skew the facts to incite their users and arm them with misinformation," and "it's very difficult to counter the misinformation when the disseminators also own the platform." Both acts were subsequently abandoned.

It set a precedent for tapping the internet's pervasive use among consumers (and therefore, the power of its overlords to effect change in its interests) that has since been repeated and has almost become de facto policy (without much challenge, in the U.S. at least). Uber now has an elaborate system of staging coups when it moves in to cities, using lobbying, grassroots campaigning, sending email blasts to its membership, and undercutting traditional certified taxis with cheaper fares (economies of scale—and repeated rounds of funding—means it can afford not to be profitable, even now, which puts taxis on a back foot). Uber has mastered using its members as a mass pressure group against controls on its way of working: direct messaging campaigns to drivers, new platforms and microsites dedicated to championing its cause, and engaging members and intimidating government officials.

"They're really trying to change the narrative," says Alden. "You have stultifying government regulation on one side, and liberation, freedom, and consumer choice on the other. They've done a really good job of framing that. I think it has really restricted the willingness and ability of governments to constrain their activities to a great degree."

The role of "Hero" vs. "Big Bad Government" is one that Silicon Valley continues to actively cultivate in its marketing and messaging. One case in point is that of Apple vs. the FBI following the December 2015 terrorist attack in San Bernardino, California, in which Apple, in its defiance of the government, became the arbiter of privacy rights. And the government became the distrusted prying eyes. Following a mass shooting that left fourteen people dead and twenty-two seriously injured, the FBI in its investigation approached Apple to unlock an iPhone discovered at the home of one of the shooters to extract allegedly important information. Apple refused to create new software that could unlock the shooter's personal password on the grounds that it would create a back door to abusing the privacy of all citizens.

"The implications of the government's demands are chilling. If the government can use the All Writs Act to make it easier to unlock your iPhone, it would have the power to reach into anyone's device to capture their data," wrote Apple CEO Tim Cook in a letter to Apple customers. "The government could extend this breach of privacy and demand that Apple build surveillance software to intercept your messages, access your health records or financial data, track your location, or even access your phone's microphone or camera without your knowledge." The Apple chief said the firm didn't take lightly the decision to oppose the order, but "we must speak up in the face of what we see as an overreach by the U.S. government."

The same rhetoric has been used to protect encrypted WhatsApp data in the UK. In April, Home Secretary Amber Rudd called on the company to allow messages to be intercepted, after it was discovered a terrorist had used the messaging platform before the 2017 attack on parliament. "We need to make sure that organizations like WhatsApp, and there are plenty of others like that, don't provide a secret place for terrorists to communicate with each other," Rudd commented on a BBC TV show.

The rise of technological civil disobedience grows every day, and is being propelled by the notion that government does not understand innovation and should not hold it back.

"Innovators and organizations are essentially bringing an end to the traditional regulatory process, and even traditional forms of democratic regulation," says Adam Thierer, a senior research fellow with the Technology Policy Program at the Mercatus Center, George Mason University. They're just doing their own thing, says Thierer, because the world we now live in is so highly decentralized, decontrolled with democratized innovation. "It confronts us with the hard choice about who makes the law for this new world that we're living in. What is law? What is governance?"

Social Politics

Barack Obama was, in many ways, America's first Facebook president, using the popular platform to connect to audiences. He was aided by Facebook cofounder Chris Hughes, who played a key role in Obama's election with Facebook as a mobilizing platform. By 2016, there was even an Obama chatbot, designed to let users contact the president via Messenger. The Clinton campaign continued in the same vein.

Social media has become integral to both political and government communications, and within that engine has made the state dependent on Silicon Valley as a vendor. It's also decentralized the traditional, verified means of communication such as the press. (See Trump and his use of Twitter.) In essence, Silicon Valley platforms have become the government's biggest intermediary to its audiences. And candidates' biggest marketing tool.

As our media consumption becomes digital, and mobile, and government advertising efforts migrate to these platforms, Facebook and Google are the beneficiaries of government's major advertising purchases through campaigns for the military, health, and other various services. Federal government spending on advertising totaled $996 million a year, according to a 2016 study by the Government Accountability Office (GAO). Coca-Cola spent nearly four times that the same year. Substantial portions of the government's ad spending now go to Silicon Valley, though it's hard to measure, as GAO commented: "The total scope of federal public relations activities is largely unknown. A number of factors make it difficult to quantify the resources the federal government devotes to public relations. These factors include the expanded use of web-based platforms, such as Facebook and Twitter." In 2014–2015 the *Guardian* reported that the British government spent £289 million on all marketing activity—with a significant increase in the digital and social media budget, a big chunk of which presumably went to Facebook and Google. (Though, the British government was one of a few organizations that withdrew advertising from Alphabet companies in 2017, after ads appeared next to extremist content on YouTube.)

But there's little transparency on how much of this money goes to platforms like Facebook, Twitter, and Google for promotion.

Social media has transformed politics in a few ways. It is now a primary channel of promotion, because all of our media consumption is becoming digital. But it is also measurable and even predictable via algorithms, allowing for new insights and incredibly nuanced understanding of consumer sentiment and the messages people receive. Data analytics teams and programmatic adverts are now part and parcel of elections—putting Silicon Valley once again in the driver's seat as experts. It also gives them a unique understanding of the electorate. Decentralizing what were once formal communication channels and processes has made a big impact on how we interact with politicians and government. It's made them more accessible, modern, and human, but at the same time has undermined their stateliness.

Macon Phillips tracks the use of Facebook by the U.S. government back to 2008. "Facebook was a big part of the 2008 election campaign," he says.

"It was focused on organizing on college campuses . . . Early on, social media was seen as having an impact on politics and campaigns, but was not as much something people thought about in terms of governance. That changed with Obama and other leaders, but really with Obama."

Today, that change is even more prevalent: "You've seen all the social media companies develop Washington, DC offices, trying to work with people in government on how to use their platforms and how to advertise on their platforms," says Phillips. President Obama, Hillary Clinton, and President Trump all have active social media accounts with millions of followers. Clinton, in a move of PR mastery, created a Twitter campaign during the 2016 presidential race that generated donations to the Clinton campaign from Donald Trump's tweets. Having a social media presence has become part and parcel of being a modern candidate with millennial appeal.

These platforms and search engines are not just fully integrated into politics, but almost, like the press, seen as another "estate." "In a debate, Hillary Clinton said, 'Donald Trump said these things, just Google it.' I think that's really interesting . . ." relates Phillips. "It's like 'don't trust me, trust a third party.'" Google, in other words, has become the ultimate fact-checker.

Live-streaming video is another powerful new tool with the potential to change political conversation, one that is being used as a virtual citizen-policing tool of police and government activity. Civil rights activist De-Ray McKesson live-streamed his arrest at a Black Lives Matter protest in July 2016; the video was rapidly viewed more than 650,000 times. In October 2016, 40,000 watched as actress Shailene Woodley live-streamed her arrest for protesting against the Dakota Access Pipeline. Woodley's Facebook page was viewed 4.7 million times and the video shared over 88,000 times just ten days after it was posted.

In 2016, J. Walter Thompson charted this in a study dubbed "The Political Consumer." We examined how celebrity culture, millennials, and brands were becoming more political generally, driven by social media. A nationwide survey of 1,000 U.S. consumers revealed interesting results. Young people view live-streaming on platforms like Facebook Live as more authentic than other media. Fifty-one percent of Generation Z respondents and 56 percent of millennials in the study said live video on social media played an important role in political discussions. (Gen Z is the teenage generational cohort defined by marketers as being born somewhere between the mid 1990s and early 2000s. Today they span roughly twelve to nineteen years old.)

Which again gives Silicon Valley platforms such as Twitter, Facebook, and YouTube a unique vantage point in the political landscape. "I think we're starting to land on a real power dynamic in terms of these companies. They make those choices, they control those algorithms," says Phillips. And so, they control the conversation.

Trans-border Systems

In many ways, focusing on geographic governance when it comes to Silicon Valley is beside the point, because this group of businesses transcends geographic legislation and boundaries. While headquartered in the U.S., these businesses move beyond borders and are functioning as transnational communities.

Amazon has already become its own global government system. It sets its own laws, pricing, and terms—the consumer is always first. It is building schools, postal networks, and entertainment from the ground up. It is a truly global commerce company, too, expanding to Japan, India, and beyond. And, as it starts to co-opt every single aspect of how consumers interact with the internet, it is becoming a highly intelligent, highly personalized shopping machine. There's Amazon Look, which lets us snap our photos of our new and old wardrobe pieces and get crowd-sourced recommendations while recording what we've worn every day (and Amazon noting whether we've gained weight using photosensitive technology). There's Amazon Echo being used to fact-check the president's birthday (inching ground from Google) as well as help consumers shop. There's Amazon Dash buttons, connected to any given number of household brands, that then informs Amazon how much soda or detergent we need how often. (Little wonder, rather than giving this business to Tide, Coca-Cola, or Colgate, they're now producing their own private label versions of these products. Amazon is becoming all-seeing and all-knowing. It is also, increasingly, more trusted than the government.)

In 2016, Jane K. Winn, an outspoken professor of law at the University of

Washington, published the paper "The Secession of the Successful: The Rise of Amazon as Private Global Consumer Protection Regulator." It addressed the potent combination of scale and consumer-centric approach within companies such as Amazon. (Winn is an expert in cyber, digital, privacy, and e-commerce law.) She argues that, as the ultimate global consumer-centric company, Amazon has essentially become its own nation-state, serving the needs of its "people," but, as a result, also harming providers, brands, and, increasingly, governments, too.

Winn describes Amazon as acting like a "private regulator" in this respect: "The rise of global platforms, such as Amazon, Google, Apple, Facebook, and Microsoft, that own global online marketplaces and simultaneously act as their primary regulators, calls to mind the idea of the 'secession of the successful,' as described by Robert Reich in 1991—the withdrawal from civil society of the wealthy and powerful into private gated communities."

This melding of marketplace and regulator is good for consumers in many ways, for now, but bad for suppliers, which are losing control over their prices or terms because of Amazon's scale. "Amazon's status as the primary de facto regulator of the marketplace it owns, combined with its single-minded pursuit of customer satisfaction, contributes to relations with its employees and suppliers that are often profoundly problematic," Winn explains in her paper. "When a platform operator is also the primary regulator of the market it creates, negative spillover effects may occur: squeezing employees and suppliers to ensure that consumers get whatever they want merely pushes conflict from one part of the platform 'ecosystem' to another."

This ultimately does not make online commerce fairer overall, she concludes in her paper. Which could be prophetic. Amazon is consumer-first right now because it's still trying to win us over. But when it becomes a monopoly, we too will become like its suppliers—forced to abide by its rules, systems, and practices, much like the evil dominating corporations that took over banana republics or dictatorships.

Consumers might be in the driver's seat at Amazon in the short-term, but the company is set upon monopoly of all consumer purchases. When it owns every category of consumer spending, and every other outlet has been destroyed, it will fully set its own terms. Left with no other options, the consumer will be forced to abide by them.

Winn believes the digital nature of these companies enables them to be much more responsive than governments as civic systems. Unlike governments that are paper-heavy, person-heavy, and still resolutely analog in many instances, digital companies—particularly ones that we interact with constantly—these are living, breathing, measurable, and instantly readable organisms that are extremely agile. They could apply this ability to governance and many government systems.

"There's a reason why Amazon is the world's most progressive and effective consumer-protection regulator—everything's happening in a fishbowl," says Winn over the phone from Washington one afternoon. "They have all the behavioral data . . . It's like the old Roman Catholic canon law, or the *lex mercatoria* of the City of London. Google is a regulator for the Google platform; Apple is a regulator for the Apple platform; Amazon is a regulator for the Amazon platform. And, because everything is happening in the Cloud, and everything is 100 percent transparent, they have the most breathtaking enforcement capacity at practically zero cost. That's why they're more effective [at ruling] than governments."

After all, Uber is able to mediate commissions based on the size of its audience, driver membership, the weather, demand, and any number of factors at rapid pace. Even when it works against drivers. Uber famously tiptoes around the language of employer to avoid having responsibility for worker benefits—they are "partners"! Yet it exerts extraordinary controls over their income and rights. It has flouted the law on frequent occasions, propelled by the endorsement of consumer buy-in and scale.

The use of algorithms, and the fact that we effectively live on these platforms, enables Silicon Valley companies to respond in not just real time but on an anticipatory basis, because they know our behaviors, desires, faults, and positive actions, and they cross-pollinate behaviors in new ways that the government cannot. Under their regime we are constantly measured and monitored beings. All of this, putting privacy to one side, is right now helping us as consumers. It's creating highly personalized recommendation lists. It's anticipating when we might need to purchase shampoo and what brand we might like. But as their power becomes all-encompassing, our ability to control their reach will disappear.

Attempts have been made to marshal the borderlessness of this group by creating global trade agreements with the World Trade Organization, but those have been largely unsuccessful. Regional book and entertainment rights, for example, which used to be brokered and sold by geographic area (the reason you cannot watch a movie in a certain country), are becoming less easy to enforce.

GAFA is eroding these rights in a variety of ways. "We call it statutory obsolescence or creeping deregulation," says Winn. "There is hard law and soft law. Old-fashioned command-and-control mandatory regulations, such as the speed limit, are hard law. Over the course of the last thirty years, more and more forms of international cooperation, incentives, and collaborative frameworks have emerged—that's soft law. The government uses the law to invite people to behave in a certain way, but it doesn't mandate it and it doesn't punish them for not doing it." So, they don't.

Richard Hill, principal of Hill & Associates in Geneva, Switzerland, and a tech policy consultant, believes the reason Silicon Valley's power on an international stage has been allowed to get so out of hand is that, historically, it's been linked to America's geopolitical strategy for dominance. Their strength has been good for business and America's interests, so it's not made sense to curtail them—until now.

"You can't blame Google, you have to blame the government for not doing its job, which is reining these guys in. That's really the guilty party," he says. "And to some extent you can't even blame the U.S. government because this is tied in with its geopolitical and geo-economical strategy." In other words, these companies have become synonymous with the future, progress, and money for America. Who would want to fight that? Who has the power to?

Efficiencies That Erode

As Silicon Valley's power grows, government is getting weaker.

The Brookings Institution, a nonprofit public-policy organization whose mission is to "conduct in-depth research that leads to new ideas for solving problems facing society at the local, national, and global level," conducted a sobering study titled "Local Government 2035: Strategic Trends and Implications of New Technologies." It shows that many of the technologies being created by Silicon Valley will either put more pressure on government resources or radically reduce revenues. And this change in lots of ways puts Silicon Valley in prime position to take over and provide privatized versions of government services.

The Brookings study paints a picture of local governments whose legislation is behind the times. Regulating drones in terms of privacy and airspace control is just one example, as it requires investment in both technology and year-round resources. There are new privacy rights to protect as more and more aspects of the way we live become powered, and readable, by technology, sensors, and more. Helicopters and airplanes are all tightly controlled. What does it mean when we're getting Dominos pizzas delivered by drones or autonomous robots on the street? And what guardrails should you put around it? Amazon and Google have reportedly already started creating their own air traffic control system. Where is the state? These are entirely new mediums and behaviors, with real civic implications that governments need to find ways to monitor effectively.

Elsewhere, new technology could displace much-needed revenue. Automated cars will (in theory) eradicate parking tickets, speeding tickets, and other fines: "Cities in California collect, on average, $40 million annually in towing fees that they divide with towing firms. Simply put, the hundreds of millions of dollars generated from poor driving-related behaviors provide significant funding for transportation infrastructure and maintenance, public schools, judicial salaries, domestic violence advocacy, conservation, and many other public services," the report states. Mobile phones are helping late-running consumers dodge fines by paying for parking meters remotely, further displacing revenue. And if automated cars mean fewer accidents, it will impact revenue to insurance agencies. Silicon Valley technologies, through automation or by creating new things that need regulating, will collectively run down the state even further.

Then there's the massive job loss due to automation: 47 percent of jobs in the U.S. are at risk of being automated within twenty years, according to the Oxford Martin School at Oxford University's 2013 study "The Future of Employment: How Susceptible Are Jobs to Computerization?" Robots will replace more workers. The result of all this will be budget deficits and unemployment. "Smart leaders are realizing this 'inconvenient truth' about the changing roles of government in the society of tomorrow and are beginning to look for solutions," says the report. "Finding solutions won't be easy, but it is a step in the right direction for local governments to take control of their destiny instead of allowing their role to be usurped by technology, citizens, or private entities."

There is an urgent need for comprehension and foresight on the part of the government, which could course-correct, take advantage of, or mitigate against some of the more troubling effects of all these new products, innovations, and services. After all, with new technologies, historically, new taxes and revenue streams have always emerged. As the car industry boomed, parking and driving regulations became a source of income. New tax structures could be introduced for digital platforms and services. While governments are not fully exploring the long-term impact of innovation, consumers are also propelling them forward. Let's not forget, most of these new products and services are beneficial and money-saving for people. But would they like them so much if they knew the consequences? Will it take skies, greyed by flocks of drones carrying Dominos pizza boxes, to make people think again? Quite often, these things take a jarring event, or a tipping point, to create clarity. In the UK, the disastrous tragedy of the fire at Grenfell Tower in 2017, which killed seventy-one low-income residents, shone a light on privatization and its pitfalls in replacing the state. It prompted a collective debate about Britain's national values, and a resurgence of its social conscience. Perhaps something similar will need to break, not bend, to illuminate the power shift happening because of technology.

Hacking the Government

Will the nation-state fight back against Big Technology's practical and ideological creep on its sovereignty? Part of the reason tech is winning is not simply about money and innovation, but cultural influence. Does government, the state, and even democracy need a rebrand?

Silicon Valley has become part of the American narrative for innovation and invention, and we're bombarded by the tech-friendly press with the idea that the iconic brands and leaders of Silicon Valley have been the spearhead of innovation, not the government. Yet Silicon Valley was started, and originally funded, by the government in collaboration with Stanford University. But this fact can't compete with the mythology of bootstrapping Silicon Valley deities leaping on unicorns and saving the world.

In his book *The Secret History of Silicon Valley*, Steve Blank explains that "In the 1950s and '60s, the U.S. military funded about a third of all technology research in our research universities, a big number. For example, at Stanford in 1966, 35 percent of all the funding in electronics came from classified programs. And Stanford was not unique. MIT, University of Michigan, Georgia Tech, Caltech, you name it, all were funded by U.S. federal government military programs of the Cold War."

We don't give government the credit for any of this because governments aren't built to promote themselves. Or communicate their achievements unless it's in the run-up to reelection. Perhaps the government should start a rebrand making the case not only for all it does, but for all the innovative things it has achieved.

An interesting case study is the nonpartisan voter registration and turnout organization Vote.org. Rather than rebranding government, it's trying to rebrand democracy itself, encouraging people of all ages and backgrounds to vote. Backed by Silicon Valley fund Y Combinator, Vote.org seeks to use technology, mobile messaging, and targeted offline campaigning to encourage people (particularly low-turnout groups) to vote and participate in democracy. Founder and CEO Debra Cleaver has spoken extensively of the need to make democracy and voting habitual and normalized among people of all ages—by approaching it as a marketer. "If Democracy had a CMO, I'd fire them," she has joked. Meanwhile, her Twitter bio reads: "Voter turnout is low because we live in a country where Columbus Day is a holiday and Election Day isn't."

Vote.org's campaigning was seen as a key driver in the record black turnout in the 2017 Alabama state election. It spent $658,000 in the final four weeks of the race in a targeted campaign. The group bought 140 billboards around the state. It also sent black voters direct mail and over 600,000 text messages with information on their local polling locations. Maybe government should take a similarly proactive approach.

Megan J. Smith, former CTO under Obama, tried to correct this disconnect between young people and government. Smith, the White House's third CTO and the first woman to take the job, is a former Google VP. She's also the woman who, perhaps more than any other, sought to claw back some of the power balance between the government and Silicon Valley—while making sure the government does a few things that Silicon Valley is not doing: one, making itself accessible to a more diverse workforce. And two, giving credit to women in the story of innovation.

Smith has enjoyed none of the adulation that Silicon Valley's male leaders do, though perhaps she doesn't court it. She is a genuine tech nerd and completely at odds with how pop culture and media has come to paint the stereotypical type-A cocky Google employee. She's frequently found at conferences championing the positive sides of technology. I've attended tours around the Consumer Electronics Show in Las Vegas led by Smith—gamely and enthusiastically showing a gaggle of women the latest tech innovations. She favors simple grey pantsuits, has bobbed hair, and speaks in a generous, soft-spoken way that belies her massive influence.

During her tenure with the government, Smith led key initiatives to open up STEM careers to more diverse socioeconomic groups and regions in the U.S. She created fast-track training programs and introduced programs to promote STEM subjects to girls and women. She actively tried, through speeches and interviews, to write women back into the history of U.S. tech innovation, a field still largely attributed to lone-wolf male figures.

Strange that Smith herself has never ended up with a *Bloomberg Businessweek* cover feature akin to her male counterparts. But then she's not digging a hole in a parking lot like Elon Musk. And she's not a man. (Musk's new venture, Boring Company, was formed after he got frustrated by L.A. traffic and decided to start digging in a SpaceX parking lot to develop a new tunnel system to solve it. Rather than being regarded as crazy, this wound up on the cover of the business rag—as seems to be the way with anything Musk does.) Though to be fair to Musk, this tunnel system now actually seems to be under way.

Much is made of the "revolving door" between the White House and Silicon Valley, and in some instances as a response to the power of Silicon Valley, it has been strategically driven by the U.S. government. It's pragmatic—if you can't beat them, join them. Or get them to join you, even temporarily.

Smith, who spent eleven years at Google, introduced "tours of service" at the White House, bringing in tech talent to work on digital platforms, strategy, and systems, a project framed almost like the Peace Corps. She led efforts to embrace Silicon Valley in new ways: getting the White House access to startups and innovation with a venture-capital-type fund, allowing the government to invest in new technologies quickly, without a lengthy procurement process. She also made sure technologists were more involved in the early stages of developing government platforms.

"She's done more than anybody else I know, certainly in the last eight years, to encourage people who ordinarily spend their whole careers at Google or Apple or Tesla or Uber to take a year or two off and come into government and be a part of a team," says Chris Kirchhoff, then partner at the Department of Defense's Silicon Valley office DIUx (Defense Innovation Unit Experimental), who collaborated closely with Smith. We talk one afternoon in late 2016, amidst the transition into the Trump administration. His phone is pinging, doubtlessly with inquiries about what the future holds for the unit, but he's calm and upbeat. "Her fundamental insight is the right one, which is that the commercial technology world is booming right now, and if we don't have people from that world who do what she calls 'term tours' in government, as a part of our policy teams, we're really going to be falling behind. So many public-policy challenges today involve technology either as an opportunity or, frankly, as a threat or a challenge."

In May 2016, Secretary of Defense Ash Carter announced expansion of the DIUx Silicon Valley office. A White House statement explained: "In this new era of distributed innovation, many federal departments are working on the major challenge and opportunity to reinvent how they engage with the technology industry, so that many more technologies developed by commercial firms and startups are acquired and adopted by government.

"This is especially true in national security, which must adapt from a Cold War–era posture of having a near-monopoly on funding advanced technology, to a world in which the commercial technology market is now many times larger and making major innovations in commercial space, robotics, data science, and many other areas of relevance to national security."

The office would "help recruit more Americans from the tech sector into government, so that more of our best and brightest innovators have a chance to join with talented colleagues in government to serve a tour of duty in government, collaborating to solve our toughest national-security challenges," it said.

The office where Kirchhoff is partner is designed to explore this part of the tech sector. It has special acquisitions authority that allows it to interact in very rapid fashion with startup firms. The unit is looking at five areas: artificial intelligence; the commercial space; network technology and cybersecurity; autonomy; and life- and bio-sciences. At the end of the government fiscal year in 2016, the fund had made investments worth $36 million.

It's difficult to tell the extent to which Silicon Valley has a genuinely different or superior approach to innovation than government does, or if it's simply money and hubris. Kirchhoff thinks there is a fundamental difference. "Unquestionably, the tech economy is one of the few sectors of the economy where somebody will literally hand tens of millions of dollars to a group of young and eager people that are trying to do something new, and wish them luck. And really try and support them as they try to pull off something grand," Kirchhoff says. "That's just not true in most of the other industrial sectors of our economy and certainly not true in the public sector, where that kind of risk-taking is not part of the culture."

Though Mariana Mazzucato, notably outspoken economist, has argued that it's precisely because the government doesn't rely on immediate profitability that high-profile experiments and breakthroughs have occurred during its time. And that to over-fetishize Big Tech's ability will only result in less funding for these pursuits, which will be damaging.

But there are obvious conflicts with Silicon Valley's role leading innovation: one is relying on Silicon Valley for its expertise in order to make judgments about policy. "Governments are using multi stakeholders," observes Richard Hill. The narrative is that "problems are too complicated to be solved by government alone, so governments have to work with private companies," he explains. "OK, fair enough. But then private companies get to participate in the decisions."

CTOs, like chief digital officers (CDOs), are part of a new segment of hires at both federal and state levels, since Aneesh Chopra became the first U.S. CTO in 2009. They are cropping up everywhere. Most international governments have them, and so do most brands. Even beauty giant L'Oréal, which is trying to position itself as a tech brand, opened a "tech incubator" in San Francisco in 2016. In essence, it's because tech is everywhere and has become everything. Entire sectors have to consider the User Experience (UX) and ease of navigating its websites. Meanwhile, technology is being employed by consumer packaged goods (CPG) and beauty companies to create new channels to consumers, new diagnostic and personalization tools. We now expect to interact with every brand and every sector with the same ease we do Silicon Valley's platforms.

There are other projects establishing closer ties between government and Silicon Valley innovation. In 2016, the Obama administration invited Silicon Valley experts to Washington to brainstorm ways to fight the militant group Islamic State online. The State Department created the role of representative to Silicon Valley in 2016, appointing Zvika Krieger, who was also director of its Strategy Lab.

Code for America founder and executive director Jennifer Pahlka—who worked as U.S. deputy CTO under President Obama—has started working with President Trump to find new ways to enhance government's use of technology. She's advising the government on a range of issues, such as procurement reform, cloud computing, and user-centered design. Pahlka, like Smith, is a believer in technology's ability to do good in civic life. She has spoken about California's switch from an online food stamp application that took an hour, and was only accessible on desktop computers, to one that can be completed with a smartphone in seven minutes.

What's clear is that in the hands of the right stakeholders, government can use technology to make itself more accessible and user-friendly but also more current in the eyes of young people. Two courses, "Hacking 4 Defense" and "Hacking 4 Diplomacy," were introduced at Stanford University in 2016, also reinvigorating the university labs' legacy of working with government to innovate. These are led by innovation guru and author Steve Blank, with Zvika Krieger teaching the courses.

It's a strange moment as Donald Trump, perhaps one of the most analog and demonstrably anti-modernity presidents, continues to rule. (Antimodern ideologically and in the sense that he still messengers documents and referred to cyber attacks as "the cyber," which would indicate a lack of understanding of complex technology issues. His proficiency in tweeting, on the other hand, is well-known.) Whether this open spirit toward techno-logical innovation continues remains to be seen. Elon Musk, Trump's most controversial backer, has abandoned his position as an advisor, following the president's decision to leave the Paris Climate Accord. Thiel's role in the Trump administration, at least visibly, seems to have been diminished. Many of the programs spearheaded by Smith were publicly funded, and now gov-ernment funding cuts seem to be the mandate. Trump's 2017 budget sliced funding by $3.2 trillion in ten years, cutting all public programs, including many safety net and education programs, while increasing spending on in-frastructure, home defense, and the military. Trump may not be a techie president, but he may need to work more closely with tech companies to en-sure the future of government, and the future success of the U.S. economy.

Puneet Kaur Ahira has worked in both the public and private spheres as a former Googler, and more recently, as special advisor to Megan J. Smith, the former CTO for the United States. She is reflective about her tenure with Smith and President Obama. "I keep coming back to this notion of time. It actually takes a tremendous amount of time to undo everything that's been done. If the next president has four years, how deep will the impact actually be?" she says. "But equally, I also think that in the eight years of President Obama's administration, we only scratched the surface of augmenting gov-ernment services and capabilities with tech and innovation. If you think about all of the areas where there was deep focus—for example, Data-Driven Justice, Computer Science for All, Net Neutrality—these efforts are all still fairly nascent. And increasingly, if you look at the shortlist of priorities, the focus is fixated on survival and security—all these other longer time horizon investments get left lower down on the list."

Ahira was program director for Google's Solve for X community at Google[x], the company's moonshot laboratory focused on developing tech-nologies that could "positively impact billions of people." Before Google, she was a portfolio analyst at Goldman Sachs. She served on the board of directors for Colin Powell's America's Promise nonprofit and cofounded an NGO called Freedom's Answer. She coauthored a book on civic activism under the same title. She was recruited from Silicon Valley to join President Obama's elite tech team inside government.

Alternative training programs and a widened geographic focus for tech training remain crucial, Ahira says: "There's a much larger candidate population who don't look like your typical tech entrepreneur or have a conventional tech background. They don't come from families with a long lineage of engineers; they didn't do computer science as an undergrad. And they might not know anyone else who did." Ahira believes STEM education should be fully integrated into all our education systems, rather than relying on advocacy organizations such as Girls Who Code, to take it to a wider cohort. "We need widespread literacy. We've seen computer science education successfully integrated across the curriculum in the UK. And the most promising spaces are those where the kids are being stretched to apply themselves creatively, critically, and technically," she says. "I think that kind of technical skillset and technical mindset is going to become a prerequisite if we, as citizens, want to have a better handle on what's happening and how it's happening." She adds, prophetically: "Because ultimately, most of this is going to become very political, very quickly."

Indeed. Training people from all walks of life for technological revolution is arguably one of the most urgent huge challenges facing governments. And yet, restricted to government's four-year terms, it's a difficult issue to tackle decisively.

What does she think of Big Tech taking on a bigger civic role in the future? Already, with access to ample funds, it is making inroads in health and education, but also positioning itself as a civic force with Smart Cities and infrastructure. "Lack of diversity becomes an Achilles heel for any team. When you don't have that diversity of background, diversity of thought, diversity of privilege, it leads to incomplete problem solving," says Ahira. "I think the issue of diversity is something that on a surface level is being acknowledged, and there's certainly a lot of painstaking effort given to sourcing the best talent from all over the world. But again, we're just importing this talent into a very ideal scenario, busing them back and forth across an idyllic California landscape. I don't know, it becomes difficult to retain a real empathy for what's going on outside the bubble."

This is shown in the kinds of problems Silicon Valley tackles, as well as its approach to civic projects. We discuss Airbnb's new Samara project in Yoshino, Japan, a community center built in the blossom-laden hills in a small village to revitalize it. The house, a beautiful mixed-use property (you can stay in the attic and take part in tea rituals by day), is an example of Airbnb's aspirational approach to marketing and social-good projects. It's also part of its philanthropic program. "It's more exotic to go to Japan and try to solve a problem outside of any real context you can relate to than it is to look in your own backyard and confront a complex history that has led to homeless veterans and aged-out foster kids camping out every two blocks," says Ahira. "And yet there is such enormous opportunity to deploy our innovation communities and tech platforms on some of these stagnating systemic issues."

Does Silicon Valley care about the whole world? It claims to. That's the narrative it espouses and the one it's using to obtain a greater and greater stake in the way we live. Not just as services but as architects of the future. And the narrative it is using to co-opt new nations on a global scale.

Narrative in all this therefore becomes incredibly important in Silicon Valley's agenda. Despite its famed lack of diversity, Silicon Valley, as intermediaries of news and media, is rapidly becoming the lens on all things and the means to mobilize audiences against government. Its filter is already writ large on our newsfeeds, one that claims to be the voice of "everyone," yet the "everyone" it defines is inherently skewed and narrowed by virtue of this group's privileged makeup. It's also shown, as Ahira observes, in its skewed approach to problems and its general perspective.

Silicon Valley's expanded control of media is now another tool in its soft power arsenal reinforcing this group's powerful cultural influence in avoiding questions and legislation. It has grown key in shifting the power balance with government—as Silicon Valley becomes the vendor, but also controls political dialogue. And in its rapid growth, supplanting media, Silicon Valley is controlling what used to be a check on power itself.

What happens when the lens on power, the media, is diminished and possibly replaced by one of the most powerful sectors that has ever existed?

3

The Fifth Estate

The World's Most Powerful Editor." It's a grand title, and one that Mark Zuckerberg has curiously been running away from since it was awarded to him by Espen Egil Hansen, the editor in chief and CEO of Norway's biggest newspaper, *Aftenposten*, in an open, front-page critique of the Facebook founder. Hansen had penned an outraged letter to Zuckerberg after Facebook took down a post by Norwegian writer Tom Egeland that featured historic images of war. Egeland's offense was posting the Pulitzer Prize–winning photograph "Napalm Girl" of Phan Thi Kim Phuc by Nick Ut, an iconic picture of an anguished and terrified young girl fleeing a napalm attack, widely considered emblematic of the horrors of the Vietnam War. It was removed from Facebook because the nudity in the image was considered indecent. (Less indecent, apparently, is the fact that the pictured women and children were in agony after liquid fire was dropped on them by the American military.) Zuckerberg was charged with censorship and cultural insensitivity. Hansen's letter accused Zuckerberg of thoughtlessly abusing his power over the social media site, which had become a key distributor of news around the globe. "I am upset, disappointed—well, in fact even afraid—of what you are about to do to a mainstay of our democratic society."

In many ways the incident showed what we all know: Facebook, Twitter, and Google are more than social media platforms. The editors of Fleet Street and the news buildings in New York may have been the "Fourth Estate," the check on power before, but today Silicon Valley is supplanting them. They are the new media magnates. (In the case of Amazon's Jeff Bezos, he now owns *The Washington Post*.) With Amazon Echo, we are verbally asking Alexa for the daily news, or scrolling through Apple News. Live events, award shows, and more are being streamed via platforms from Twitter to YouTube. Bloomberg has even launched a built-for-Twitter, twenty-four-hour news platform, TicToc, with a dedicated news team, demonstrating the importance of the platform to news consumption. Facebook is launching original entertainment. Will a news show be next? It's already signed deals with news and entertainment companies Vox Media, BuzzFeed, ATTN, and Group Nine Media. What would a Facebook show look like? Would it be mediated by "likes"? Would global news correspondents and bureaus be replaced by virtual reality headset–wearing avatars, transported to natural disasters as cartoon characters (à la Mark's virtual visit to the wreckage of Puerto Rico)? Would artificial intelligence be used to report basic news stories without the need for verification? And be brought to life by AI presenter bots? Maybe presenters will be done away with altogether. Or perhaps each viewer will be faced by their very own tailored AI-powered avatar presenter based on their likeness, delivering news and angles on coverage skewed to each person's preferences. Will appropriate news content be restrained by the curious and often arbitrary moral dictums already present on Facebook platforms? (Which have become the stuff of comedy BuzzFeed "listicles." During the 2017 Christmas period, a holiday card featuring a painted robin was banned for being too sexual in nature. A picture of a woman giving birth was also banned. Both might easily have appeared in news items on traditional media, in the right context.) It's all possible.

But in this encroachment upon journalism, the Silicon Valley empires are also impeding one of the biggest and most important historic checks of power. One that checks on governments, and one that might have checked on them. One in which professional, fact-checked journalism now sits alongside unverified stories and user-generated content. These companies have become the mediators and curators of the news. The primary channels of the news. And, increasingly, the generators of the news.

The majority of Americans (62 percent) now get news from social media, including 18 percent who do so "often," according to Pew Research Center.

Meanwhile, consumers are cutting the cord from traditional media. Forty percent of millennials are choosing to rely solely on streaming services or the internet. This has democratized access to information, but also put the emphasis on algorithms to prioritize the information when we search for it, or the order within which we see top stories (often powered by how many clicks it has already received, how often it has piqued people's interest, or just advertising). This kind of news, therefore, is dependent on populism and shock value.

Facebook's audience size alone is the same as many media outlets combined. And yet, there's an ongoing tension as this outsized influence collides violently with laissez-faire, automated, or crowd-sourced checks in place of the traditional responsibilities of its newspaper predecessors. It's rapidly getting an audience that leapfrogs any newspaper or credible journalism outlet, but has none of the due diligence or policies of fact-checking that traditional organizations have. However, as horror stories emerge of live videos broadcasting real-life murders, there's an emerging debate about power and its liability.

After a murder was live-streamed on Facebook's video platform in 2017, Facebook blamed the three-hour time lapse in taking it down on users not alerting them to it sooner. Reputable publications such as *The New York Times* and *The New Yorker* still publish corrections even if a company name is misspelled. They are attached to the responsibility of journalism, to the discovery of truth and accuracy.

As media consumption becomes digital, the ability to create highly targeted digital advertising and positioning on platforms like Facebook and Google is packing a powerful punch. It's one which is eroding revenues from traditional media. It's been estimated that in 2016 Facebook absorbed more than $1 billion from the newspaper industry. As they get more influential still, will their own indiscretions hit the top of our newsfeeds?

There have been signs of pushback. In March 2016, brands including Walmart, General Motors, JPMorgan Chase, PepsiCo, Starbucks, and Johnson & Johnson pulled out of YouTube after their ads appeared alongside extremist hate-speech videos and unverified user-generated content, prompting the parent company to review its policy about controls over amateur video. Facebook has hired CNN anchor Campbell Brown to build better relations with news organizations in the wake of the fake news onslaught in 2016. And many have taken comfort in the rising sales of *The New York Times* in the early days of the Trump presidency, celebrating the reinvigoration of good reporting and journalistic values. CNN experienced its most-watched year in 2017 while launching a pro-"facts" campaign championing its journalistic rigor. Culturally, traditional journalism is experiencing a renaissance as iconic news-breaking moments are celebrated (see 2018's *The Post*, starring Meryl Streep, which features *The New York Times* and *Washington Post*'s coverage of the Pentagon Papers, charting America's involvement during the Vietnam War in the 1970s). *The Times, Post,* and *New Yorker* have also had record years, breaking stories on Russia's connection to the U.S. election, and the Trump administration, as well as groundbreaking reports exposing the litany of sexual abuse accusations against Harvey Weinstein, Alabama politician Roy Moore, Vice Media, and others.

But all this is to try to rebel against a tsunami, one in which newspaper organizations are dying. Supporting the best ones, which are still staffed by trained, fact-checking journalists, and seasoned writers, has become positioned alongside the ACLU and other nonprofit organizations almost as a form of benevolence and social good. Not the profit-making business it once was.

Look forward five years, particularly as all media consumption goes digital, and it's difficult to imagine any editorial brand reliant on advertising having a future. It belongs to Facebook, Apple, and Google. Stronger beloved publications will be saved by paid-for subscriptions, but in an era of ubiquitous free content, that will involve a brutal period of Darwinist competition and consolidation. Softer lifestyle categories of media, such as fashion and luxury titles that might have possessed a faint veil of authentic cultural journalism, have already become akin to branded content because of dwindling sales and advertising revenues, and a slow adjustment to the digital space. Or they have been replaced by social media "influencers."

"Fake News," the slogan, the movement, has impacted the credibility of the press. Meanwhile the collective misreading of U.S. election sentiment by respected newspapers has led many to question the continued relevance of journalism as we know it. In fairness, outlets such as *The New York Times* have tried to shake off their elitist, coast-ist progressive image. The wider wave of groundbreaking political stories led by traditional journalists has helped. Still, there have been times when this endeavor has drawn criticism, too. In the wake of the Charlottesville, Virginia, clash between tiki-torch-carrying white nationalists and anti-fascist activists, *The New York Times* sought to shed light on to the pro-Nazi sympathizer mindset by profiling white nationalist Tony Hovater. It was accused of gross insensitivity and of normalizing racism for presenting Hovater in too kind a light. National editor Marc Lacey wrote in a response: "We regret the degree to which the piece offended so many readers. We recognize that people can disagree on how best to tell a disagreeable story. What we think is indisputable, though, is the need to shed more light, not less, on the most extreme corners of American life and the people who inhabit them. That's what the story, however imperfectly, tried to do."

In a poll of 1,000 U.S. consumers conducted by J. Walter Thompson in January 2017, the majority of respondents felt that journalism will be less valuable ten years from now. Fifty-three percent said their perception of television has changed since the presidential election, 48 percent for social media platforms, and 45 percent for online sites. Of those whose opinion of sources has changed, most said it has changed for the worse. Specifically, 69 percent said their opinion of television has changed for the worse, 69 percent said this of social media platforms, and 66 percent said this of online sites.

This echoed Gallup's 2016 poll, which showed trust in journalism at an all-time low. In 2017 it rebounded slightly, moving from 20 percent to 27 percent of people saying they trusted newspapers, but this is still far from the newspaper heyday in the 1980s and 1990s, when 37 percent of people trusted them.

What's clear is that traditional journalism is being challenged, both symbolically and economically, by outside aggressors. It's being positioned as untrustworthy, and irrelevant, while also having its audiences disintermediated (and monetized) by tech giants. But to lose journalism—journalism as we know it—is to lose a critical layer of consumer protection. We lose dialogue, contention, questioning, and investigation, and we end up with a simulated branded-content universe of unchecked influence and action. It could happen sooner than we think. Some believe it already has.

Silicon Valley and the Media

For all the claims of openness, Silicon Valley sees very little media scrutiny. This favorable treatment gets increasingly dangerous as its role becomes more all-encompassing, unchallenged, and amorphous. It's ironic that while undermining the strength of traditional media organizations, coverage celebrating Silicon Valley in newspapers, TV, and magazines is still key in this group's continued dominance as consumer brands and cultural influencers. It's a central component in its relevance and connection to millennials, and in elevating its philosophy and personalities, and pivotal in amplifying Silicon Valley's narrative. In killing traditional media, it's essentially killing one of the chief architects of its mythology.

After all, Silicon Valley doesn't get beaten up by the media often. Many of these companies publish press updates on their websites, although they rarely need to engage in meaningful dialogue or external critique about their practices. Save for the enjoyably quippy irreverence of Recode or the more outspoken newspapers such as the *Guardian* and *New York Times*, many publications praise technology unceasingly. Critiques have ramped up recently in the wake of fears about Big Tech, European Union fines for tax evasion and privacy breaches, Amazon's purported antitrust moves in acquiring Whole Foods (Target, Twitter next?). But this dissent sits within countless websites, print magazines, and bookshelves filled with books venerating tech. Even *Vanity Fair*, a magazine whose roots lie deep in Hollywood, has rapidly expanded its attention on the new celebrities, the techerati—from launching its Hive platform to hosting its New Establishment Summit in Los Angeles, with attendees including Shervin Pishevar and Snapchat CEO Evan Spiegel.

The media historically has been soft on tech companies, and tech companies frequently circumvent the media and issue statements rather than have a dialogue with journalists, which runs squarely counter to their purported openness. "There's a very strong veneration of the founder and the notion of change," says Ravi Mattu, former tech, media, and telecoms editor at the *Financial Times*. "Think about *Wired* magazine, which ran a whole issue with Mark Zuckerberg on the cover, asking if Mark Zuckerberg is going to change the world ... The American Dream becomes personified in the founder of a tech startup, and, fair enough, he's done some amazing things. But the problem is, the construct is bad, because it means people don't ask serious questions of this industry, the way they should do." A more recent *Wired* magazine cover features a beaten-up Mark Zuckerberg following a year of scandal about its role in elections. But this sits within a bigger picture of countless covers, from *Wired* and other titles, celebrating white male tech founders.

Indeed. There's an extremely powerful founder narrative, linked to the American Dream, which drives the sentiment that "who are we to critique these guys?" They have bootstrapped it to become extremely successful as entrepreneurs. Success is inherent to the American DNA; so is entrepreneurship. In the wake of the 2008 economic crisis, millennials faced career stagnation, little opportunity, and economic malaise. These founders, many of whom are millennial-age, have gone out on their own, built businesses, and triumphed despite these challenges. That's an incredibly powerful message to receive—and the reason many millennials cite tech founders as their key influencers (as opposed to, say, celebrities). It also makes questioning them seem, at times, unnecessarily negative.

This bias can also be seen in the initial veneration of Theranos's Elizabeth Holmes. (For the uninitiated: The Palo Alto–based health tech company gained fame for attempting to develop blood tests that required only a few drops of blood and were conducted quickly using proprietary technology at a fraction of the cost of a professional lab. Holmes, only nineteen when the company was founded in 2003, became a celebrity of the tech circuit, attracting major funding, before it all collapsed when the *Wall Street Journal* revealed the company doctored its research.) Prior to these revelations, Holmes was presented as Steve Jobs reborn. "People weren't asking basic questions about that stuff and *Wired* is emblematic of that," Mattu continues. "Do tech publications really question enough of what's going on in that world? I don't think so. *Fast Company* is fun to read, but how much are they just puffing up the dream that we all want to believe in? I'm not talking about mass media and newspapers—the *Wall Street Journal* broke the story on Theranos. But, day-to-day, there's not enough stopping and saying, 'Hold on a sec.' You see it in the way funding rounds are covered. Someone raises X amount of money and is valued at Y. All of a sudden it becomes a breathless story, not someone saying, 'OK, this company just raised a massive amount of money, but it's bullshit.'"

Access to Silicon Valley is strictly controlled, and there is a belief among tech figures that talking directly to audiences is better than being mediated by media (this they have in common with President Trump). But that again becomes a broadcast rather than a dialogue. Facebook now blasts announcements directly on its network. Product launches are tightly controlled. Rhetoric is wildly poetic and self-aggrandizing.

The growing impulse for founders to present themselves as thought leaders is worth noting. From publishing think pieces on Medium, to using Twitter to create followings, or launching popular podcasts and newsletters that chart the latest tech news and events—this is, in its own way, a one-way street, establishing their content and output as a form of media. Andreessen Horowitz (a16z) has long understood the triangle of exposure, visibility, and startup value. It hosts annual summits for executives that feature its companies heavily. These enable a16z to support companies they are invested in yet control the conversation around them. Many tech media companies host events that are reliant upon tech execs taking part, further celebritizing tech founders, but also putting pressure on moderators not to ask tough questions. (Access to these highly private companies has become so difficult that their participation in a panel or discussion alone is enough of a feat for many high-profile events. Jargony, circular, political answers are often given to questions and rarely followed up on by interviewers, lest they burn bridges with the company.)

It's a long walk from the 2010 movie *The Social Network* and its portrayal of Mark Zuckerberg as an unlikeable brat to *Vanity Fair* profiling this group as rock stars. "They have become celebrities as well as geeks who run companies. But they're not geeks. They're now part of the establishment," observes Mattu.

Silicon Valley responds to criticism about its policies, its tactics, and its massive power by simply reiterating its own narrative louder and louder, framing critique as antagonistic to values such as freedom, access to the internet, and human rights. In response to threats of regulation, it claims the internet is "free" and should not be regulated. The message is about "connecting the world," not the reality of "connecting the world in a commercialized space for financial gain by selling your information." In response to calls for more responsibility, critics are called "luddites."

"It's so easy to label somebody who raises issues [or criticism under this mythology] as a luddite, or a critic, or a raging Communist," jokes Julia Powles of the University of Cambridge, who specializes in the interface of law and technology. Powles is also one of the most outspoken opponents of Silicon Valley activity. "If you sat down with anybody—I speak about this stuff as much with people who are not experts as experts—everybody feels the same way," she says, referring to Silicon Valley's all-pervasiveness in our lives. "But then you do feel like you're being a bit paranoid or a bit hypocritical, whatever sensation is needed to start to question it."

One of Powles's critiques is that companies like Google try to frame individual cases within bigger conceptual issues to win public debates. For instance, a case about someone removing outdated, damaging personal information from the internet becomes, in the media, framed as "anti–free speech" and the internet portrayed as an engine of truth. In this "right to be forgotten" case, it was a Spanish lawyer who—when his local newspaper digitized their archive—found that the top search result on his name was a reference to his house going into foreclosure several years prior. The result was defamatory, beyond his control, and no longer relevant. He made a reasonable request to take it down—he'd not given permission for this piece of information to live online forever. But the case spurred a wider debate, engineered by Google, about the right to have access to all information online, and the freedom of the press.

"Google benefited from keeping the debate in abstract terms, ensuring continued support from the media and the loudest members of the public, and provoking knee-jerk, often elliptical, and dehumanized reactions," Powles wrote assessing the case in her 2015 paper "The Case That Won't Be Forgotten." In other words, rather than considering privacy cases individually, the discussion became a question of "Do you want free speech or not?", which isn't exactly the point. It's not like this house listing was in the public interest. It's not like it was even relevant to his abilities as a lawyer. It was about the level of unconscious information that is now accessible to the public due to search engines like Google and their ability to control what information is prioritized. In logistical terms, for Google, it might simply have been the issue that if they allowed this one case to become precedent, it would open up the need to create newly staffed teams to monitor this kind of case. Facebook has already been forced to hire teams of workers to monitor terrorism threats on its social platform. Much as Silicon Valley's platforms and their success is predicated on algorithms to scale and create a massive impact, there are growing instances where, by the sheer magnitude of their audiences, they're being held to account for their actions. If you are the world's only search engine, it can ruin someone's life if the only piece of information about them that comes up in a search is something from a troubled and now bygone period of economic hardship. Especially if they are not public figures. The commercial internet in this way is making us all public figures.

The mythology machine also helps Silicon Valley circumnavigate regulation. In creating a sense of exceptionalism to what they do, the internet becomes viewed as something special and alive that should not be constrained—at least not by government. This can be seen most patently in the debate surrounding net neutrality. In the U.S., before the Federal Communications Commission (FCC) voted to repeal it in 2017, net neutrality legislation introduced under Obama barred ISPs like Comcast, AT&T, and Verizon from paid prioritization or blocking internet traffic, allowing for free search for new businesses and startups. Without it, discovery of new brands, items, and websites becomes commercialized. Interestingly in this instance, Amazon, Facebook, Reddit, Netflix, and Microsoft through the Internet Association (IA) have historically supported keeping net neutrality rules—in part, perhaps, because without them, it gives too much power to the telecoms rather than them as gatekeepers to paid ad searchers.

In almost every aspect of society, we are comfortable with regional regulation. We accept that some drugs are not permitted in the UK. Some food ingredients are more regulated or taxed in one country than another. But the internet is "borderless," aligned with the air and the ocean. And therefore should not be constrained.

Gawker founder Nick Denton believes Silicon Valley won't always be so celebrated. "I actually think it has a high volatility," he says. "When Silicon Valley's on the up, the coverage is breathless and reverential, and when Silicon Valley falls on its face . . . Remember the press coverage after 2000 [the bursting of the tech startup bubble]—it was not generous. There were tech heroes like Carly Fiorina or Elizabeth Holmes at Theranos; women seem to get this more than men, being built up and being knocked down later. It corrects itself rather violently, so the whole process is unhelpful. These people should not have been elevated to the extent that they were, nor are they such terrible human beings that they deserve the humiliation that is visited upon them if they disappoint." (This was evident in the media coverage of Zuckerberg's 2018 Congress appearance.)

Matthew Belloni, executive editor of the *Hollywood Reporter*, gave a talk at TEDxHollywood about the shifting notions of power, influence, and damages in the digital media realm with the rise of Silicon Valley media giants. To an audience of techies, local execs, and me, he pointed to the mistrust of media in our current climate. "At the same time, people are consuming media like they never have before, they're just consuming it in different ways," he explained. "Everything under the sun is media and we're looking to it more than we ever have before."

Belloni talked about a new paradigm, pointing to the instance of country singer Blake Shelton suing *In Touch Weekly* for defamation when it ran a cover falsely claiming he was going to rehab. "What's interesting to me is that defamation law is premised on the need for a mechanism for individuals to stand up to the 'powerful media.' Because for many, many years there has been a powerful media and people had little recourse to respond to that. These days, I would argue that's not the case. Blake Shelton has 17.9 million Twitter followers, most of whom he has been informing repeatedly that this is not true. *In Touch Weekly* has 194,000 Twitter followers. In print, *In Touch Weekly* has a circulation of less than 400,000. So Blake Shelton's message, denying what this outlet is saying, is reaching an audience probably fifteen to twenty times as big. Question: where are the damages?"

To Belloni, notions of power are being completely upturned in this space. "For all that is made about the ubiquity of social media and power of the digital media environment, individuals have much more power now than they did pre–social media. Anyone's message can, on their Facebook or Twitter or Medium or anywhere else, become as powerful as anything said in *The New York Times*. Should the laws reflect that?" In a world where the lines between what is journalism, what is marketing, and what is privacy are so distorted, do we need to find new ways to define right, wrong, and fair? Because it's increasingly nuanced and complex. Or blurred altogether.

There's no doubt that the "power" of traditional media, like that of the government, is being eroded by Silicon Valley and its economic headwinds. Yet, its critics continue to lampoon media and entertainment brands, reasoning not only unfair treatment but their brainwashing influence. Donald Trump has often tweeted against *Saturday Night Live*'s satirical depiction of him—in particular by Alec Baldwin—while also claiming an unfair landscape. *SNL* has around ten million live viewers, Trump has 18.3 million Twitter followers (dependent on how many fake followers he does or doesn't have). Trump is also shutting down critical journalists in news conferences and has held only one press conference after over a year in office. (Though again, as with *The New York Times*'s increased readership, Trump's public criticism of *SNL* seems to have prompted a ratings high for the show.)

Belloni also discussed Hulk Hogan's infamous trial against Gawker Media. Hogan was funded by Peter Thiel and won thanks to those limitless legal resources for a case that might normally have had a very different outcome (more on this later). When a billionaire tech icon like Thiel can affect the course of justice by funding a lawsuit to shut down a media brand, where's the power? Not with the media. Increasingly so.

The current state of publishing and media is reflected in the wide gamut of websites which run from pop-up-dominated sites where unwanted images, videos, and slogans appear like a rash you can't get rid of; or worse, that still the page and movement, from the *Guardian* to Wikipedia, which has gone for a schoolmarmish approach—"If you use it, if you like it, then why not pay for it? It's only fair. Make a contribution"—right through to the *Financial Times* and the *Wall Street Journal* which have instant paywalls. More recently the *Guardian* has taken this begging further: "Unlike many news organizations, we haven't put up a paywall—we want to keep journalism as open as we can. The *Guardian*'s independent investigative journalism takes a lot of time, money and hard work to produce. But the revenue we get from advertising is falling, so we increasingly need our readers to fund us. If everyone who loves our reporting, who likes it, helps fund it, our future would be much more secure. Support the *Guardian* for as little as £1." Between the constant headlines about layoffs, not to mention seeing millimeter-thick magazines in CVS, it paints a sad tale.

Events, summits, and conferences have become a cash cow for media organizations. Editors are wheeled out. Stale coffee, stale pastries, and stale wine served for a few hundred dollars a ticket. Or, in the era of rising ad blocking, many have set up creative branded content "shops" which offer brand advertorials that look and feel like editorial but come priced like ads. For example, *The New York Times* has created T Brand Studios, a branded-content suite that puts branded video documentary content and features alongside traditional content. It's labeled accordingly, but subtly, and the lines are increasingly blurred. Now movies, feature journalism, and podcasts are all being offered in branded form to clients, sitting alongside regular editorial content, as a new revenue stream. Branded "experiential" content has become the latest avenue, seeking to appeal to experience-loving millennials. Media companies such as Refinery29 have started creating ticketed immersive experiences, which combine genuine installations by artists with brand "activations" for companies from Dyson hairdryers (standing in a room of blowing hair devices) to Casper mattresses (jumping on a pile of pillows) to Juicy Couture (standing in a full-size snowglobe). All are mandatorily selfie and Instagram designed.

All this, even before the automation of journalism en masse begins in earnest—in other words, algorithms generating the news stories. This has already been occurring in basic sports reporting. Increasingly, says Richard Hill, a Geneva-based technology consultant, there's "not even a human being involved. There's no value added and that's very dangerous because it's eliminating, basically, investigative journalism. A lot of automated feeds are produced off of the official information that you get from the government or the company.

"There's no more revenue models for the traditional press because the only way you get money is from advertising and online media, but all the advertising is controlled by Google," says Hill. "I see my local newspaper, which has a nice website, they have advertising and they're trying to get money out of that, but you know it's pathetic in the print edition, the number of advertising pages has just dropped."

Denton and many others believe that part of the reason for its shifting fortunes is media's own lack of diversity. It's lost touch with the audience. "Everywhere the media has been looked at as being a national institution, the fourth estate, some mechanism for the dissemination of news and the arbitration of differences. That role has now been lost or superseded," says Denton. "The media is seen by a very large number of people as being not one media, but general liberal media, which is part of, not even the whole of, the elite, progressive viewpoint—an urban, cosmopolitan, internationalist mindset that is probably shared by 5 percent or 10 percent of the population."

The lack of diversity in the media could be viewed as having less to do with self-selecting white privilege and nepotism than with its dwindling position. In many instances, only independently wealthy people can afford to be in journalism anymore. The average salary of a reporter is $43,640. Many millennial twenty-somethings trying to make it in media are having their rents supplemented by their parents. According to a 2016 study by the Institute for Social Research at the University of Michigan, as many as 53 percent of American twenty-somethings in creative careers receive financial help from parents.

Even obtaining a job in journalism, as with TV and many of the creative arts, requires being able to work for free as an intern, ad nauseam (and be cheery about it), live in an urban center, and then work for low wages. It is true that certain segments of the media, especially book and magazine publishing, are overly peopled by the white, liberal elite. But that's also true of Silicon Valley, the de facto new media curating our stories.

And this new media is about as elite, white, and privileged as you can get.

The Valley Wag

Nick Denton arrives at Sant Ambroeus, a little Italian place with red leather banquettes and wood paneling in the Nolita neighborhood of New York City. It's just days after the presidential election in 2016; the timing is fortuitous for me, given tech billionaire Peter Thiel's connection to President Trump and support of his ascent to power. And it's not that much farther—a few months—from the infamous lawsuit that saw Gawker shuttered, and Denton personally bankrupted. Denton walks in as I order coffee.

Denton, a Brit, is an Oxford graduate. In 2002 he founded Gizmodo, a site that covers consumer technology. He created Gawker the same year and eventually Gawker Media housed a group of popular websites, including pop-feminist Jezebel, sports-centered Deadspin, and auto site Jalopnik. His early career was spent reporting on Silicon Valley for the *Financial Times*, where he grew frustrated by the overly fawning coverage of tech entrepreneurs. Denton also founded Valleywag, a blog owned by Gawker Media and edited by Denton for a time, which was, in its day, the Page Six of Silicon Valley, chronicling tech founders, companies, and venture capitalists. It famously exposed that Google founder Larry Page and then high-ranking Google employee Marissa Mayer had dated in the late 2000s, and that Eric Schmidt was in an open marriage. Denton broke such stories as Salesforce.com CEO Marc Benioff's attempt to detain a *Wall Street Journal* reporter, claiming that reporters were sitting on this story. Some of its more antagonistic headlines chastised Peter Thiel, among other tech luminaries. Of all people, Denton has a unique vantage point on Silicon Valley's relationship with media and in particular on Peter Thiel's relationship to media.

Peter Thiel and Donald Trump are aligned in their distaste for the traditional media, and both use platforms to express their opinions. Thiel achieved revenge against Denton's Gawker Media by funding the Hulk Hogan lawsuit against the company. This, Thiel revealed, was in retaliation for his being outed as gay by the publication several years before. Gawker Media was forcibly sold after the judge awarded Hogan $140 million in damages. Denton declared personal bankruptcy.

But Denton's connections to Silicon Valley go wider than the Hulk Hogan case. As founder of Gawker and editor of Valleywag 2006–2007, he was privy to the resurgence of Silicon Valley, its characters and companies, after the dot-com bubble to the birth of what it is now. He continues to watch tech closely.

Denton sips his coffee. He is remarkably sanguine, even disconnected in his comments, given the circumstances. He seems to have intellectualized the whole Hogan lawsuit as a parable, almost. (Ironically, in 2018, Thiel made overtures to buy what was left of Gawker, a move that could either amuse or enrage Denton.)

Denton believes the filter bubble and echo chamber goes wider than we as consumers really understand. It's not just about our newsfeed, he thinks, it's about all the information we receive online. "If you think about the news business, the incentives for news organizations and writers are determined by the Facebook algorithm. They give us little hints of how it works now and again, but really, not that much more," he explains. "You have more and more of our daily lives, and more and more of our professions and economic activities, governed by terms and conditions, and the algorithms of these platforms."

Look closer, and tech companies' relationship with media criticism has always been thin-skinned, certainly in comparison to industries such as the financial sector that are frequently critiqued in broadsheets or tabloids.

"That's why Valleywag existed," Denton says of his now-defunct website. "It's a one-industry town, Silicon Valley, and it's a relatively new industry. It's not like New York and to a lesser extent Los Angeles, where there is a relatively full ecosystem of media, with magazines that do puff profiles and nice photographs of celebrities and ask softball questions, and plenty of journalists that give good reviews to movies in exchange for invites to parties and screenings and stuff like that. There's also a gossipy press, a radical press, and to a greater or lesser degree there are other voices. In Silicon Valley they could never really hack it."

Many Silicon Valley companies, with effectively gated-community campuses, use access as the primary carrot for control. In attempting to secure interviews and access for this book, presumably because it was a) not entirely about one tech brand (and would not celebrate it), and b) obviously going to be somewhat critical, and c) because the volume of requests they receive is overwhelming, I was flat-out rejected by the cornerstone companies. Or ignored. I was also an unknown quantity, outside what would likely be their usual roster of known tech journalists.

Denton's access, even back then, was similarly constrained: "Certainly if you're a journalist in Silicon Valley and you criticize, you're likely to lose access, and Silicon Valley is run by twenty people; ten venture capitalists and ten others who are prominent in the big five tech companies," says Denton. "There isn't a huge amount of alternate access. They keep strong, powerful control of their employees; NDAs and confidentiality agreements all over the place. There was a brief moment of freedom when the internet came along and this was a tech-savvy group of employees who would leak. And I think the companies have put a lid on that to a large extent."

Even outside of the Hogan case, there were always consequences if you ran against Silicon Valley egos. "We had consequences back then. We were never banned from Facebook, but we were barred from Apple events just after our iPhone 4 story that was probably one of the biggest," he explains. "That was back in 2010." (Gizmodo acquired a prototype iPhone 4 and revealed details ahead of the official launch.)

Press interviews for products are now pre-planned and carefully orchestrated. Op-eds are placed in prestigious newspapers, sidestepping the questions of an interviewer.

Denton points out that Amazon's Jeff Bezos stands apart from the rest of this crowd. "In the media, he is regarded the most favorably because he supports *The Washington Post*, allows them to do independent journalism, and has criticized people like Peter Thiel for being overly sensitive. He seems like a new tycoon that the existing media establishment can be OK with."

Silicon Valley's unwillingness to engage in meaningful critical dialogue could be seen as unwise, but Denton thinks it is actually key to its continued success. "How can anyone say it's unwise, when the five most valuable tech companies in America all adhere to some version of this policy?"

But these are isolationist policies that disconnect the companies from objective feedback, criticism, and debate. These brands are all about remaining popular and relevant to consumers. Silicon Valley's tone-deafness and lack of empathy is well storied, and has led to massive PR gaffs. Letting a critical voice in, and being genuinely open to it, might make them look more human.

Truth and Narrative

To Silicon Valley the media is simply a tool for amplifying the message about their companies and the narrative of wonder attached to what they do. This stems, in part, from the abstractness of technology—they need it explained and deified by the press. Without the story, they're nothing. But they also want to control the story.

These are information businesses, after all. They're conceptual businesses, they're not steel mills. Lots of things hinge on their narrative. "Oftentimes people don't understand the product, so how the story is told is completely critical to hiring employees, to getting the right number of investors, to getting customers to sign up," says Denton. "Everything depends on it, even more than it does in the analog world. If there's any disruption in that story, a leak, a critical voice internally, it can be very disruptive." As a result, Silicon Valley cares more about maintaining a pristine image than most companies—oil or gas we buy as essential commodities without need for consistent consumer buy-in.

The media has become a powerful promulgator of the narratives employed by Silicon Valley. It's also been used to imbue them with emotions that foster attachment from consumers and places them in a moral framework. These companies foster the image that they are not just platforms. They are sentient, moral beings that do amazing things.

But creating this image has complicated results, especially when it comes to tensions arising from their role as stakeholders in news, and as the new guardians of media. By rendering these companies moral, human, and superior, we're attaching a moral framework to what they do, rather than a business framework. We are more connected and loyal to them for this reason (which is good for them), but then we also feel more betrayed when they behave like corporations or act cynically. It's a double-edged sword. This does vary within the group. Consider Amazon as opposed to Facebook. Amazon has never oversold itself as a moral being, or anything other than an incredibly good retailer. We're not shocked that it uses robots and is ruthless as a business operator. It's so efficient, and seamless, and despite all the headlines about its treatment of factory workers and its undermining of local businesses, it's everyone's not-so-guilty pleasure. Facebook has told us for years that it is solving world problems and connecting the world. As such, we feel much more affronted, and violated, when negative stories come out about it.

"Nobody thinks the big telecoms are 'good guys' and I think people are neutral about big hardware manufacturers like Hewlett-Packard, IBM, or Cisco," observes Richard Hill. "But when it comes to the internet companies [Apple was not, of course, an internet company], somehow all these guys are just doing this out of the kindness of their hearts, for the benefit of humanity. And I think it's only now beginning to sink in that maybe it's not that simple."

These are for-profit companies, after all. They don't have moral codes, they have business interests. "The sooner we get away from the notion that they are sentient beings who have their own moral frameworks separate from the financial interests of their shareholders, the better off we'll all be," says Joe McNamee, executive director of the European Digital Rights (EDRi) international advocacy group. The problem, he says, is that collectively "everyone seems to think that those companies should magically work out what each individual thinks the correct level of censorship or content is, but that's not the case. They work out, at any given moment, what is most profitable for them to do or not do, and then do it."

It's revealing in the dialogue surrounding Bitcoin and blockchain technology in general for example. Bitcoin, a cryptocurrency, is framed as the ultimate symbol of libertarianism, an escape from government and decentralized engines of democracy to enthusiasts, rather than simply another form of digital currency whose stock market value still only exists, ironically, in relation to traditional currencies (i.e., it does not exist in a silo—its valuation exists from being compared with U.S. dollar values, not as an independent thing). Blockchain, the real-time, constantly updating program that measures digital assets, is also being framed with the ideology of seizing power back from meddling banks and governments, allowing for trading and exchange free from interference. But in many ways, it's simply a more advanced accounting system.

It's another example of how Silicon Valley, tech, and the internet paint themselves as something more special than what they are, and that the tech insiders are more special then all of us other laypeople.

David Golumbia discusses this in *The Politics of Bitcoin: Software as Right-Wing Extremism*. Golumbia, an associate professor of English at Virginia Commonwealth University, looking at the media language specifically, argues that the rhetoric surrounding Bitcoin and blockchain technology places it on an ideological pedestal—any criticism is simply people not understanding the technology. "The implication is that this lack of technical expertise disqualifies the critics from speaking on the topic at all," he says.

Now many techies are starting to talk about blockchain elections being the most accurate way to achieve democracy. "The world is not going to turn upside down because you can suddenly cast a vote on your computer instead of going down to the voting place. Similarly, I think blockchain does have legitimate potential uses, but they're all like improved record-keeping and things that are mild improvements on technology that already exists or functions."

In other words: it may make the stock exchange or election faster or more efficient, but it will not upturn what voting is, or what currency is. Yet visit a tech conference, or a Bitcoin event, and the die-hard fans have a cult-like belief in its transformative powers. Bitcoin's founders are famed for their deep libertarian beliefs, championing this decentralized, unregulated currency as the ultimate escape from government interference. Since then, it's been watered down, but the broad belief in blockchain's democratizing influence is still strongly embedded in rhetoric. Maybe this will evolve as Bitcoin and other cryptocurrencies start to be used wholesale by innovative countries. (Several nations, including Estonia, are experimenting with uses for cryptocurrencies.)

But all this rhetoric has become part of a powerful force in tech's favor. A way to, at once, make its powers and tools seem more special. A way to sidestep criticism and steamroll opposition.

Fake News and the Future

The issue of real and fake news will become more important as Silicon Valley platforms like Google, YouTube, Facebook, and Twitter become central to the news cycle, placing generated fake news alongside fact-checked, legitimate content. And it gets harder to differentiate between real and artificially generated posts. Video coverage, particularly live video, was viewed at one point as a way to cut through this, appreciated for its unfettered, instant, visceral, and immersive properties. As we have seen, it has proven to be particularly effective in citizen journalism.

But even live video and images will soon have the potential to be doctored. In the past two years, researchers have made massive advances in manipulating pictures, images, and sound with machine-learning, artificial-intelligence programs. These can continually refine their output. Initial success suggests that within the next decade, highly sophisticated moving and still visual output might be possible, making it difficult to believe our eyes, as well as what we read.

The issue of fake news is already a pressure point for Silicon Valley tech giants, as brands and big media companies withdraw advertising following the discovery of those ads being placed next to extremist or fake content. But this has only been discussed in the most overt and controversial cases. What about the grey space in between? Branded features and partisan "news" content. Or inaccuracies in AI-generated written news reports. Or, even more gravely, the content that affects public opinion in elections using online propaganda, as has been done by Russia in the run-up to both the American and French elections, as revealed by intelligence reports. The British government has also asked Mark Zuckerberg for evidence of whether Russia-backed accounts affected the EU referendum and its general election.

Fake news is becoming a key political issue. French advertising giant Havas, as well as the UK government, in partnership with the *Guardian*, BBC, and Transport for London, all withdrew ads from Google in 2017, following Google's lack of guarantees when it comes to ad placement. Havas attributed the withdrawal to Google's inability to "provide specific reassurances, policy, and guarantees that their video or display content is classified either quickly enough or with the correct filters."

France has taken action a step further. In January 2018, President Emmanuel Macron announced a new law to combat fake news. During elections, social media would face tougher rules over the content that they allow online. And deliberate attempts to blur the lines between truth and lies were undermining people's faith in democracy. Macron's new rules include tougher regulation about showing the sources of apparent "news" content, and limits on how much could be spent on sponsored news material.

In his announcement, Macron talked about the lowered cost of such activity; he said it was now possible to propagate fake news on social media for just a few thousand euros. (Which rather puts the scale of Russia's $1.25 million per month during the lead-up to the U.S. election, and its potential impact, in perspective.) "Thousands of propaganda accounts on social networks are spreading all over the world, in all languages, lies invented to tarnish political officials, personalities, public figures, journalists," he said.

But there's a question of how to resolve these tensions.

In the wake of revelations about Facebook staff curating its newsfeed in 2016 with more liberal stories, what was more concerning to Microsoft's Danah Boyd was not that the feed was curated, but the widely held misconception by consumers that an algorithm's sorting and listing information would be less biased than humans doing the same thing. That a code was somehow more neutral than a human in curating a newsfeed of stories. In a May 2016 piece on *Data & Society*'s platform dubbed "Facebook Must Be Accountable to the Public," also published by the *Huffington Post*, she wrote: "What is of concern right now is not that human beings are playing a role in shaping the news—they always have—it is the veneer of objectivity provided by Facebook's interface, the claims of neutrality enabled by the integration of algorithmic processes, and the assumption that what is prioritized reflects only the interests and actions of the users (the 'public sphere') and not those of Facebook, advertisers, or other powerful entities."

She added: "There was never neutrality, and never will be . . . I have tremendous respect for Mark Zuckerberg, but I think his stance that Facebook will be neutral as long as he's in charge is a dangerous statement. This is what it means to be a benevolent dictator, and there are plenty of people around the world who disagree with his values, commitments, and logic. As a progressive American, I have a lot more in common with Mark than not, but I am painfully aware of the neoliberal American value systems that are baked into the very architecture of Facebook and our society as a whole."

The Facebook and napalm photo incident, while well-intended, revealed the cultural blindness in Silicon Valley's perspective.

Which comes down to a paradox as Silicon Valley captures more and more control of the news cycle and online speech. If we expect them to take more control of content online, protect us from fake news, from abuse, what guidelines do we set? Is it better if an algorithm does it, or if a Facebook-selected group, with their own personal biases, does it? Then there's the question of what, really, is Facebook. A media company? A social network? Because that has implications for the responsibility it holds.

"The German justice minister has said Facebook should deal more with hate speech. It's illegal—why don't they do more? Well, because they're not a law enforcement authority," says Richard Hill. "They can delete content, but unless you're happy for there to be absolute impunity, then they can't do all you want them to do. The problem that we have in this society is that, as long as you have politicians saying, 'Why doesn't Facebook take more power and be more efficient in regulating our free speech?' you can't simultaneously say that they should also have less power."

In many ways, Google and Facebook are caught between a rock and a hard place. "Google can be trained to be racist as hell," Boyd tells me. "Does Google have responsibilities once it's been identified? Yes. But that responsibility is actually very easy to be done in terms of public shaming . . . Take what's gone on with Facebook and how they should be modifying the News Feed. Is the answer for them to make it such that it's whatever is in your feed, that's populism, or is it to curate, which has been the history of democracy and republicism? If so, which values are going to be structured? . . . No matter what, they're damned for any choice they make, so it's one thing to talk about regulating them, but what values do we actually want? We can't agree as a public on what those should be, so the question to me is, is the right answer for them to be regulated through legal structures that are themselves pretty corrupted? To be regulated by public shaming, which is what is really working right now for some of them?"

Maybe it comes back to that original conflict—that these companies have intentionally and strategically placed themselves within a broader symbolic framework in our lives. As such, we attach more expectation to them than simply being businesses. They benefit from this, but this stance also creates new pressures that other commerce might not carry. Silicon Valley companies have fostered ideological and moral personas which may begin to work against them as issues of fake news, trolling, and the filter bubble become more prevalent in popular discourse. Do we want them to take responsibility or not? They, of course, do not.

There's a growing dichotomy between Silicon Valley's outsized, world-dominating ambition and the way it tries to present itself. The world's biggest media companies—a global taxi company, a global hotelier, planting anchors in harbors around the world—are masquerading as "technology companies," "platform solutions," and "community driven hospitality companies," attempting to absolve themselves from any of the messy checks and balances that have slowed their predecessors. It fooled everyone in its stronghold markets, until it didn't. Armed with a slew of cheerful, ukelele-soundtracked intro videos and tropes about empowering communities, Silicon Valley is now trying to sneak in—and conquer—new territories far and wide. Will these new territories also be fooled?

4

Connecting the World

t could almost be a Benetton ad. That, or a Unicef campaign. Or both. Visit the website of Internet.org, Facebook's pseudo-philanthropic organization dedicated to bringing low-cost internet to underdeveloped countries, and there are pictures of hijab-wearing girls laughing, children smiling in national costumes from various corners of the earth, cycling in villages, and more—except instead of holding buckets of water or baskets, they're clasping mobile phones. Optimism and worthiness are laid on with a trowel. There are case studies about the positive impact of Free Basics, Facebook's limited, free version of the internet that gives users access to a selection of websites and content without data charges. Children have been able to study. Fathers have been educated about how to be better parents. Facebook partners with six internet and mobile companies including Samsung, Ericsson, Nokia, and Qualcomm, as well as regional operators, to offer Free Basics. There are other more ambitious Internet.org projects, too, such as the Internet.org Connectivity Lab, exploring lasers and lightweight aircraft to bring internet to remote areas.

"Through our connectivity efforts we've brought more than 25 million people online who otherwise would not be and introduced them to the incredible value of the internet," it says. "They're doing better in school, building new businesses, and learning how to stay healthy."

After conquering the U.S. and other mature markets, Silicon Valley has its sights on colonizing the remaining corners of the world, and in many instances is raising the banners of altruism to do it.

Africa and its 1.2 billion population has been one major target. In 2017, Google CEO Sundar Pichai announced plans to train ten million Africans in digital skills and increase funding to African startups. It's hired a CMO for Sub-Saharan Africa. It's also launching YouTubeGo, a version of YouTube designed to stream with weaker internet. In the same year, Facebook announced plans to lay 500 miles of fiber-optic cables in Uganda. Both giants are launching tech hubs and various initiatives to expand their reach in developing African markets.

The internet here, like Christianity before it, is presented as the great civilizer, unlocking economies and empowering (that word again) people to achieve their potential. Free internet infrastructure is being built as a gift in exchange for ownership of the consumer population's digital universe, which of course is infinitely more valuable.

As it enters these markets, and other dynamic emerging economies from Southeast Asia to South America, Silicon Valley is discovering new challenges. For one, it's going head-to-head with Chinese tech giants such as Alibaba and Huawei. In 2017, Alibaba CEO Jack Ma announced a $10 million African fund. In fact, Chinese tech companies are doing battle with Silicon Valley in a number of lucrative markets, including India and Brazil. Alibaba has made large investments in Paytm and Snapdeal. Didi Chuxing, the equivalent of Uber in China, has invested in Ola. Smartphone maker Xiaomi led a $25 million funding round in content provider Hungama Digital Media Entertainment in April of 2017. Web services company Baidu is also exploring India.

Who will win?

The axis of influence is starting to tilt. Silicon Valley may have owned innovation culturally, on a global scale, for the past two decades, but new vibrant tech hubs are emerging and challenging its dominance. They're also creating new competitors. Opponents are emerging from vibrant new tech scenes in Israel, India, and Bali. Emerging leaders are "building apps and services that respond to local needs, and in doing so, they're building products for the future of the internet," Caesar Sengupta, Google's vice president of product management, told the *Wall Street Journal*. "The next generation of global tech companies is just as likely to come out of a local coffee shop in Bangalore or Ho Chi Minh City as they are from Silicon Valley." His sentiment was echoed by former Uber CEO Travis Kalanick. Commenting at a Beijing tech conference, he said: "In the next five years, there will be more innovation, more invention, more entrepreneurship happening in China, happening in Beijing, than in Silicon Valley."

Still it persists. Like Hilton, McDonald's, and Coca-Cola before, Silicon Valley is attempting to roll its American brands out globally, hoping their primary colored–pizzaz will win over nations and deflect comparisons to the more cynical corporate behemoths and imperialists that came before them. But in this enlightened and transparent digital age, that's getting harder and harder to do.

Silicon Valley's famed tone-deafness is being further exposed as it enters new markets. The nineteenth-century Imperialists may have been able to freely and brutally invade island after island, but Silicon Valley's missteps as it moves into new markets are, ironically because of the internet, reported on and critiqued live. Silicon Valley giants no longer enjoy the consumer innocence of their early years, where childlike music and startup rhetoric let them swoop into any market they chose and appear smaller than they are. Their role as famous, bold-faced, global corporations is inescapable. And the trajectory from excitement to cynicism about them as a result has also been exponentially accelerated.

It's getting tougher for Silicon Valley in its key strongholds, too, as opinions about it change and the extent of its gargantuan impact becomes apparent. Silicon Valley enjoyed a successful decade-long rollout across most established Western markets from the UK to Europe, but it is rapidly being challenged. In some instances its outsize role and dominance is spurring outright backlash in the form of fines, bans, and lawsuits by governments. Among consumers, the sheen and early innocence that saw these companies welcomed and often adulated is fading quickly toward collective suspicion or worse—for businesses built on soaring earnest tropes—irreverence. As the impact of Silicon Valley companies in distorting competition, society, property prices, and employment becomes truly apparent, it's also reawakening collective social consciences in many countries. European nations are starting to protect their values, taxation systems, and regulations from rapid encroachment.

Silicon Valley's ride until now may have been smooth, but its plans for global expansion face choppy waters.

European Revolt

Europe has always resisted Silicon Valley ideals, despite its massive success there (Google has a 90 percent market share in Europe, compared with roughly 64 percent in the U.S. thanks to competing players). French and Spanish taxi drivers went on strike against Uber. The Cannes Film Festival thumbed its nose at Netflix by creating a new rule that stopped films without cinema distribution in France from entering the competition (movies shown in theaters in France are subject to taxation to support the French movie industries and release-date regulations, which Netflix had sidestepped). Despite this, Apple, Google, Facebook, and Amazon have thrived in Europe. But things are starting to change. In the past year, European Competition Commissioner Margrethe Vestager has ordered Ireland to recover €13 billion in taxes from Apple. She has fined Facebook €110 million for misleading regulators during its purchase of WhatsApp. Amazon was ordered to pay €250 million to Luxembourg for illegal tax benefits. Google, meanwhile, was fined a giant €2.4 billion for flouting competition laws and abusing its dominant position in the search market at the expense of challenger versions. The European Union also recently ruled that Uber should be regulated as a transportation company, not as a technology solution or any other mask it's attempted to apply to itself in a bid to skip the rules faced by regular taxi services.

The move has garnered Vestager considerable celebrity. In a profile with the *New Statesman*, she commented: "There's no economic rationale behind the way some of these companies are set up . . . It's not to serve the purpose of the company; it's to serve the purpose of avoiding tax." Elsewhere, commenting on tech company monopoly power, she added: "You can be big, and you can be successful . . . but you cannot abuse your power to stop others from challenging you from being the next big thing in five or ten years."

In May 2018, of course, the General Data Protection Regulation (GDPR) came into effect, enforcing new privacy laws, strict new rules about using people's data and their personal control of this. It was "designed to harmonize data privacy laws across Europe, to protect and empower all EU citizens data privacy and to reshape the way organizations across the region approach data privacy."

This follows rising dissent at the behaviors of these companies. The free-flowing back-and-forth exchange of staff roles between Silicon Valley giants and European government is growing in public awareness. The Google Transparency Project, initiated by the Campaign for Accountability, an American ethics organization, has identified at least eighty revolving-door moves between Google and European governments since 2005, set up in a bid to safeguard against antitrust legislation. These moves included Tomas Gulbinas, a former ambassador-at-large for the Lithuanian government, and Georgios Mavros, an advisor to a French member of the European Parliament, who now both work as lobbyists for Google. Uber hired Neelie Kroes, formerly the European Commissioner for Digital Data, in 2016. In 2017, the Transparency International EU released a report that 50 percent of Google's registered lobbyists used to work for the EU.

On the surface there's nothing wrong with this—Barack Obama hired lots of people from Google to equip his administration with a better understanding of technology. As these giant companies continue to grow, and they brush up against regulatory issues, it's also normal to hire heads of policy to navigate these waters. Still, too much crossover raises conflict of interest questions. Who's being influenced by what?

"All organizations can benefit from the experience and insights that former politicians bring, but there is an issue with those who one minute are drawing up EU laws and the next are lobbying their former colleagues on the exact same issues," Daniel Freund, head of advocacy at Transparency International EU, said when its study was released. "We need rules that prevent conflicts of interest or the capture of the institutions by lobbyists."

Legislation to combat the influence of Silicon Valley has been mounting for a while. In 2016, a Berlin court upheld a ban on users of Airbnb (and similar agencies) renting out more than 50 percent of their apartments on a short-term basis without a permit from the city; rule-flouters risk a fine of up to €100,000. The city authorities have even set up a website where users can give anonymous tipoffs about Airbnb usage. The reasoning was that services like Airbnb distort rents and therefore affect availability of affordable housing. Regulations in Amsterdam and London prevent hosts from renting their properties for more than sixty and ninety nights per year, respectively, and at the end of 2016, Airbnb agreed to support this by limiting the number of nights its hosts could rent out their properties, the first time it has made such a concession.

Efforts at regulation have also taken on the gig economy: in 2015, Germany came down on Uber, demanding that its drivers obtain the same license as regular taxi drivers, causing the company to suspend its services in Hamburg, Frankfurt, and Düsseldorf. In France, Uber was fined €800,000 for operating UberPop, its service using unlicensed taxis. Two of the company's senior executives were fined a total of €50,000.

The same year, the European Commission opened its antitrust investigations into Google over various competitive issues, from manipulating their search results to highlight Google shopping options, to practices in search and advertising in which advertisers are prioritized, to varying search engine speeds in Google's favor.

Finally, privacy has been a rising concern in Europe. After the Edward Snowden revelations about the American government's mass surveillance in the U.S., it became clear personal data from European users of services like Google, Microsoft, and Facebook—also passing through servers in the U.S.—was potentially at risk. This created great controversy in Europe, including a subsequent case brought by Austrian lawyer Max Schrems against Facebook for privacy invasion, which resulted in a European Union court declaring invalid the Safe Harbor rule, which allowed U.S. tech companies to store EU personal data in the U.S. for processing. A new agreement has been reached—though it's a moot point whether that really matters when it comes to the UK with the introduction in 2016 of its Investigatory Powers Act, a counterterrorism initiative allowing the British state to indiscriminately hack, intercept, record, and monitor the communications and internet use of the entire population.

In 2018, new privacy rules are going into effect, giving regulators in European countries more power to fine technology companies for improperly collecting or sharing user data.

It started, at least in the public mind, with the landmark "right to be forgotten" ruling in 2014 by Europe's highest court, which declared that individuals had the right to request removal from searches personal information they felt was misrepresentative, no longer accurate, or irrelevant. As Julia Powles, of Cambridge University, commented in a paper on the case: "In some modest but incomplete way, the case recognized and protected our fundamental rights over personal data—those meaningful, yet intangible links that are the building blocks of our identities and relationships, and that have become the substrate of the digital economy."

Why is Europe stronger at tackling Silicon Valley influence? It's linked to its collective strength, says Powles. In other words, the European Union has authority over numerous countries and packs a big enough punch not to be scared. "That makes it able to engage with something more societal and at a scale that matters. The only language that companies talk is value to shareholders, so it's a significant enough market that withdrawing or bulldozing just doesn't work. It [Big Tech] has to pay attention."

The Special Relationship

Big Tech's experience in mainland Europe stands in contrast to the UK, where Silicon Valley companies have thrived.

"The UK has consistently undermined the European project. It's the most pro-business," says Powles. "There's no moral, cultural compass on the seizure of more communal values, which you feel most strongly in European countries. You see it in all sorts of regulations, like the [European] regulation of working hours, insuring the way public services need to accommodate people with disabilities."

When Silicon Valley giants started planting their London offices around 2012, much as it would pain stoic Brits to admit, the locals were deeply excited. Overcome by the glamour of these American tech brands, they flocked to them. They tweeted about the free food in the lobby ("It really is free!"), and took selfies by their logos. Doors were flung open to executive offices. Meanwhile, any invitation to present to or meet with Silicon Valley company employees was greeted with enthusiasm. Since then, Silicon Valley companies have established a bigger and bigger stronghold in the UK. And their mystique has been propelled by the relative distance these brands—Facebook, Apple, and Google—kept from British media.

The UK's tax rules have also made it an attractive place for Silicon Valley giants to plant major operations. London may become a bigger tech hub yet, if the European Commission continues to crack down on the tax breaks given to tech giants. Prime Minister Theresa May has said she would "welcome" Apple to the UK after it was hit by the European Union with its €13 billion tax bill. And, as Brexit prompts a migration of banking and other sectors to European cities, more incentives are likely to be introduced to lure the tech giants to London in search of headlines about new jobs and trade. Signaling this in 2017, UK Chancellor of the Exchequer Philip Hammond announced a budget allocation of more than $674 million to boost innovation and technology. Theresa May has doubled the number of visas available to specialist tech workers. Meanwhile, Foreign Secretary Boris Johnson, in an interview with Britain's *The Times* newspaper, suggested relaxed legislation was on the horizon for tech companies. "We have a very original economy, very different from other European countries—tech sectors, bioscience, bulk data, this is a very innovative place to be. We may in the future wish to regulate it in a different way from the way that Brussels does."

London is already, in many ways, a Silicon Valley colony, a loyal outpost floating alongside a grumpier Europe now clamping down on Big Tech. The lavish headquarters built in the San Francisco Bay Area are swiftly being replicated near the River Thames. By 2020, Google's King's Cross campus will transform the area into an urban Google village and take on 3,000 new workers, bringing the total employed at the London HQ to a potential 7,000 people. In fact, King's Cross may soon become known as Silicon Cross—Facebook recently announced it would be planting its headquarters in the area, according to the *Times* UK. It will span 65,000 square meters, tripling Facebook's presence in the capital. In 2017, Amazon employed 15,500 in the UK, and Facebook an estimated 1,500. Snapchat established its international HQ there. And Apple will be the biggest tenant at the vast $10 billion

Battersea Power Station redevelopment in south London, due for completion in 2021. "Here in the UK, it's clear to me that computer science has a great future with the talent, educational institutions, and passion for innovation we see all around us. We are committed to the UK and excited to continue our investment in our new King's Cross campus," Google Chief Executive Sundar Pichai said in a speech announcing the plans.

The close relationship between tech companies and British government goes back to Tony Blair. Talk to many of those involved in the government's digital programs, and they describe an almost fan-like relationship between government and the London tech world in the early days of Silicon Valley expansion and with the emerging "Silicon Roundabout." Matt Biddulph jokingly coined the term Silicon Roundabout as early as 2008, describing the area of tech startups around Old Street tube station near the City of London. The area has since seen a growing presence of Silicon Valley tech companies. Tech companies accelerated further during David Cameron's era.

"The government were very keen to ensure that they were seen to be supporting the UK tech industry," says Tiffany St. James, former head of public participation for the UK government and an executive director of the British Interactive Media Association (in 2004 she was one of the architects of Directgov, the British government's first consolidated information and services website).

Tech was identified as a major new sector for economic growth with lots of emphasis on investment in the tech startups and programs. Google and Facebook, as well as new startup founders, were a frequent presence at Number 10 in the Cameron era, mirroring Barack Obama's close connections to the tech world. Martha Lane Fox (or rather, Baroness Lane-Fox of Soho), founder of lastminute.com, an early digital travel disruptor in the UK, has in many ways been the face of "digital government" and digital championship in the UK, having led the centralized digitization of its platforms with the Government Digital Service. She's also on the board of Twitter.

But there's rising dissent about tech's influence in the UK and new discourse about the purported economic benefits they bring. Despite attempts to make the UK a digital media hub for homegrown businesses, much of digital ad spending, a growing market in the UK, is going to Google and

Facebook. GroupM, WPP's media group, estimated UK ad spending in 2017 at £18.8 billion. While traditional media advertising is declining, the UK has established itself as the most digital-centric advertising market in the world. GroupM found that digital display demand continues to rise strongly and predicted a 15 percent rise for 2017, particularly into social media, and, within digital, from static to video. "The largest driver is paid search which is accelerating again. It benefits from rising automation, geo-targeting capabilities, and the point-of-sale immediacy of mobile for performance-minded advertising," it said. As noted earlier, it's estimated that as much as 99 percent of that growth worldwide is going to Facebook and Google.

The close ties between tech and the UK government are also under growing scrutiny.

In April 2016, *New Scientist* published the findings of a leaked document that revealed the extent of Google-owned DeepMind's collaboration with the National Health Service, which had not been publicly announced. The Royal Free London NHS Foundation Trust (responsible for three London hospitals) gave Google's artificial-intelligence company DeepMind access to health-care data on more than a million patients to build an app to alert doctors about the risks of severe kidney injury. Sensitive information including HIV status, abortion procedures, and drug-use history was included in the data. The NHS was reportedly paying DeepMind for use of its Streams app, which alerts clinicians' smartphones if a patient's condition deteriorates. It also allowed them to view patients' medical records and see where patients are being cared for. The partnership generated criticism and debate, as evidenced by a paper authored by Julia Powles and former *New Scientist* journalist Hal Hodson, attacking the deal's "lack of clarity and openness, with issues of privacy and power emerging as potent challenges as the project has unfolded." It was argued that there was a lack of transparency about how the data would be used, and lack of clear consultation with involved patients.

DeepMind issued a rebuttal, and said that no data was shared with parent company Alphabet and it is normal for the NHS to share data with third parties. Medical professionals were quoted citing the app's efficiency benefits. The app is being investigated by the UK's Information Commissioner's Office.

Other voices have joined the mix. Labour party shadow minister for Industrial Strategy, Science, and Innovation Chi Onwurah called for regulation and greater transparency of Facebook and Google's algorithms. "Algorithms aren't above the law," Onwurah, who studied electrical engineering at Imperial College London, told the *Guardian*. "The outcomes of algorithms are regulated—the companies which use them have to meet employment law and competition law. The question is, how do we make that regulation effective when we can't see the algorithm?" Onwurah also wrote a letter to the *Observer*, the *Guardian's* sister paper, calling on Google, Facebook, and Uber to "take responsibility for the unintended consequences of the algorithms and machine learning that drive their profits."

More recently, in a challenge to Facebook, Google, and Twitter, Prime Minister May has called for tech companies to take faster, greater action in removing extremist content and information that aids terrorism. Tech companies have responded with statements about the "millions" of pounds they are devoting to developing machine learning that will automate this.

How that progresses will be interesting to watch. What's clear is that UK consumers, at least, are starting to view this group more critically. But recent incidents have also exposed sometimes paradoxical demands on tech companies and how we feel about them. When it comes to private technology companies having free access to medical records, there's discomfort. Even if it does create efficiencies—despite how willingly people give data to Weight Watchers, Fitbit, and others for their tailored fitness regimes. When it comes to companies sharing personal consumer data with police, or counterterrorism services, the answer is less certain. No one wants to help a terrorist, do they? These questions are going to continue as artificial intelligence, technology, and data transform and become symbiotic with every aspect of the way we live, and more times than not, new services and systems are created by private companies, not the state. What do privacy and ethics look like in an era where technology is, effectively, everything? And how should the state protect us?

Deep-rooted cultural differences in many instances dictate how we respond to these questions. As Silicon Valley touches all these things with its products and services, it's colliding with sets of values that vary greatly from market to market. In Europe, for example, Germans have a long history of attachment to data protection because of spying during the Communist era. So do the Dutch, and the French to some extent. Contrast that with Singapore, where famously people assume that the government knows everything about them.

It plays out in a similar way when it comes to employment rights—independence, self-determination, and flexibility, save for the heavily unionized industries in the United States, are running themes. Uber lost a UK ruling regarding minimum wage for drivers. In France, the URSSAF—a network of organizations that administer the country's social security system—has also brought a lawsuit against Uber, which has been accused of practicing what can be translated as "hidden wage labor" or "disguised employment relationships."

In December 2016, a network of European and North American unions (including groups from Seattle and Washington, DC), labor confederations, and worker organizations went head-to-head with the gig economy. They issued a call for "transnational cooperation between workers, worker organizations, platform clients, platform operators, and regulators to ensure fair working conditions and worker participation in governance in the growing world of digital labor platforms, such as Clickworker, Amazon Mechanical Turk, Jovoto, and Uber."

Europeans are taking a very different approach to ideas of employment because their experience of it is different from America and even the UK. The U.S. has historic widespread at-will employment, but a market like France has well-entrenched employee protections and principles of employer responsibility. That context is inevitably going to shape the view of a platform like Uber, which offers very little protection to its "members." It runs counter to fully baked and historic national values.

The different attitudes toward data in the U.S. and Europe are shaped by national histories. According to Jane K. Winn, "Americans are really invested in the idea that 'I can reinvent myself; I am the author of my own destiny.' Consumer credit in the United States is linked to that American sense of unlimited possibility and urgency." She adds: "That's why Americans don't believe commodification of personal information is bad. Commodification of personal information is essential to the way that the credit economy works in the United States. And Europeans don't support the commodification of personal information, in part because it supports consumerism and consumer finance and consumer debt."

They also differ in attitudes to government "at a deep, deep structural level," says Winn. "How does the United States feel about government? Mistrust. How does the United States feel about the market? Trust. Americans mistrust their government and they trust the market. Europeans trust their governments and they mistrust the market, so data protection law, as in Europe, reflects this . . . I don't know of any other country in the world that would want the American system. It is totally unique to American culture."

Which would be fine if Silicon Valley were only in the U.S. But it is rapidly expanding in Europe, Asia, South America, and beyond, and each nation has complex, culturally rooted relationships with data and privacy. Understanding these cultural mores is crucial to Silicon Valley's success. Thus far, it has proven to be challenged in cultural sensitivity.

Golden Arches

Of all of the international prizes, China is the biggest and most tantalizing for its scale and value, but remains the most elusive to Silicon Valley companies. And China is now rapidly competing with Silicon Valley for lucrative emerging markets.

China has deeply rooted and entrenched native tech brands. They wield large internal influence, supported by the Chinese government, which historically has reinforced their entrenchment by banning foreign platforms that don't comply with their rules. Chinese tech firms work in close, transparent symbiosis with the government on privacy and censorship.

Outside their national borders, China's tech brands have yet to achieve quite the same cultural mystique and soft power of Silicon Valley companies. While often notably absent from Western tech and business media, Chinese brands are gaining greater visibility in the international press. Chinese tech and social media brands such as Alibaba and Tencent have been investing in Hollywood and Chinese movie projects (developing promotion, ticketing, and product placement tie-ins), all enhancing the visibility of these Chinese brands in mainstream cultural outlets.

Recently China's been on a soft-power offensive. At the 2017 Lions International Festival of Creativity (advertising's annual hurrah by the beach in Cannes, in the South of France), Alibaba showed off its Uni Marketing advertising platform and its deal with France's Publicis Groupe.

Jack Ma, CEO of Alibaba, pledged to create a million jobs in the U.S. after a meeting with President Donald Trump in January 2017. He has also said he intends 50 percent of Alibaba's business to come from outside China. Alibaba has also been investing in Hollywood entertainment, Magic Leap technologies, and more. Singles' Day (the world's biggest online shopping event), which started in China as an anti–Valentine's Day celebration for the unattached back in the '90s, has arguably been Alibaba's biggest global export. In 2016 the festival, which generated around $17.7 billion in sales, made headlines for having a Pokémon GO–style augmented reality mobile game, which gamified shopping around physical malls. Katy Perry performed at the launch concert. Singles' Day has since been adopted by other international retailers.

Ma has been making overtures to American businesses, positioning Alibaba as the gatekeeper to the lucrative Chinese market. At Gateway '17, a June 2017 Alibaba conference in Detroit, Ma said his company could help one million American businesses sell to China and the rest of Asia in the next five years. Alibaba was also present at New York Fashion Week in 2017. Its partnership dangled access to Chinese consumers. Meanwhile, Tencent wooed Western marketers with its vast trove of consumer data at Cannes.

As the world looks to emerging markets for growth, China's tech companies may have the edge, since these areas, like China, are all mobile-dominated and have a native understanding of leapfrogging to mobile-first life. Didi Chuxing announced a $100 million investment in Brazil. It raised $5.5 billion in funding in 2017, with sights set on massive expansion. Alibaba has already made inroads in other markets outside China, with partners including Southeast Asian online retailer Lazada. If Chinese brands can successfully rebrand for the West, they're poised to make a huge impact on the tech landscape.

Chinese tech is also starting to lead on innovation. Former Alphabet boss Eric Schmidt warned that China is poised to close in on the United States' lead in artificial intelligence by 2025. At a conference in Washington in November 2017, Schmidt stated the power shift will be caused by the Trump administration's funding cuts for basic science research at a time when China has unveiled a national plan to develop AI.

Meanwhile, a few Silicon Valley brands continue to try their luck in China. Amazon, having been slow to grow in the market, announced it is offering Amazon Prime for free. Others have thrown in the towel. After a long-fought battle against ride-hailing rival Didi Chuxing, Uber sold its operations to the company. Google shut its operations in 2010 after a cyber-attack from within the country targeted it and dozens of other companies. While investigating the attack, Google found that the Gmail accounts of a number of Chinese human rights activists had been hacked.

Nevertheless, the size of China's immense market remains alluring. Six years later in 2016, Google moved back in, opening an experience center in Shenzhen. Very little was released about the opening or the exact function of the center, but one detail reported by the media was the attendance at the event by a relatively high-ranking national government inspector, something that many read as significant.

Each passing year only makes conditions tougher in China for Western companies. Silicon Valley giants now face fierce local competition from Chinese companies that have not only massive user bases but a dense, multifaceted string of services incorporated into their offer. Google equivalent Baidu has 80 percent of all web searches in China, the country's biggest search engine. Like Google, the site offers popular vertical search-based products such as image search, video search, news search, and maps. (Through Baidu's mapping app, users can do everything from ordering a taxi and making a restaurant or hotel reservation to ordering in food and finding local stores.)

Mark Zuckerberg's attempts to woo China are now famous. He has learned Mandarin and has courted the government, and he even invited Chinese president Xi Jinping to name his first child. Facebook, despite these persistent efforts, continues to fall short compared to competitors such as Tencent QQ and Sina Weibo. Sina Weibo, once seen as a cut-price Twitter, has quickly become a rejuvenated platform with sparkly market-leading additions such as embedded comment threads and videos.

The most revolutionary, however, is Tencent's WeChat, a social network and messaging service that has morphed into a multi-layered platform offering everything from a free video-chat system and taxi-hailing service to bill-paying services and an extensive shopping capacity. Its environment is so rich, it's been dubbed the "one app to rule them all." That title is borne out by the devotion of 1 billion users worldwide—nearly everyone with internet access in China—and several million overseas users.

Chinese tech firms wield comparable celebrity with Silicon Valley figures within China. Alibaba (sometimes described as the Amazon of China) is by many metrics the world's biggest online commerce site, made up of three main sites: Taobao, Tmall (the premium shopping site), and Alibaba.com (the company's business-to-business platform). It was founded by Jack Ma, a charismatic local hero whose singular focus has taken the company from an enthusiastic idea to one of the world's most valuable tech companies. "He's on the cover of every magazine, everybody knows him, they watch videos of him, they're imitating him," says Kevin Kelly, a renowned futurist who recently finished a book tour in China, comparing Ma's media presence to that of Mark Zuckerberg.

Part of the issue for Silicon Valley companies is that China has very established, and mature, players as well as culturally divergent approaches to the internet—and to counterfeits and intellectual property as well. Chinese tech firms famously, and freely, copy one another's features. "Chinese companies approach the internet in a different way," writes *New York Times* contributor Paul Mozur. "In the United States, tech firms emphasize simplicity in their apps. But in China, it's three major internet companies—Alibaba, Baidu, and the WeChat parent Tencent—who compete to create a single app with as many functions as they can stuff into it."

Silicon Valley may also be moving in this direction, adding density and new functions to each of their offers and replicating the scrappiness of Chinese tech firms, even if it means blatantly copying rivals. Facebook-owned Instagram recently added "stories," another version of Snapchat. They are cannibalizing each other's services.

Will it be able to fight off China when it comes to the rest of the world? Imperial battles are sure to follow. And in many instances, it's in regions where China might have the upper hand, given its inherent understanding of emerging market behaviors in technology (or in some instances, its pure scrappiness, as was witnessed with Uber's experience launching in China). The fight for global domination might mark the next highly public humiliation for Silicon Valley.

Connecting Cuba

"You're gonna feel the sun on your face in two hours." The portly JetBlue stewardess winks, clasping her buckle as the plane prepares for take-off.

CNN and HGTV are playing on monitors during the flight. *Fixer Upper*'s Chip and Joanna Gaines are unveiling another rustic industrial barn makeover (isn't it always?) as the plane descends into Havana.

How strange to fly such a short distance and land in such a radically different place. A married Texan couple are crying with joy when getting the first look at their distressed chandelier and marble kitchen island (again, isn't it always?) as passengers are invited off the plane. Into a land that is, mostly, without internet. Or at least, a radically different version of the internet than we're all used to. All internet service on the island is controlled by the state-owned telecom company ETECSA and primarily provided through crowded, government-approved wi-fi hotspots around the country. There are 237 paid public hotspots on the island for 11 million people to use. Home internet connections are rare, and public access wi-fi at the hotspots costs CUB$2 an hour—which is expensive for average Cubans who earn only 17–20 of these "convertible pesos" per month. It's also very slow. Yet, demonstrating the desire for connectivity, the hotspots are recognizable for the crowds that gather around them. Most are in parks, international hotels, and other public places and are swarmed on Sundays, everybody's day off, with crowds beneath the shade of trees, sitting on benches, and looking intently at their screens.

This does show signs of changing, thanks to Google, which was recently granted permission in partnership with ETECSA to install servers on the island, increasing internet speeds as signals no longer need to travel through Venezuela, where the nearest Google server previously was. The servers store content from Alphabet-owned properties Gmail and YouTube, making their apps up to ten times faster. Washington, DC has no direct data link to the communist island.

The Google agreement reportedly contained a clause that ETECSA will not "censor, surveil, or interfere with the content stored as cache on those servers." The content is encrypted, meaning the Cuban government cannot hack it. The Google deal follows a concerted effort on behalf of the company since President Obama announced the reestablishment of relations with Cuba in 2014. (Trump has promptly rolled this back.) But Google's efforts, for now, seem unthwarted. Even so, there's a long way to go before Cuba has anything like the internet that most established or even emerging markets experience. And the internet is faster if you're using Google-owned products.

Cuba has emerged as a hotspot in recent years, an exotic time capsule withheld from Americans by a long-standing trade embargo, a new and alluring destination for intrepid tourists. Momentum has been fueled further by new surveys in favor of lifting the trade embargo between the U.S. and Cuba, Obama's relaxation of travel restrictions, and a historic presidential visit to the island in 2016. On cue, the headlines have been full of brands announcing new travel routes to Cuba (not least JetBlue, with direct flights from New York). Starwood Hotels, now merged with Marriott, manages a hotel in the city. Movies, like *The Fate of the Furious* (part of the Fast and Furious franchise), are being filmed there (Vin Diesel even took part in a music video). Chanel hosted its fashion show in Havana, flying luminaries from around the world to cruise the ruins of crumbling Old Havana in open-top cars, Instagramming to their heart's content. Will Trump's actions reverse this? He's already introduced tighter travel restrictions, which—combined with the devastation wrought by Hurricane Irma—has prompted a slide in tourism. Still, the groundswell of international interest in Cuba, and the rising ambition of its residents, might prove its forward momentum unstoppable.

Much of Havana feels like a promise of the future paused in motion, as communist rule came in to place and U.S. blockades ensued. Casinos and movie theaters, thrown up with unbridled exuberance in the 1950s economic boom, have remained under a bell jar since diplomatic relations were severed. Vedado, the neighborhood built at the peak of Havana's casino prosperity, is practically a precursor to the Jetsons in its unbridled, star-spangled enthusiasm for the future. Today, water parks, stadiums, movie theaters with modernist lines, swooping arrows, and curves are sprouting weeds and crumbling at the edges. Their bright colors faded like a vintage T-shirt. It's like watching a holiday home movie on an 8mm.

Havana was built for Instagram—and yet, try to Instagram its crumbling pastel Beaux Arts ruins, its 1950s open-top American cars, and you'll likely have to wait till you're back with JetBlue.

Cuba may not have easy access to the internet, but it doesn't act like it. There's a palpable desire for connectivity, and its residents are as connected to pop culture as any New York millennial.

Walk the streets of Old Havana and pretty much every young person has an iPhone or a Samsung smartphone. R&B music blasts from vehicles. Smartphones are replete with apps (about 2 million Cubans own cellphones). Youths are clad in knock-off Nike sneakers. There's a thriving app startup scene—except the apps are designed to be used with very little or no connectivity. There's even a bootleg version of iTunes, with the latest magazines, games, movies, and TV shows, distributed on a physical external hard drive via a network of entrepreneurs to Cuba's residents. It's called *El Paquete* ("The Package") and includes not only international magazines but the burgeoning raft of new local magazines coming out of Havana.

Little wonder that Silicon Valley's companies, primarily Google, have zeroed in on the island as ripe territory for expansion. Not only as a humanitarian prospect (not to mention a sexy headline) but as a lucrative untapped market of some 11 million new consumers. They're meeting with startup founders there. Sponsoring galleries—with free wi-fi! Courting politicians and finding ways around the lack of connectivity or easy payments. (Airbnb's biggest challenge in Cuba was getting a digital marketing and payment platform to work on an island with such poor connectivity and limited banking services. It set up a system where someone using a wi-fi hotspot manages Airbnb reservations for multiple property listings and remittance services. Cuban hosts receive their payments in cash from a courier on a motorcycle, usually within a week of the booking.)

Yet here again, China is not hanging back. Chinese phones, like Apple's, are common in Cuba. Like Google, Huawei is courting the communist government to ramp up telecommunications on the island. And, while Cuba is closer in proximity to the U.S., China as a communist country shares historic trade links with Cuba.

Silicon Valley's Cuba initiative sits as part of a wider strategy in emerging markets: presenting internet infrastructure as a gift and part of a wider humanitarian mission. But one with obvious commercial incentives—a fresh market with pools of consumers to reach. And this time, because they're laying the cables, bringing phones, and offering payments, they're able to claim a much more holistic set of data from consumers than when they were simply a search engine. All they need to grapple with are the governments.

Cuba is on the brink of a lot of change, but at the same time is very aware of its historic animosity with the U.S. and the implications of American tech behemoths infiltrating and spying. But in this borderless age, even this concern, as my local guide explains, is becoming irrelevant: "Most Cubans have Gmail already. Most have Facebook." Though without easy connection to high-speed internet, the lucrative monetization of online searches and interactions has yet to start flowing to these companies.

The servers are the latest development for Google in a concerted effort to bring internet to Cuba. It has partnered with Cuba's Museo Orgánico de Romerillo to offer free wi-fi. (Drive by on a weekend and this too, a quiet garden on the outskirts of Havana, is surrounded by residents. There are benches on the side of the road, near no residential developments, yet here people are hovering over their phones.)

The signs weren't promising for Silicon Valley giants at first: Google offered to install wi-fi antennae throughout Cuba for free in 2015 and was rebuffed by the second secretary of the Cuban Communist Party, José Ramón Machado Ventura, who commented at the time: "Everyone knows why there isn't more internet access in Cuba, because it is costly. There are some who want to give it to us for free, but they don't do it so that the Cuban people can communicate. Instead their objective is to penetrate us and do ideological work to achieve a new conquest. We must have internet, but in our way, knowing that the imperialists intend to use it as a way to destroy the Revolution."

Fast-forward to 2016 and it's a different picture, but not for many Silicon Valley companies. Google and Airbnb stand as isolated success stories in this instance. Amazon started laying the groundwork to ship packages to Cuba by adding a "ship to Cuba" button on its website in Havana. But the option didn't go live (and as of 2017, still hasn't), prompting an error message that reads: "Due to export controls and economic sanctions laws and regulations, we are unable to process transactions from your current location." Mark Zuckerberg has yet to bring Free Basics, Facebook's emerging-markets free app, to Cuba but has said Cuba "definitely fits within our mission."

Airbnb moved into Cuba in 2015 with a listing of 1,000 homes. A year later that had grown to 4,000 homes, which, according to Jordi Torres, Airbnb's general manager for Latin America, makes the island the fastest-growing vacation market ever. Speak with homeowners in Old Havana, and many have been able to restore their homes using income generated from Airbnb lettings. The Cuban government is now seeking to regulate and tax this.

It's strange that while Cubans themselves desire connectivity, and tourists might express frustration at not being able to post Instagram shots until they've departed—for outsiders, the rush to Cuba is being driven by its exotic standing as one of the last internet-free time capsules. Once internet and universal payments arrive, everything will change.

Cuba's Disconnected Tech Scene

It's remarkable in a place like Cuba that there are tech entrepreneurs at all. Several conversations are illustrative of the dynamic in Cuba now, and what might happen as Silicon Valley expands in Cuba.

A community of young entrepreneurs on the island have built apps designed to work around patchy access to the internet. These ingenious apps hold gigantic and detailed maps of the island created by local entrepreneurs, offering the benefits of Google Maps without requiring internet connectivity. There are apps that allow users to review restaurants, just like Yelp, only the review doesn't post immediately. It's stored, and programmed to post when the phone receives sufficient internet signal. It's like a simulation of the Internet. Map guide Isla Dentro and lifestyle guide Conoce Cuba are two examples of sophisticated restaurant guides and commerce hubs with astounding levels of design quality and internet-like detail. These founders are the young face of Cuban ingenuity.

Would they be excited about more connectivity in Cuba? The answer is yes and no. After all, if high-speed internet arrives, anyone can simply access Yelp or other international websites. They won't need a proprietary local map, and a gigantic file, clogging up their phone. Many of their apps thrive on the challenges that having no internet creates.

There's a curious official black market to the tech world in Cuba. It's almost like the government knows young people crave technology, U.S. brands, and connection, but don't want to acknowledge or condone it in a formal way.

Around Havana, the streets are replete with tech repair shops. Many are luxuriously appointed with Apple branding, demonstrating a further appetite for Silicon Valley brands. These tech repair shops will unlock phones and install apps, sidestepping location restrictions. Everything has been conceived to look like official Apple stores. Technology is carefully repaired for maximum life, too. In the same way they continue to lovingly tend to their cars, Cubans will never throw their phones away like Americans do.

El Paquete is a highly known and evolved bootleg operation. It costs CUB$5, roughly $6.50, a week. "People want to consume the same way they consume in America. All the time. We have to keep up," says one dealer I speak to (they preferred not to be named). *El Paquete* now sells advertising. And little wonder. The whole of Cuba is its audience.

As with Cuba in general, the island's disconnected tech founders are also familiar to Silicon Valley companies. Many refer to Google's local rep by his first name. They all own iPhones or smartphones. Many founders were selected for Obama's 2016 Global Entrepreneurship Study and have visited Silicon Valley or New York. But they say they are committed to Cuba.

Do they mind if American internet companies come in? "The internet is like the ocean. It's free. You cannot control it," says engineer Jorge Enrique Fernandez. In Cuba still—as in its early, uncommercialized days in the U.S.—the internet is viewed with a degree of innocence as a liberalizing force. The gateway to freedom, in other words.

Fernandez's statement is illustrative of the paradigm shift happening in all the new digital frontiers—from Kenya to the streets of Havana. One where connectivity, seeming so precious to those without it, is beside the point to others. It is freely given but only in return for data, which is much more precious.

Digital Rajas

The noise of Jaipur, Rajasthan, is that of any thriving, dense city. It's a constant whirring and beeping, with car exhausts revving into action. This place, like many Indian cities, is surging frenetically into the future, yet grappling with narrow streets, dirt tracks, and roads built in previous eras for half the traffic. Drive through the streets past haggling traders and rickshaws, and there are pigs, cows grazing on garbage, and the crowds. Cars, mopeds, and lorries are all swarming through bottleneck junctions, around its beautiful Pink Palace, City Palace, and bustling stores. Somehow it all works.

Yet for all the chaos and humanity, there's a rising common thread too: tech. There are billboards for YouTube. Oppo, a Chinese-owned smartphone brand, is advertised high above the markets. Ubers are operating on main roads. India is in love with technology, digital platforms, and more important, social media.

Few countries hold more potential for Facebook than socially minded India, and today the company is growing rapidly (it boasts 166 million users). But in 2015 it suffered a major setback when a scandal erupted over the roll-out of Free Basics.

"Connecting the World" is a frequent headline. The project is part of Facebook's wider mission to invest in new businesses and introduce new methods to connect the world. It invites governments, nonprofits, and local companies to partner. But it is also a business development tool for Facebook, allowing companies to access new audiences in tough-to-reach landscapes.

Facebook has been researching new ways to deliver this mission, too, at what the company calls its Connectivity Lab, looking at unmanned aircraft, lasers, and more: "The team is exploring a variety of technologies, including high-altitude, long-endurance planes, satellites, and lasers," according to the project pages on the Internet.org website. The SpaceX Falcon 9 rocket that exploded in 2016 was carrying a leased satellite (which was also lost) intended for use by Internet.org's project in Africa. The $200 million satellite was expected to extend social media access across the continent.

Free Basics has been successful in Africa, but critics have been quick to point out the issues of violating net neutrality through the limited internet included in the service, and for potentially discriminating against companies and competitors not on its lists. Some countries wanting better connectivity but with scant state funds to build it are grateful; but some are not.

India is a good example of the latter, and is a case study in Facebook's blindness to cultural nuances in its attempts to introduce Free Basics there unchecked.

Facebook unveiled Free Basics in India in 2015, following a much-publicized visit by Mark Zuckerberg, with great fanfare and platitudes about connecting the world and unlocking potential for poor or rural communities. But it was swiftly met with a backlash that caught Facebook off guard. Critics of the closed—and therefore seemingly anticompetitive—nature of Free Basics dubbed it another form of tech imperialism. A grassroots campaign criticizing the app, made up of lawyers and a group of coders, sprung up calling itself Save the Internet. At the same time, a viral video made by All India Bakchod, a group of popular young comedians, exploded immediately online and raised awareness of the issue, explaining why net neutrality was important. In response, in February 2016, regulators banned the Free Basics service in India based on "Prohibition of Discriminatory Tariffs for Data Services Regulations." Facebook swiftly withdrew Free Basics but has since returned with a paid-for platform in India.

Zuckerberg was clearly offended, penning an op-ed in *The Times of India* in response: "We know that for every ten people connected to the internet, roughly one is lifted out of poverty. We know that for India to make progress, more than one billion people need to be connected to the internet.

"That's not theory. That's fact.

"Another fact—when people have access to free basic internet services, these quickly overcome the digital divide," he said.

He was quickly met with angry op-eds in response. "Zuckerberg is on the defensive because he doesn't understand the culture and values of Indians. He doesn't realize that Ganesh cherishes the freedom that India gained from its British colonizers in 1947 and doesn't want a handout from a Western company. Ganesh may be poor, but he doesn't want anyone to dictate what sites he can visit, what movies he may watch, or what applications he can download," wrote Vivek Wadhwa in *The Washington Post*.

Adding fuel to the flames, accusations of imperialism were exemplified by a tweet from the venture capitalist Marc Andreessen who, after the ruling that made Free Basics illegal in India, commented: "Anti-colonialism has been economically catastrophic for India for decades. Why stop now?"

Where did Facebook go wrong? What's wrong with free internet? In presenting the internet as a gift, Facebook tapped into deep Indian cultural sensitivities about imperialism, having been occupied and "civilized" by the British Empire for many years. Also India, unlike many African developing economies, has a rich native digital industry and landscape of tech companies.

There were other missteps. Tensions were heightened during the peak of the conflict by a misjudged and heavy-handed messaging campaign. Facebook appealed to its Indian user base with a message in response to the imminent ban: "Free Basics is a first step to connecting one billion Indians to the opportunities online. But without your support, it could be banned in a matter of weeks."

Macon Phillips, former head of digital strategy to President Obama and later coordinator of U.S. international programs, remembers when the Facebook story broke. He was in India as the controversy unfolded. "It was remarkable to see it play out on a day-to-day basis there. No one in the media, the government, even the activists, had any expectation that things could have happened that quickly. It really surprised everyone. We have an expression, 'the dog caught the car'—dogs are forever chasing cars and they finally catch one, and that's what it felt like."

Of Facebook's messaging campaign, Phillips highlighted another issue: control of information when it's a sole internet provider. "They pushed messages telling people to advocate with its policy. But for me the question is, how many people learned about the original video through Facebook? And at what point do you start seeing Facebook not only promote its viewpoint, but perhaps suppress other viewpoints that have to do with its own corporate interest? Or, when it's promoting its viewpoint to its users in India, does it have a responsibility to also let them know about a super-popular counterpoint? What's its role as an open platform versus a self-interested company?"

Indeed, people can visit other websites for news and content. But what happens when Facebook *is* the internet? It is swiftly becoming so in many developing markets.

Google's experience in India stands in contrast to Facebook, from a PR standpoint. Google has been quick to step into India, but with a much more open approach. Various figures are quoted but essentially, to meet a government target of adding a further 100 million internet users in India, state-run carrier BSNL announced it would set up 2,500 public wi-fi hotspots across the country by March 2017. In 2015, Google CEO Sundar Pichai also announced a partnership with Indian Railways and RailTel to install 400 wi-fi hotspots at railway stations, making wi-fi available for the more than ten million people who pass through the stations every day. Once this is fully operational, it will be the largest public wi-fi project in India, and one of the largest in the world. Crucially it will also be fast and free, with the long-term goal of making it self-sustainable. One would assume that access to Google-owned sites will be faster.

Google's wi-fi project has largely been welcomed, and highlights the fundamental flaws in Free Basics. While Facebook was trying to sell the idea of a limited "Zuckernet" to India, Google was giving away the entire internet, and at fast speeds and a level of service that most of the connected world already enjoys. In short, Google has attempted to address the key issue of connectivity, rather than condescending to Indians as Facebook's Free Basics had done.

"The thing that I've come back to as I've looked at a lot of these questions is that competition's a really good thing," says Phillips. "Competition requires a level playing field, which is why we need some government regulations. You also have to have multiple players on the field. And so I wonder what end game Facebook has in mind when all services and internet traffic for consumer things are on Facebook? When you start to not have any competitors, that's when Facebook becomes lazy. And that's when their services start falling apart."

Silicon Missionaries

Facebook's mission, though, continues apace. Beyond lucrative territories like Southeast Asia and India, where the focus is on rising affluents joining the middle-class, poorer developing and frontier markets have also become a key focus. Here, bringing internet to people who have never before had it is again being positioned as a philanthropic mission. And in weaker countries, Silicon Valley is finding governments much more amenable to their encroachment.

"The story is rather familiar, from a historical perspective. Google, Microsoft, and Apple will come to India to say, 'We will offer you enormous benefits. We bring you capital, we bring you technology,' but of course, they're asking for something in return . . . You can see clearly from China's perspective that their idea for their e-commerce was largely to block international and the global domination and to carve out a territory for their own companies, for their own political control. So far, it seems that they've been successful," says Dongsheng Zang, an associate professor of law at the University of Washington. In larger economies, the tech companies are increasingly facing pushback, says Zang. "Look at emerging economies like China, Brazil, and India, not even to mention Russia. They're not just being passive and waiting for domination—rather, they have their own strategies. There are enormous efforts to talk back to the imperial projects."

But it's not that simple, especially with poorer countries. In Africa in particular, a lot of evidence suggests that the biggest barrier to development is weak institutions. It's long been identified that well-functioning state institutions are a really important factor in development. If companies are allowed to come in and build and own their infrastructure—like Google offering to build fast internet infrastructure and put up all the masts, give everyone broadband, but in return for less regulation, all the data it wants, and a very, very lax regulatory infrastructure—the governments are effectively over a barrel. They've got a choice between going for an important free thing that they really want for their people and will make them very popular, but this meaning they are essentially giving up control of governing the internet in return. What that's actually doing is undermining the state. It also means that, while the access supports local businesses, the data gathered, and the value of that data, goes back to the U.S.

Bill Gates was perhaps one of the earliest proponents of Silicon Valley's dual approach to philanthropy: that social good could also be entrepreneurial. "In the next fifteen years, digital banking will give the poor more control over their assets and help them transform their lives," Gates has since said. "By 2030, two billion people who don't have a bank account today will be storing money and making payments with their phones. And by then, mobile money providers will be offering the full range of financial services, from interest-bearing savings accounts to credit to insurance."

He pointed to the high penetration of mobile phone users in economies like Africa and the opportunity for micro-lending and banking for "unbanked" consumers through money transfer services such as Safaricom's M-Pesa in Kenya. M-Pesa essentially turns the cellphone into a portable bank account, allowing users to deposit and transfer money via SMS text message to other people, and redeem money, too. It's been praised for allowing millions of people without bank accounts to be part of a formal financial system.

Facebook's Internet.org is the next incarnation of this mission of entrepreneurism mixed with philanthropy. And in Africa, it's welcomed. It was first rolled out in Zambia in July of 2014. In 2016 Myanmar became the eighteenth nation to sign up. By November of that year, forty million people (0.5 percent of the world population) were estimated to be using the service. The company was also in talks in late 2016 with the U.S. government to bring the Free Basics program to the United States. The latter could be a significant move as net neutrality laws, put in place by the Obama administration, are rolled back in the United States, allowing Free Basics–type models to operate in home territory.

Will low-income U.S. citizens become the next banana republic for Silicon Valley?

"The United Fruit Company was the original, evil, global multinational corporation that destroyed governments in developing countries for profits. That's what Google, Apple, Facebook, Amazon, Alibaba, Visa, and MasterCard look like to developing countries now," says Jane K. Winn. "It's like the newest chapter in imperialism. First, it was colonialism, second it was global multinational companies, now it's these platforms."

But there is a key difference. Where older colonial markets exploited local labor to extract or produce commodities that would then be exported, the new colonial model is based on providing services to emerging markets. Or as Winn describes it, "The fundamental architecture is consumer empowerment."

In other words, ironically, digital media platforms are actually creating a way for people to question the motives of the tech giants that provide them. "The calculus of how these platforms are going to play out is going to be very different. The citizens are now consumers and participants in an active way that they weren't a hundred years ago or fifty years ago. So this time when the story is told, there's hope that it's going to turn out to be less exploitive and more transparent and fair," Winn says.

India's backlash is a forerunner example of what Winn is describing—a market mediated and regulated by digitally informed local audiences and businesses. In 2015, the government of India launched Digital India, a nationwide project to connect rural areas with broadband internet. Microsoft pledged to provide broadband connectivity to 500,000 villages in the country. Amazon pledged to invest $5 billion in the country, while homegrown e-commerce company Flipkart is determined not to cede territory to the global behemoths. Alibaba is signing up Indian partners including Kotak Mahindra Bank, IDFC Bank, DHL, and Aditya Birla Finance, according to a report from online news publication Quartz. Stakes are high: India's potentially lucrative B2B e-commerce market is expected to grow by two and a half times through 2020.

"The Indian government is thinking in an extremely farsighted and shrewd way about having open technology environments, but the government controls the fundamental infrastructure because they paid for it with taxpayer dollars as public goods," explains Winn. "The government of India is building an open, interoperable architecture so that all consumer payments run through the government-controlled architecture, and the payment-services providers compete head-on and give consumers better services. But there's never the possibility that the infrastructure is being controlled by a private company."

A key revelation for India is that financial inclusion is paramount for the next ten, twenty years in terms of economic development. "They're absolutely paranoid about global multinational corporations encroaching on government control. So they have bitten the bullet and they have built the infrastructure," says Winn. "The Reserve Bank of India created a research and development institute in Hyderabad in 1996 precisely so they could start doing things like this."

The reason it works is that "it maximizes consumer welfare, it promotes innovation, and it completely eliminates the possibility of walking into a proprietary system. The Indians figured out an innovation ecosystem which is compatible with Indian social values." And therefore, they've retained control.

So where next? Governments are proving sticky. Foreign cultures, history, and nuance are at times unintelligible. Virgin territory, free from controls, criticism, and limitations is much more alluring. And it doesn't get more expansive, or ungoverned, than outer space.

5

Moonshots

It could easily be the opener of a Steven Spielberg movie. But that, perhaps, is the point. High production values meet high drama as the SpaceX Interplanetary Transport System rocket appears in the frame, emitting bursts of steam, almost like it's alive. It launches into space accompanied by majestic classical music. Moments later, in a dramatic sequence, the ship approaches Mars. Suited astronauts open the spacecraft's doors revealing a glowing, utopic Martian landscape. The brave new world.

"What I really want to try to achieve here is to make Mars seem possible, make it seem as though it's something we can do in our lifetimes." Elon Musk, moments before, is speaking onstage to an enraptured audience at the International Astronautical Congress in Guadalajara, Mexico, September 2016. It's part celebration of the endeavor to inhabit Mars, and part pitch for investment.

"History is going to bifurcate along two directions. One path is we stay on Earth forever and then there will be some eventual extinction event. I don't have an immediate doomsday prophecy, but eventually history suggests there will be some doomsday event. The alternative is to become a spacefaring civilization and a multiplanetary species, which I hope you would agree is the right way to go."

The whole presentation is theatrical. Musk, standing on a stage, has a planet Mars spinning behind him. There are sleek CAD drawings of complex designs combined with evocative visions of life on Mars—at one point, a rendering, like some teen fantasy, shows a silhouetted Lara Croft–type figure against a glass biodome with a glowing Mars backdrop.

For someone describing the astounding feat of actually colonizing a new planet, Musk's tone is markedly blasé. The selection of Mars over other planets was logical—you know, because Venus is an acid bath. Mercury is too close to the sun. Musk makes it sound like picking a summer house . . . but affordably. Life on Mars will eventually be achievable under the $100,000 mark, he says, and because so few people will go in the beginning, it will be really easy to get a job.

"The main reason I'm personally accumulating assets is in order to fund this," Musk says in conclusion. "I really don't have any other motivation for personally accumulating assets except to be able to make the biggest contribution I can to making life multiplanetary." It's his gift to humanity. He's continued to project his future visions of life in space at subsequent conferences and events, culminating perhaps in one of the most widely watched launches; in February 2018 Musk successfully rocketed a Tesla into space toward Mars and beyond, propelled by SpaceX's Falcon Heavy rocket. The launch was a global media sensation and described by CNN as a symbol of a "new space age"—one in which Elon Musk, celebrity and visionary, is at the forefront (even if he is backed by government grants and tax breaks). Over two million viewers tuned in to watch the event livestream, which was further brought to life by a video camera inside the car, showing a dummy pilot in the driving seat (and with David Bowie's "Space Oddity" playing in the background). The affair reportedly cost $90 million. For many Musk fans, and for the media in general, it was a wet dream, propelled further by humorous Twitter exchanges with rival space visionary Jeff Bezos wishing him luck. (Musk returned with a kiss emoji.)

Strange to think that not long before Musk set his sights on conquering space, his entrepreneurial vision was as prosaic as facilitating online payments. But such grand ambitions are increasingly prevalent in the tech world.

With growing fortunes, and a strong sense of manifest destiny, Silicon Valley's leaders seem determined to leap beyond industry and business to transforming the universe, life as we know it, and our future. They are doing so with an egocentric lens on their legacy, but also with an eye to long-term, potentially lucrative markets. In being the ones to lead the charge, they are also driving an important cultural shift, at least optically—one in which Silicon Valley, not government, is the architect of the future.

Musk isn't the only one with his sights on space. "We need a dynamic, entrepreneurial explosion in space, just as I've witnessed over the last twenty years on the internet—thousands of companies and tens of thousands of startups doing interesting things online," Amazon founder Jeff Bezos told the BBC in September 2017. Bezos has also founded Blue Origin, a private spaceflight services company that has promised to take tourists into space by April 2019. Meanwhile, Richard Branson's Virgin Galactic received a $1 billion investment from the Kingdom of Saudi Arabia to make a reality of its dreams to create "the next generation of human spaceflight."

The glamour (and potential imminence) of space travel is also capturing the popular imagination, paving the way for on-the-ground experiences inspired by space. Future Valley, a space-themed park in Hangzhou in China, is developing a balloon tour to take passengers on a comfortable near-space experience fifteen miles above the Earth's surface.

Silicon Valley's move into space travel is emblematic of a wider expansion in the scope of their ambition. Moonshots, as they have become known, are synonymous with Silicon Valley—defined as incredible feats, experiments, and attempts to change the world or solve an insurmountable problem. And moonshots are now being explored everywhere. Silicon Valley's center of expertise has expanded to all specialties of invention and research from material science, to biochemistry, to robotics, medicine, genetics, data science, blood testing, engineering, machine learning, and DNA sequencing. And beyond. And they are all intersecting in new ways to create new, daring products. Often these are in such unchartered territory, or moving so quickly, that the potential ethical quandaries are an afterthought or not yet understood from a regulatory point of view. But they could change our world, fast. Or, in the case of outer space, give Silicon Valley leaders control of a vast new territory, becoming architects of how human exploration works.

With these innovations, they are taking on audacious challenges—space exploration, flying cars, new pneumatic transport systems—and approaching them with a long-term vision and unprecedented resources, including government backing. If it's not Mars, then it's the Moon, and certainly orbit. Such is their belief in their abilities, with no limit to self-aggrandizing statements, and not much public scrutiny either. They're building the future! Stepping in to solve humanitarian crises and shaping scientific advances! A tweet from Musk generates breathless headlines from tech and business press. Jeff Bezos joining Instagram was breaking news. His subsequent posts sharing favorite inspirational novels, shipping supplies (in an Amazon Prime airplane, no less) to Puerto Rico following Hurricane Maria, and developments at Blue Origin are widely followed. Musk sent solar panels to the island. Both moves to aid Puerto Rico were notably outside of government efforts. These men, with previously unseen wealth and influence, don't need government. Bezos's net worth is now more than $105 billion, making him the richest person in the world.

Silicon Valley leaders are theorizing about the future of civilization with the rhetoric befitting of prophets (Musk has stated that he thinks it's likely we're all, unbeknownst to us, living in a computer simulation—this in addition to predicting doomsday extinction of the planet). Or they're building apocalypse bunkers for when society, impoverished by automation from robotic devices and artificial intelligence, turns against them. With experiments in applying everything from biotech to AI to extend our lifespans, augment our bodies, or replicate them with technology, they are also hacking humanity with a degree of irreverence reserved for people who believe they are clearly above it, and nature itself. Or believe our civilization is merely another system, something that can be disrupted (repeatedly referencing works of historians and philosophers, perhaps they see themselves within a greater arch of history now).

It started with figures such as Peter Thiel, famous for his interest in longevity research, and futurist and singularity theorist Ray Kurzweil reportedly ingesting record numbers of dietary supplements in a bid to "solve" aging. Martine Rothblatt is cloning human minds virtually, in an attempt to make us immortal. Meanwhile, a latent human cyborg movement is giving us entirely new senses, embedding our human flesh with connection to the internet.

All this started out on the fringes, an indulgence for billionaires, or as the topic of SXSW Interactive fireside chat. But changing humanity is becoming an industry. Consider Alphabet's portfolio. Consult the project list of Verily, its life sciences company, and it's pure science fiction. There are clever contact lenses that can detect changes in glucose levels. There's Galvani Bioelectronics, creating bioelectronic medicines with GlaxoSmithKline to tackle chronic disease. "Bioelectronic medicines will be designed to treat disease by modulating electrical signals in peripheral nerves using miniature, implanted devices. They may provide an entirely new toolkit for control and reversal of disease, and could complement pharmaceutical and other therapies," says Verily.

There's also Debug, a program to combat disease-spreading mosquitos by releasing sterile ones to eliminate them.

"Our team is developing new technologies that combine sensors, algorithms, and novel engineering to raise millions of these sterile mosquitoes and quickly and accurately sort them for release in the wild. We're also building software and monitoring tools to guide mosquito releases and new sensors, traps, and software to better determine which areas need to be treated and re-treated." Verily isn't Alphabet's only venture. Calico, a biotech company, is trying to solve diseases associated with aging. There's DeepMind, a London-founded company applying artificial intelligence to solve a variety of problems, particularly in health. A recent project includes using machine learning to enhance mammography screening for breast cancer.

Theirs is a world of unbridled enthusiasm for the future, but one—in its lust for the virgin territory of pastures new, and correction of all of nature's seeming "inefficiencies"—that is also revealing of their outlook.

"There is a creator phenomenon," says Puneet Kaur Ahira, a former executive in Google's Moonshots division. Indeed. Much like the tech missionaries civilizing Africa with internet, Silicon Valley is planting new seeds, envisioning its own futuristic utopias in space—ones that run much more efficiently because of their holistic control. "We're in such a rush to go to Mars; I think that's fascinating. Why are we in such a rush to go to Mars? Why are we pouring billions of dollars to get ourselves there?" asks Ahira.

In part it's that Mars is a tantalizingly blank canvas. On Earth, Silicon Valley technologies have to grapple with messy things like cities, older infrastructure, and the law. So while getting to Mars is undoubtedly a great scientific achievement, setting up completely new communities from scratch is remarkably more simple than grappling with integrating into today's fabric. They can design the universe in their image without having to adapt to anything, unlike Earth where there are towns, infrastructure, and societal norms that simply will not vanish. To hark back to Obama's Pittsburgh address: Government is "hard and it's messy, and we're building off legacy systems that we can't just blow up." In space, they can build a new cradle of civilization from the ground up. But will their futuristic vision, unfettered by the constraints of cumbersome existing systems, be the perfection they envisage?

Silicon Valley's ideal version of life is at odds with the "mess" of life on Earth, which is only going to become more imposing as inequality, globalization, and technological innovation grow more advanced. But the problems on Earth don't involve Lara Croft in a jumpsuit.

"Maybe in our pursuit of an off-planet future, we'll discover the panacea to our on-planet complexites; but maybe not," echoes Ahira. "And then what? So much of all this is a matter of attention span and the messy process of figuring out how to work together in a coherent way."

Nevertheless, it seems a missed opportunity for an industry that draws incredible talent, incredible minds from the highest caliber universities around the world, not to mention dreamers, thinkers, and seemingly limitless pools of money, and not focus that on the toughest problems on the ground. Still, perhaps these innovations developed in space could be repurposed later on Earth.

Income inequality continues to grow. In America, one of the richest countries in the world, 41 million citizens struggle with hunger according to Feeding America, a food bank charity. Mass unemployment is on the horizon thanks to the widespread application of robots and AI in everything from retail shop floors to offices. Opioid addiction is a nationwide crisis. There are gigantic problems facing us, at home and abroad. To be fair, many of Silicon Valley's moonshot endeavors are aimed at creating products that help honorable significant causes, such as affordable sustainable energy and more efficient health care, but they're usually attached to a degree of commercial motivation (more valuable consumer data). They're tech-based. Or they're extreme, headline-driven, loud, and un-nuanced. They're about only the great feats, not the small ones, or even the medium ones. And they seem to distinctly avoid issues relating to poor people in their own backyard.

Which raises the question: Why is Mars a priority in the first place? For all the rhetoric about civic action, Silicon Valley's world-bending endeavors can feel more about hubris than humanitarianism.

Silicon Systems

Silicon Valley companies and individuals are starting to think systemically, like governments—except usually without the practical considerations of funding, existing infrastructure, and bureaucracy that hamper local authorities. Uber is imagining the future of transport as flying cars in a metropolis. Hyperloop One is redrawing the planet with trains transported on vacuum tubes and maglev (magnetic levitation) tracks that move at the speed of sound.

In so doing they are constructing a new vision of energy, human bodies, and newly designed space enclaves. Rethinking infrastructures. But reimagining modes of transport for the first time with a futuristic lens, the way that trains, planes, buses, and bicycles (evolved and iterated over the years) operate, in an attempt to add something bold and new. How much of this is really plausible?

Which is not to say that things do not need fixing. And one thing that this group shares is a proactive vision for the future that, in some cases, the government (and governmental systems) has lost, locked into a four-to-eight-year elective leadership cycle. Where the focus from transport to energy is on incremental change, Silicon Valley is looking to space to solve the energy crisis and is evolving twenty- to fifty-year plans. Where innovation in transport, the sexier kind, perhaps stopped with Concordes, Silicon Valley is attempting to transform this with sci-fi visions. As for its bid to solve aging and disease, time will tell. While many governments still cling to fossil fuels, Silicon Valley is pioneering to make sustainable energy affordable.

Which is in many ways exciting. But it's a future increasingly being led by commercial interests. It's new big ethical decisions being made by individuals free from constraint. It's new frontiers being defined by Silicon Valley leaders, and all their inherent biases. Schools, trains, health-care systems, life itself.

It's important to consider how this future will manifest—it is being built, and decided, faster than ever and in a very real way may come to re-place the rapidly diminishing state. Just because they got to the future first, should they be the ones to decide what it looks like?

Forces of Tech

"We're living in a time where moonshots can happen faster than at any other time in human history. And the evolution of the engineering skills, the entre-preneurial skills, and the access to resources and capital is in place where an idea like Hyperloop can go from concept to breaking ground and moving atoms within twenty-four months," says Pishevar, Hyperloop One's controversial for-mer executive chairman and former managing director of Sherpa Capital.

Hyperloop One has recently rebranded as Virgin Hyperloop One after joining forces with fellow visionary entrepreneur Richard Branson. Pishevar resigned from his role at Hyperloop amid sexual assault and misconduct al-legations that emerged in October 2017 (which he continues to deny). Bran-son took over as a board member, attracting $50 million more investment. Suffice it to say, when Pishevar and I met in late 2016, such troubles were far off in the distance. #MeToo was not yet a global movement. And he was all bombast, bravado, and confidence.

Pishevar at his peak was perhaps one of Silicon Valley's biggest moon-shot evangelicals. But his mantle of world-changing ambition continues to be taken up by other enthusiastic leaders. Meanwhile, the vision presented by Virgin Hyperloop One, and other Silicon Valley ventures from super-sonic flights to driverless cars, seems to be making progress.

Sherpa Capital's sleek offices sit a few floors above Market Street in San Francisco. In 2016, Sherpa Capital raised $470 million for two new funds, Sherpa Everest and Sherpa Ventures II. The company is behind Uber and Munchery, among others. In person Pishevar, like Musk, has the tendency to make statements such as "bend space and time" and "transport is the new broadband" with a degree of ease normally applied to giving street directions or ordering a beer.

A private company landing on the moon is just "proof that the next set of superpowers are going to be entrepreneurs, not nation-states," agrees Naveen Jain, exuberant Seattle-based entrepreneur and founder of Moon Express, a space mining venture, and well-being artificial-intelligence company Viome, among other ventures. Jain is not one for understatements. This is a speech he's become accustomed to making at events, in part, waving two fingers at what is usually a buttoned-up corporate audience. "So far only three countries have landed on the moon, and all three have been superpowers. Now we've become the fourth superpower. It doesn't matter what the industry is. Entrepreneurs around the world are going to eclipse nation-states, and the things that used to be in the domain of nation-states are going to be accomplished by entrepreneurs."

Jain is another walking soundbite, beloved for statements such as "It's easy to predict the future when you're building it yourself." He often refers to an entrepreneur-built future where disease is "optional" or "elective." (Jain may be based in Seattle but has a long history in Silicon Valley, and embodies its ethos.)

Jain even believes Silicon Valley and its like-minded entrepreneurs could contribute to world peace: "Think about all the things we fight over. Water. Energy," he explains. "All we have to do is make that accessible, affordable, and democratize and demonetize that. Once you do that, once things are in abundance, they lose value and people stop fighting over them. For example, we don't fight over oxygen, because we believe it's in abundance. The only time we fight over things is because we believe they are scarce, and scarcity is what creates value." And this is where Silicon Valley and commercial forces are so powerful, he believes. "Cellphones started out as things only for the rich and famous and the Wall Streeters. And now the poorest person in Africa has a cellphone."

On the subject of innovation, the government is not without its defenders. Outspoken economist Mariana Mazzucato, again, has frequently talked of the need to revise the damaging image of government as a sluggish Leviathan. She has pointed out, in fact, that like the internet itself, many revolutionary innovations in pharmaceuticals and the smartphone industry (from GPS to Siri to touchscreens) were government-funded. In her 2013 TED talk, she warned against underestimating the important role of government in innovation (particularly risky long-term innovation) and of the danger of fetishizing Silicon Valley's transformative abilities. In other words: we've been giving Silicon Valley too much credit. She also said the juxtaposition "has huge implications even with this whole notion that we have of where, how, and why we should be cutting back on spending."

But she's pushing against a narrative in pop culture that seems only more drawn to Silicon Valley prowess. As well as a rapidly changing landscape in which Big Tech's limitless millions for innovation are dwarfing that of the state.

This is partly due to an evolution within the Valley itself, Pishevar says, explaining that more private funding is now available to tackle big projects: "If you looked at the generation before—that's Tesla and SpaceX—Elon had to personally finance and almost bankrupt himself and borrow money to pay rent to be able to save those companies," he says. "Those companies went from 2002 to 2014–15 in terms of the full arc of execution. Whereas if Elon had started SpaceX, or even Tesla, now, he wouldn't have had to finance it himself completely and would have been able to move things a lot faster than what was experienced. We're seeing this generational change in the expansion of the speed at which you can execute really big ideas, and that's exciting."

And the thing is, many of these feats might now actually be achieved. Virgin Hyperloop One, at least visibly, seems to be rapidly coming together at a test site in Nevada. Its PR machine is in full swing—not a day goes by without a new proposal being announced to transform commutes from the Middle East to Europe. And these moonshots are being regarded with more reverence than before, too. But for all the headlines, Hyperloop has yet to truly materialize. At CES 2018, the annual Las Vegas consumer electronics show, a much-vaunted app simulating Hyperloop's booking experience was launched.

Shernaz Daver is a Silicon Valley veteran, chief marketing officer at Udacity, and advisor to Google Ventures, the venture-capital arm of Alphabet, Inc., which focuses on transforming life science, health care, artificial intelligence, robotics, transportation, cybersecurity, and agriculture. Daver believes technology and DNA sequencing will now be able to prolong the quality of life in later years. And this has all become possible only recently. "It's been amazing to watch."

Space is a fast-growing frontier in private enterprise. SpaceX grabs headlines, but Blue Origin is also winning contracts from NASA. Beyond headlines about colonizing Mars there are plans to mine asteroids for minerals and to commercialize space travel with reusable spaceships. Sending satellites into space for a variety of applications is a similarly growing market.

VR expert and NASA collaborator Jacquelyn Ford Morie explains that "there's a huge network of companies: The Space Experience Economy, the Space Tourism Society, Virgin Galactic, Jeff Bezos's company—they're all connected. They all share stuff but they're in competition too . . . Everybody is trying to raise the awareness and the speed at which these things are going to happen. All of that gives us a critical mass where things are going to happen. I think we'll be on Mars in ten years."

That's just the beginning, she says. The Space Tourism society is looking at a multi-tiered, fully fledged space-travel industry, from Earth-based experiences and low-orbit excursions to actually constructing hotels and destinations in orbit—on the Moon and on Mars.

"There's a theme park called Mars World which will be a jumping-off point for that," says Ford Morie. "That's going to be constructed west of Las Vegas. They've got their first $75 million and they need about five times that to do this entire thing." It will, she says, not only be informative for the general public but raise awareness and excitement about space travel in a way that hasn't been done before. "The space-tourism efforts are much broader," she explains. "It's not just sending someone up there for $40,000."

Aside from tourism, the commercial applications are big. "Asteroid mining is going to be huge. It is going to help us with the fact that we're digging up all the rarest metals at an alarming rate here on Earth. I believe we'll be sending our garbage out there, too."

In all of this, SpaceX in particular seems to have captured the imagination of many. Says Kosta Grammatis, an award-winning engineer and scientist whose first job was at SpaceX: "I graduated at twenty and wanted to be a rocket scientist. I wrote to SpaceX so many times about an internship. Everyone that works for Elon Musk works all hours—they believe in a bigger mission. It's a joke often made, but it's a bit like a cult. They're all funny, smart guys. They remind me of what the young staff at NASA must have been like in the Apollo years—the average age was twenty-five to twenty-seven. They're obsessed with getting to space and that's why they work like dogs."

And much of it is starting to become all the more real in the public mind, especially following Musk's much-Instagrammed test over Los Angeles in late 2017, a bright-firing orb that on first sight many took to be a UFO.

Grammatis says Musk is impressively focused. "He was on a total mission not just to change the world but to bend nature." Musk, says Grammatis, "takes too much credit for space travel and what he's achieved, when one considers the government were big investors. But he's had the ability to pick and back winners, so in essence he's a king-maker in some ways . . . that, itself, takes vision."

Bezos, like many others in Silicon Valley, sees space as the answer to environmental issues. We need to protect the Earth, he said at the 2016 Code Conference, one of the many tech summit shindigs populated by Silicon Valley execs, this one staged by tech news site Recode, "And the way we will is by going out into space. Energy is limited here. In at least a few hundred years . . . all of our heavy industry will be moved off-planet."

Which raises another potential meta what-if question. Forget Earthly geopolitics. How will the universe world order be organized if there's a space resource grab and a new wave of Silicon Valley energy power magnates vying for asteroid territory? Does jurisdiction even exist in space? What happens when the Silicon States sets their eyes on the stars?

The Way We Move

Violet light bathes the sidewalks of Eighth Avenue at 6 a.m. as Manhattan stirs awake. Neon coffee shop, BBQ, and diner signs are flickering to life. A hunched army of commuters exit taxis, slamming doors with laptop bags forcefully lop-siding their gaits as they trudge to the illuminated escalator, descending into the heart of Penn Station. Is there anything worse than Penn Station at dawn? A line starts outside Dunkin' Donuts as workers hustle to assemble chemical-laden carbs and warm caffeine stimulants. Penn Station's gourmet options, much like its interior, are stuck in a time warp. Climb aboard the Acela express to Washington, DC and customers are delivered at high speed to the grander Union Station, via bridge and swamps, for the immodest fee of around $200. The unfortunates who cannot afford this joy are faced with the bus—lurching along the freeway for several hours longer, pulling into random parking lots along the way. To be dropped at unsavory points often at a time barely resembling the scheduled arrival at their destination.

America doesn't have the exclusive on awful travel experiences. London's District Line for a long time delivered some of my most favorite horror stories—an hour of being forcibly Gecko-shaped against condensation-covered windows, rattling from West London to groovy Shoreditch for around ten dollars per day—compare that to New York's $2.75/ride subway. Trying to get onto the train at Clapham Junction, or the Northern Line in Clapham, the south London commuter belt during rush hour, is like a human game show. People actually jump against walls of human flesh, attempting to fit within crevices between bodies to make it onto coaches. And that seems tame by Tokyo standards where people are willingly shoved onto crowded trains as a matter of custom.

And that's just the things on rails.

Somewhere along the way transportation got pretty awful. There was some innovation. Trains got faster. Planes got charging cords and individual entertainment stations. And in the Nordics, people luxuriate in clean, fast, efficient train systems. But the modes themselves largely stayed the same. (OK, if you travel on a Middle Eastern airline you can have a private four-poster bed with a hot tub, butler, and personal gym. But the rudimentaries are still there. It will still take fifteen hours to get from Dubai to New York.) Nothing, in other words, is reinventing what transport is.

An elaborately tiered system of domestic air travel has developed in the U.S., commodifying all aspects of comfort, space, or preferable location, and of course this is not unique to America alone. (Oxygen could be a five-dollar offering of the future. Meantime, anything other than the back-row aisle seat, toilet-line central, has an additional price tag.) That's if you can get to the airport. In many cities you'll need to pony up for a taxi or a bus ticket.

Cars, then, remain one of the easiest ways to get about, but they can be costly once gas, insurance, parking, and repairs are factored in—not forgetting the expenses and impracticalities of owning a car in urban centers. New alternatives to owning one are emerging. On weekday mornings, young millennials can be seen lining the streets of Manhattan, smartphone in hand, picking up ride-share services such as UberPool and Via. Uber has tested a $100 unlimited monthly subscription offer in Manhattan. It has become a credible commuting service for those who can afford it. (Interesting to consider what the displaced revenue may be doing to the beleaguered subway, which is reportedly planning to increase fares from $2.75 to $3 per ride. That's happening alongside delays, headline-grabbing accidents, and breakdowns. It was estimated by the *New York Times* that the New York subway system needs a $100 billion investment to be repaired and rebuilt, ensuring its survival.)

The Pew Research Center released some interesting demographic data on Uber. It found that 29 percent of college graduates have used ride-hailing services and just 13 percent are unfamiliar with the term. Among those who have not attended college, just 6 percent have used these services and over half (51 percent) have never heard of them. Overall, 26 percent of Americans with an annual household income of $75,000 or more have used these services. For those living in households with an annual income of less than $30,000, just 10 percent have used these services and 49 percent are not familiar with them. The same study found that while prominent in urban centers, services like Uber are still relatively latent nationwide. Yet in areas where they are concentrated, their influence is powerful.

In other words, Uber may feel like a replacement to public transport in cities, but it is still used, and skewed, heavily toward young, educated, affluent consumers.

At SXSW 2015, Bill Gurley, a venture capitalist at Benchmark and another investor in Uber, spoke about the untapped market for transport in the U.S. "For eighty years, we've grossly underestimated the demand for transportation services. And we limited it at a city government level," he said. He added that in cities such as San Francisco, use of Uber was five times higher than that of the existing taxi fleet. "That's new demand," he said, estimating that the full size of the market could be as much as ten times that of taxis. "At first it was just an alternative to taxis . . . But it's started to compete with other things."

The rental-car market being one. In 2017, shares in Hertz Global Holdings hit their lowest in seven years. They dropped by 39 percent in one year. Shares in Avis Budget Group Inc. declined 26 percent in the same year. In the last quarter of 2017, Uber accounted for 55 percent of ground transportation transactions expensed through Certify, America's second-biggest expense software platform. And Uber's recent reputational controversies about its ethics, internal sexism, and aggressive culture seem to be doing little to erode its revenues.

Gurley also pointed to a wider cultural shift. "Millennials don't give a shit about cars," he said. "There are kids who will turn sixteen and won't get a driver's license . . . millennials view cars as a utility, not as a social statement, which is a huge shift for North America."

Which puts Silicon Valley at a further advantage over rivals such as Detroit. Both hubs may be creating cars, but Silicon Valley's are largely designed for ride-sharing systems, not ownership.

Uber has already supplanted not just taxis but hire cars and car ownership. It's also positioning itself as the architect of the future of transportation, with automated cars (being tested in Pittsburgh) and UberPool (replacing the daily public transport commute). In addition, Uber has published a white paper about on-demand flying cars in cities. (White papers are a common form of reports on a specific issue. They are created by governments, academics, or other experts exploring or making a proposal on an issue.)

The white paper trend is worth noting. From Elon Musk's white papers to Uber's recent ninety-seven-page vision for the future, these documents—often illustrated with renderings reminiscent of 1920s urban futurism—are public challenges to the way traditional transportation operates today. Such white papers usually receive a huge amount of attention.

"Imagine traveling from San Francisco's Marina to work in downtown San Jose—a drive that would normally occupy the better part of two hours—in only fifteen minutes," says Uber's "Fast-Forwarding to a Future of On-Demand Urban Air Transportation" paper published in 2016. "Every day, millions of hours are wasted on the road worldwide," it continues. "For all of us, that's less time with family, less time at work growing our economies, more money spent on fuel—and a marked increase in our stress levels: a study in the *American Journal of Preventative Medicine*, for example, found that those who commute more than ten miles were at increased risk of elevated blood pressure."

The solution? "On-demand aviation has the potential to radically improve urban mobility, giving people back time lost in their daily commutes . . . Just as skyscrapers allowed cities to use limited land more efficiently, urban air transportation will use three-dimensional airspace to alleviate transportation congestion on the ground."

The next area ripe for disruption is postal services, as evidenced by Amazon's recent acquisition of cargo jets and ocean freight services—not to mention testing drone delivery. Many people, including Virgin Hyperloop One chief executive Rob Lloyd, are excited: "It's amazing, but the postal services are relevant again . . . I actually think you'll see private industries funding new infrastructure. An early sign of that is Amazon buying two fleets of 767s to control their own infrastructure, just as DHL and FedEx brought their own airplanes. They brought their own infrastructure because it became a part of the dynamic of their cost model. Transportation infrastructure, increasingly, could become part of the cost model that big enterprises will look for in an on-demand world." Amazon has introduced cloud computing services for businesses, enabling small companies to sidestep building their own IT infastructure systems. Its shipping infrastructure is transforming consumer expectations toward deliveries en masse. Today it's not uncommon to expect packages to arrive on the same day in major cities, or next day, and free of charge. That's largely thanks to Amazon. Will plug-and-play deliveries for new businesses be its next business-to-business service?

Silicon Valley isn't stopping there. It's seeking to reinvent energy, from cars to homes. With storage batteries, affordable solar panels, and electric cars, Elon Musk is in effect becoming an energy magnate. Amazon is investing heavily in renewable energy. It signed an agreement to buy 90 percent of the output from a new 235-megawatt wind farm in Scurry County, Texas. It has also announced an agreement with Iberdrola Renewables for a 208-megawatt wind farm in North Carolina. In 2016 Bill Gates announced the start of Breakthrough Energy Ventures, a $1 billion clean-energy fund, which he plans to chair. Other backers include Jack Ma and Jeff Bezos. The fund aims to invest in next-generation energy technologies.

Moving Mountains

While Virgin Hyperloop One originated in California, its most vociferous support is, interestingly, far from home. The most vocal backing has come from markets such as Northern Europe, where there's a well-established legacy of investing in new transport infrastructure, and the Middle East, where there's the autocratic vision to achieve a project of the magnitude of Virgin Hyperloop One, as well as a largely blank canvas in terms of relevant infrastructure. (Not to mention a general enthusiasm in the Middle East for fantastical futuristic developments—in Dubai there's a 22,500-square-foot indoor ski slope, after all.)

Pishevar's ambitions, pre-allegations, had recently extended to rethinking government and campaigning, in the wake of the 2016 presidential election result, for California to leave the U.S. Speaking to CNBC after the election, he said the state could "reenter the union after California becomes a nation. As the sixth largest economy in the world, the economic engine of the nation, and provider of a large percentage of the federal budget, California carries a lot of weight." He added that he wanted California to become the catalyst for a national dialogue, as the country needs to "confront the systemic problems that this election has exposed."

In person, Pishevar compares the lack of enthusiasm in the U.S. for his pneumatic train with the struggle of the Wright brothers to launch aviation. "They had that similar situation where the first interest in the airplane was from the French, German, and British governments. The American government didn't take it seriously. They funded their own project, which was a complete failure, whereas these two brothers with $2,000 of earnings from their bicycle shop figured it out. It's incredibly inspiring. It's also very analogous to what's happening now, where international governments are much more ahead of the game in terms of interest in deploying Hyperloop."

One of his ideas to solve this is to hold a California referendum, throwing the choice to the people. "I'd have someone run a campaign that basically says that the California high-speed rail is a complete waste of taxpayers' money at $80-plus billion, and we should vote in a referendum to replace it with Hyperloop; to take over the right of ways and then return that money to taxpayers and put it into infrastructure projects and schools."

Like Jain, Pishevar believes the future will be built by entrepreneurs. "One of the lessons I've learned as an entrepreneur is that it really does take a very small group of people to push something forward. If the Wright brothers hadn't worked so hard with a small group of people and a small budget, the history of flight might have been delayed by decades. The economic impact that has had on humanity has been massive. We feel the same way with Hyperloop. We're trying to speed up the process of the kind of important technology innovation that can become part of a whole new transportation grid. Moving people and things faster will make the global economy work faster and create growth, jobs, and opportunity." He has also been looking at companies such as Boom Technologies, trying to bring supersonic flight back with passenger airplanes (supersonic flights fly faster than the speed of sound and were initially developed for the military). In December 2017, Japan Airlines (JAL) and Boom announced a $10 million strategic partnership to bring commercial supersonic travel to passengers.

"Supersonic flight has existed for seventy years, but until now it hasn't been efficient enough for routine travel. Boom's airliner enables fares 75 percent lower than Concorde, about the same price as today's business class tickets," says Boom. "This advance in efficiency is made possible by a breakthrough aerodynamic design, state-of-the-art engines, and advanced composites."

Pishevar's original vision for Virgin Hyperloop One extended beyond the transport network itself. It has the potential to overhaul dock systems and unlock new geographies. "A lot of people don't understand that there's a real estate arbitrage play here, too. Ports around the world are sitting on really expensive real estate property. Trucks are also creating a lot of infrastructure strain and pollution. Long Beach Port alone is $200 billion of real estate value and there's 800,000 trucks a day that go there that the mayors want off the highway. We could build an offshore port that could take the cargo straight to the desert and meet the trucks there. Then you could basically have $200 billion of prime waterfront property developed for new housing and commercial properties. Multiply that by all the ports around the world and you're talking about trillions of dollars of value creation and massive pollution and environmental benefits."

As for our current cities, Pishevar is not a fan (meeting Pishevar is like meeting a live petri dish specimen of Silicon Valley stereotypes, both for his magnetic ambition and uninhibited self-belief). "Cities need to be redesigned. I look at cities now and they're based on nineteenth- or twentieth-century infrastructure. So you have depreciating assets that are seventy-five or one hundred years old, falling apart, and need to be replaced. Whole swaths of cities will have to rise up anew. You have what I call regenerative development of existing cities and completely new development of new cities. I joke that Elon has to go to Mars and terraform Mars—we have to terraform the planet." He adds that many new cities and even nations have been created in the last one hundred years, so this is not even very innovative. "It's just studying history . . . The world before had a much more straightforward process of someone saying, 'Let's go build a city.'"

Old buildings, urban settings, and a mixed layered fabric of cities are something great, and rich. Wouldn't we be losing something if we just tore everything down and started from scratch? The future and history can coexist. In Japan and in France, futuristic architecture and transport sit alongside history. But, for now, Virgin Hyperloop One is not arriving in the U.S., where there's inconvenient things like existing infrastructure that cannot be terraformed. And democracy.

But there's no doubt that Silicon Valley has its eye on transforming how we move around the planet.

Hyper Travel

"In Europe, transportation infrastructure is as expected as health care," observes Lloyd. "It's not a nasty thing to imagine that someone would spend $10 billion to make a more efficient, high-speed connection between two cities where there's frequent travel. It's actually expected. So you get that in Northern Europe, also in Dubai, where we expect that we're going to be bringing the first ideas forward."

America has a mixed history with regard to public transport, from railroad monopolies controlled by captains of industry (or "robber barons," depending on your view), to early privately run cable cars and subways in the late nineteenth century. Public transport was a profitable pursuit. Cornelius Vanderbilt built the New York Central Railroad and the Grand Central Depot, and many of the other major railroads can be attributed to industrial tycoons from Leland Stanford to Collis Potter Huntington.

After World War II, cars and gasoline became widely available. Cars also became status symbols, associated with freedom, independence, and the American dream. Highway-building programs ensued, as did suburban sprawl and urban development dependent on access to cars. Meanwhile, with the creation of efficient jet aircraft for long-distance travel, a major airport-building initiative took place. And all this public transport needed government funding to sustain it. So, from planning to execution, public transport became the realm of the state. But over the years there has been a decline in public transport overall. According to a 2016 study by the American Society of Civil Engineers, America is $1.44 trillion short of the investment it needs to repair infrastructure in the next decade.

Today, mobility in the U.S., or ease of mobility, is a tiered system based on personal income and location (unless you're in a major city, but even then, that's partly the case). Long-haul buses are a slow, uncomfortable option compared to planes and trains. For those who can afford it, the more comfortable but still painfully slow Amtrak will take you from Boston to New York or down to Washington, DC—Amtrak's Acela Express is a little faster but expensive. Amtrak is another fatality of the Trump administration, though. Trump's 2017 transportation budget slashed federal aid to America's rail systems. It cut funding for long-distance Amtrak service and drastically cut money to help expand transit lines and build new ones. The new $16.2 billion budget sees a nearly 13 percent reduction in spending during the fiscal year of 2017, about half what Congress originally allocated, including a $630 million reduction in subsidies for long-distance Amtrak routes. It's more disappointing after 2016, when Amtrak announced it would be introducing high-speed trains along its northeast corridor by 2021 as part of $2.45 billion in federal loans. Meanwhile, a series of high-profile train derailments in Washington have highlighted the urgency of updating the underfunded network.

Was Peter Thiel right? Did we lose our ambition and stop building exciting things?

Of Silicon Valley's bolder endeavors—at least those on Earth—Virgin Hyperloop One is one of the bigger bets. A mission to reinvent the horror of long-distance travel with a time-bending, planet-flattening, on-demand bullet train on stilts.

Arrive at the corner of Bay Street and South Santa Fe Avenue, a down-at-the-heels, warehouse-like area of downtown Los Angeles, and it can get confusing. This is supposed to be the location of the shiny new headquarters of Virgin Hyperloop One, the company reinventing how we, and goods, move around the planet. The street is desolate, lined with boarded-up stores save for a dusty strip club called the PlayPen, a dive bar, and a gas station.

The first glimpse there might be change afoot is the American Tea Room. It's a groovy, hipsterish island in what is currently an industrial wasteland, but it has all the trappings of a Brooklyn café—aprons, moustaches, a tea zone, polished concrete seating, and a vertical garden. Further meandering and there's Our/Los Angeles, a Pernod Ricard experiment in producing vodka in a locally run, locally adapted distillery. There's a local art gallery, and there are two more artisan cafés. There's also the Springs, a wellness center housed in a warehouse, offering a natural wine bar, yoga, juice bar, and workshops. If Los Angeles's downtown theater district is becoming a hub for hipster reinvention, then this industrial part of downtown L.A. is the new answer to London's Shoreditch and a growing hotspot for startups. And they don't get much hotter than Hyperloop.

It's difficult not to get excited stepping into the Hyperloop One offices. A regular headliner at tech conferences where drones and jargon about "social media influencers" and "being authentic" are an incessant hum, Hyperloop One has stood out as bold in its ambition and refreshing in its futurist outlook.

It's also emblematic of one of the more widely ambitious Silicon Valley private ventures.

Thiel talks about our reluctance to seize the future, and of our tendency to view that future in dystopic terms, but Hyperloop seems to have captured people's imagination. There are naysayers of course, particularly engineers and journalists, as well as doubts about how much this thing—the ultra–high speed floating tubular train system—will actually cost to build, but it nevertheless seems to be striding ahead. There are countless headlines about India or the United Arab Emirates potentially being the first location for Hyperloop, or how we'll soon be able to go from "Helsinki in Finland to Stockholm in Sweden in just twenty-eight minutes."

If it's successful, it could also be extremely lucrative. The company estimates that the market for moving things and people around could be $154 trillion over the next twenty years. That is, of course, if it ever successfully starts taking passengers and freight.

The ambition is also for it to be affordable, using what Pishevar describes as Uber's "adjacent subsidization" model. "Where black car service, which is more expensive, subsidizes UberX, and then UberX subsidizes UberPOOL, and then UberPOOL made it the price of a bus ride. Cargo is our adjacent subsidization for a Hyperloop passenger." (Will it therefore experience the same financial losses as Uber? In November 2017, Uber's quarterly losses had jumped 40 percent to $1.46 billion.)

Like Uber, Google driverless cars, and seemingly every new Silicon Valley service, Hyperloop will be on-demand. (When it comes to civic and social life imagined by Silicon Valley, everything is turned inward, personalized, and ultra-convenient. There are no timetables. No one will have to encounter anyone, or anything, at any time that they don't want to. And when they do want something, it will arrive quickly. Considering how on-demand culture has already turned urban millennials into a tribe of impatient selfish babies, unable to handle any social realities, let alone wait for taxis, thanks to Uber, dates, thanks to Tinder, deliveries, thanks to Seamless, and—er—anything, thanks to TaskRabbit, it's wild to imagine what this could do to our sense of collective social consciousness. Is it so bad to wait for a train? And pity the poor, for whom this is still largely unaffordable.)

The finished system will transport people or goods at a speed of up to 745 mph, which is just below the speed of sound and faster than an airplane. In Hyperloop's vision, passengers and freight will be propelled in pod-like vehicles through a near-vacuum tube, gliding through magnetic levitation. In July 2017, the company carried out a test in Las Vegas with a transporter that could achieve 250 mph, its self-described Kitty Hawk moment. It's now completed test runs in a fully fledged test center, with white tubing mounted in the Nevada desert. Though there have been no human tests yet, the Wright brothers would have been open-mouthed.

The idea for Hyperloop began in 2013 when Elon Musk published a fifty-seven-page white paper describing a radical alternative to public transport—capsules containing twenty-eight people could be fired through a sealed, low-pressure tube. Floating on a cushion of air, the capsules could make the journey between San Francisco and Los Angeles in thirty minutes.

The project was later taken over by Pishevar and Lloyd. The story goes that Pishevar and Musk were on a humanitarian mission to Havana, Cuba, in 2013—presumably another city that could be terraformed from scratch—when Pishevar asked if he could take on Hyperloop. Musk, after all, had space, cars, and energy on his plate. Pishevar suggested that Hyperloop could carry freight as well as people. He subsequently recruited a cofounder, a former SpaceX engineer named Brogan BamBrogan. Hyperloop Technologies set up shop in BamBrogan's garage in Los Angeles in November 2014. By 2015, the project was big enough to open its current downtown location, and it raised money from Sherpa Capital among others. Lloyd joined in 2015. Since then the company has generated $295 million in investment, signed deals with Dubai's Roads and Transport Authority and DP World, which is the world's third-largest port operator, and established partnerships with General Electric and Deutsche Bahn. But the company has continually had naysayers. Before Richard Branson came on board, it was reported to be experiencing financial problems. It has repeatedly been dubbed a fantasy project, or worse, a Ponzi scheme. Before Pishevar's legal issues, the company's slick reputation was marred by a lawsuit filed by BamBrogan, who exited his position claiming harassment and financial mismanagement—but from this at least, it appears to have moved on.

The company has enlisted BIG—the Bjarke Ingels Group, utopianist architect of the moment—to design the vision and experience. The promotional video, set in 2020, offers a teaser. The Hyperloop terminal is a sleek, futuristic circle in the heart of Dubai, surrounded by skyscrapers and gardens. Pods join and move around the circle continuously; pods contain meeting rooms, lounges, and cargo, and they are deployed in regular intervals to sealed Hyperloop tubes, where they jet off to their destinations. The video features actors portraying how it will be used for a trip from Abu Dhabi to Dubai. The entire experience is frictionless and idyllic—renderings by BIG show a light-filled terminal space. It's all very slick, with thumping digital music adding to the ambience.

Hyperloop isn't shy on futuristic rhetoric, either. Taglines include "Be anywhere. Move anything. Connect everyone. Hyperloop is the new way to move people and things around the world." Or "Hyperloop is a new way to move people and things at airline speeds for the price of a bus ticket. It's on-demand, energy-efficient, and safe. Think: broadband for transportation." And "We're not selling transport, we're selling time." Certainly one of the more enticing aspects of the on-demand loop pod system is eradicating the time currently spent in airport departures and security.

The Virgin Hyperloop One headquarters has all the bells and whistles of a startup, complete with exposed brick walls (ironically, it sits next to old train tracks). When I visit pre–Richard Branson, it's still plain old Hyperloop One and only a small discreet door sign indicates what's behind. Today, there's a parking lot with vine-covered, multi-tiered car lifts, and a full frontage with sleek grey planters and desert grass landscaping.

Engineers are walking around. Out back there are vast tubes being lifted around by cranes. Amid the noise, drilling, and commotion, Lloyd, formerly president of Cisco, is bullish about the company's future. "If you look at what we've done in a short period of time, we're going to have our kick-off moment this year and have the first full-scale Hyperloop in history working with cargo as well. That's pretty phenomenal." (Note: 2018 this has yet to happen.)

Lloyd brushes off those who question Hyperloop One's science. It's difficult to see, without a moneyed dictator prepared to flatten everything, how to build a giant network of mounted low-pressure, maglev tubes shooting trains back and forth across oceans. But the pure ambition is laudable. (Each of its proposed routes will need gigantic infrastructure built to carry the tube network, via either new tunnels or mounted monorails.)

"The good news is, the challenges we face are to just demonstrate that this system works," he says. "But remember, we expect the naysayers to absolutely resist something quite disruptive, because there's no rules around what we do. The book on transportation in the UK is this thick," he indicates a thick volume, "the rail regulations are this thick"—he indicates another huge pile of paper—"and there are about two pages that have any relevance to Hyperloop. Two pages. So we have to write a new book. Governments don't necessarily feel very good about writing new rules and regulations, so we have to help them do that. The biggest challenge, in my opinion, will be writing the playbook for how to regulate what looks like a plane, riding on a track, and in a tube—it's almost like, 'Oh my gosh, this is pipelines meet airplanes meet rail meets solar farm.'"

The vision presented by Lloyd is of a future where entire geographies are transformed. Of Virgin Hyperloop One's high-speed, long-distance capability, Lloyd commented that "it alters the definition of a city. Cities would be defined much more as regions than the boundaries of municipal government . . . Your working and living arrangements would be very different, so you would start to change property values. You wouldn't have to live in San Francisco and pay ridiculous rents to have the vibe of San Francisco."

Space saved by Hyperloop being partly underground would also mean extra real-estate development potential. It's a big, chunky, audacious project, involving miles of tubing, concrete, metal, new town planning, and new towns. And it's being led by a private company, a tech executive, and backed substantially by Silicon Valley venture funds.

Will it work? Could Hyperloop be the disruptive force that changes transport in the same way the smartphone changed telecommunications?

"Transportation has typically been the domain of governments." But, says Lloyd, innovation in recent years has been iterative and incremental— not transformative, which is where entrepreneurs have the edge. "We'll put in a metro for city transportation, we'll get our buses to be smarter and get an app for your bus, and that's all around the world. Unless something really disruptive comes around, there's no reason to expect that that would change. I think, in transportation infrastructure, the same thing is going to happen. I wouldn't expect anybody in government to actually want to accelerate a disruptive technology. It's not a natural behavior—it doesn't make sense to disrupt all the mechanisms that you feel might be working well. It's going to have to be a company, an industry, a movement."

A Silicon Valley "movement," presumably.

Tech's entrepreneurial spirit, limitless funding, and ambition is turning to reinventing every corner of our lives. Its way of thinking is lauded as a secret sauce for fixing just about everything, from disrupting a broken transport system to improving the way we learn. In all, technology, economies of scale, and disruptive business models are usually deemed the cure. But what happens when it tries to disrupt one of the most lucrative and entrenched systems around? Can Silicon Valley save health care?

6

The Future of Health

As symbols go, it was pretty potent. Amid ongoing national debate about America's broken health-care system, the future of the Affordable Care Act, sky-high drug prices, and continuous headlines about the opioid epidemic, with scant signs of resolution, in stepped not government with a decisive action but three titans of industry. One of them was Jeff Bezos.

On January 30, 2018, Jeff Bezos, Warren Buffett, and Jamie Dimon announced they were entering the health insurance business with a new joint venture. The partnership, between Amazon, Berkshire Hathaway, and JPMorgan Chase, is a new company aimed at providing their U.S. employees with a better alternative for health care. In a statement, they said the company, while still in its early stages, would be "free from profit-making incentives and constraints."

"The ballooning costs of health care act as a hungry tapeworm on the American economy," Buffett commented. "We share the belief that putting our collective resources behind the country's best talent can, in time, check the rise in health costs while concurrently enhancing patient satisfaction and outcomes."

The venture's ambition is to find a more efficient and transparent way to provide health-care services to their collective base of 840,000 employees and their respective families. "The health-care system is complex, and we enter into this challenge open-eyed about the degree of difficulty," Bezos said. "Hard as it might be, reducing health care's burden on the economy while improving outcomes for employees and their families would be worth the effort."

Reports soon speculated that this company could in time extend its services to all consumers. So much so, shares of established health insurers from UnitedHealth (UNH) to Anthem (ANTX), Aetna (AET), and Cigna (CI) took a dive following the announcement.

And little wonder. Amazon had already ruffled feathers by making key hires and acquisitions in pharmaceuticals, including buying pharmaceutical licenses and holding talks with generic-drug makers. The threat of it disrupting the pharmacy business was enough to inspire pharmacy chain CVS Health to acquire health insurance behemoth Aetna for $69 billion in a defensive move, and tout new potential services such as in-store primary care and medical follow-ups.

The perceived threat is not unreasonable. Amazon is giving many packaged goods, fashion, beauty, and personal-care brands a headache with its roll out of AmazonBasics, more affordable, private-label alternatives to branded versions. Meanwhile, a new wave of Amazon lines in fashion, beauty, and athleisure are being pitched as desirable independent brands akin to Nike, Lululemon, and Tory Burch (see Dear Drew by Drew Barrymore). All of which are promoted in Amazon search results above other brands. Then there's Amazon's grocery business. Efficiencies, robotics, and machine learning enabled it to reduce the price of organic goods in its newly acquired Whole Foods supermarket chain by as much as 43 percent. No doubt a host of private-label affordable organic groceries are on the horizon, creating challenges for Trader Joe's among others. All that's coupled with the fact that Amazon is already baked in to people's daily lifestyle and shopping habits. More online shopping searches start on Amazon than Google, according to the "State of Amazon" study by BloomReach in 2016. (Ninety percent of consumers will check Amazon even if they have found the product elsewhere.) All of this could provide big competition when applied to the world of health.

Would it be the worst thing for Amazon (along with Buffet and JPMorgan) to shake up health care? Health-care systems in the U.S. and the UK are under deep scrutiny. The United States spends more on health than any other nation. Despite this, the average life expectancy has fallen in consecutive years, according to the Centers for Disease Control and Prevention. Health inequality is an ongoing issue. A recent study in the *American Journal of Public Health* found that household spending on health care was a significant contributor to income inequality in the U.S. Meanwhile, medical expenses push millions of Americans below the federal poverty line. "Medical outlays reduced the median income of the poorest decile by 47.6 percent versus 2.7 percent for the wealthiest decile and pushed 7.013 million individuals into poverty . . . The way we finance medical care exacerbates income inequality and impoverishes millions of Americans."

In the UK, the woes of the National Health Service continue to make headlines. In 2017, the British Red Cross even warned that it was on the brink of a "humanitarian crisis" because it could not keep up with demand for ambulances and hospitals.

Perhaps Bezos, Buffet, and Dimon's health care 2.0 could have global potential.

Many Americans (unless they work in health care) would welcome the prospect of Silicon Valley's disruptive forces changing the game for creating at least a new set of competitors to the big giants, if not a new system entirely. The current health-care system doesn't seem to benefit anyone except those who can afford it—and chances are, they too would welcome a cheaper, more efficient version.

The continued specter with any of this, of course, is that it gives private companies like Amazon access to yet more intimate personal data. Do we trust them? And is the benefit of sharing this information incentive enough for a reasonable health-care system? For many, it actually might be.

In 2017, J. Walter Thompson surveyed 1,000 American adults on the future of health. Eighty-eight percent of women and 83 percent of men said they believed the health insurance system was broken and must be fixed. Seventy-five percent of consumers thought startup tech companies should be working to improve the health insurance system. In the same study, the majority of consumers said they would be comfortable sharing anonymized medical data for research, both with research institutions (69 percent) and with private companies (62 percent).

But health is not just one thing, of course. Health is pharmaceuticals, hospitals, doctors, emergency rooms, optometrists, chiropractors, dentists, sleep coaches, yoga teachers, and medical marijuana. And Silicon Valley is moving into many of these spaces and attempting new services that disintermediate traditional businesses with consumer-centric, transparent, and data-driven alternatives. Or make huge breakthroughs in life sciences, biotech, equipment, and even the way health insurance itself works.

The Chan Zuckerberg Initiative has set up a $600 million Biohub as part of its mission to cure, prevent, and manage all disease. Research is open—encouraging other researchers to feed in. Grants are given with a five-year time limit to make a breakthrough. OraSure, a Pennsylvania-based tech company, has partnered with the Bill & Melinda Gates Foundation to offer its HIV self-testing product at a more affordable price in fifty developing countries.

New equipment and hardware are also being developed, which could service hospitals, clinics, and research organizations. A San Francisco startup called 3Scan has raised $14 million in venture funding for a proprietary robotic microscope and computer vision systems to automate tissue analysis for scientists involved in drug discovery.

Jeff Bezos has invested in Juno Therapeutics, a cancer research startup.

Tech's health awakening started, perhaps, with the dual rise of trends in well-being and self-quant (the trend for using devices such as wearable Fitbits to monitor fitness levels and improvement, which have since become embedded in people's lifestyles and health regimens). Over the past few years, well-being has become a global phenomenon—the lens through which people consume everything in the attempt for a balanced lifestyle—perhaps in the knowledge that we're now all going to have to work until we're one hundred years old. According to the Global Wellness Institute, the well-being economy is now worth $3 trillion. It grew 10.6 percent to $3.72 trillion between 2013 and 2015. There are now paint colors positioned with a well-being angle. Luxury apartments with purified air and water (see Deepak Chopra's latest development in Miami). And as luxury fashion sales see challenges, a global army of athleisure-bedecked consumers continues to spend on brightly colored seasonal leggings and crop tops.

With that, consumer health tech products have exploded, promising shoppers the ability to monitor their own health. The halls of CES, the Consumer Electronics Show staged every year in Las Vegas, have started to groan with new devices that help consumers monitor everything from their sleep patterns to the lighting in their room (designed to optimize your circadian rhythms) to their pregnancy, stress levels, blood pressure, and more. The inventions continue to get more inventive. At CES 2017, several connected cars boasted well-being benefits such as mood-enhancing displays and fresh air alert "bursts"—all of which seems a bit of a stretch, given that you're sitting in a vehicle and when they all become self-driving people won't even need to exert themselves to steer. With smartphone dependence and rising anxiety and mental health awareness, mindfulness apps have exploded, helping us, ironically, to disconnect. Calm, an app that offers guided meditations, has been downloaded fourteen million times and counting. Headspace, a similar app, has been downloaded eighteen million times. There are apps for mindful eating, childbirth, and more. WeCroak is an especially morbid addition. The app reminds users several times a day that they are going to die, along with other motivational messages such as: "The grave has no sunny corners." The philosophy behind its approach has Bhutanese folk origins. Apparently there is a famous belief that to be happy you need to think about death five times a day. The instinctive response is to appreciate life and seize the day.

Some of these wackier concepts are driven by the culture in Silicon Valley itself, one defined by a relentless quest for self-improvement, turning to philosophy, history, spiritualism, and far-flung lands for ways to be better at their jobs. As Amber Atherton, founder of advertising tech company Zyper and new Palo Alto resident, tells me: "Most of my startup friends do have tutors. There's a culture of self-improvement and desire for efficiency, it's like nowhere else. You just want to optimize, optimize. How am I being more efficient? All the time."

Collectively, this sits within a growing appreciation of well-being in lifestyle as a form of preventative health care, a way to ward off chronic disease. According to Aon Employee Benefits, the number of employers investing in workplace well-being increased from 36 percent to 42 percent this year, with a view to preventing (rather than treating) everything from disease to anxiety and stress-related symptoms. Consumer tech companies have been in prime position to capitalize on this shift, presenting new services as a way to take control of personal health care and potentially avoid excessive medical costs for treatment.

There are other factors, too. New technologies are making it easier, faster, and cheaper for companies to offer what were previously highly specialized tests and personalized analyses, giving way to a whole wave of health monitoring that was previously unavailable. The cost of sequencing a single human genome has fallen from $100 million in 2001 to under $1,500 today. Low-cost sensors enable people to monitor the air quality around them or (with wearable forms) their skin hydration. Advances in AI reduce costs in health care by aggregating massive amounts of data, creating cognitive health predictions. AI is also being applied in new consumer services such as Viome's.

Affordable DNA and blood testing are now positioned as direct-to-consumer products. Personal genomics company 23andMe has launched a testing kit it sells directly to the consumer that complies with the U.S. Food and Drug Administration rules on personal genetics testing. For $199, people can order a kit that will help them understand not only their DNA and ancestry but also their health, including genetic health risks (your risk of getting certain diseases), wellness, and carrier status (whether you carry certain inherited conditions). Bill Gates and Jeff Bezos have both invested in Illumina 2016, a biotech company working toward cheap DNA sequencing. It recently launched Grail, which aims to detect cancer in its early stages through DNA testing.

Wellness is also being revolutionized with new hyper-tailored services previously only available to professional athletes. We charted these new services emerging from 2016 at JWT. WellnessFX, an at-home blood test, has advanced analysis of blood, genetics, and the microbiome alongside recommendations to improve diet and exercise. The company recently launched its first testing kit, the $111 Lifelong Vitality package, which monitors key markers of women's health.

Blueprint for Athletes is a diagnostic service that conducts detailed blood tests to measure key indicators of muscle status, endurance, nutrition, and other factors that impact athletic performance. With consumer versions of the Blueprint test priced at $225 to $500, the company is aiming toward serious and weekend athletes. InsideTracker also has at-home blood tests. It analyzes biomarkers such as vitamin levels and cholesterol to give users personalized recommendations and an "inner age" metric. Home kits start at $199.

"Health care is moving to the home," Paul Jacobson, CEO of WellnessFX, told us. "Everything we're doing is geared toward new technology that's making the experience of collecting samples more convenient. As that happens, eventually you're going to get your results on your cellphone directly. You're probably going to be able to bypass labs."

Disrupting the diagnostic testing industry alone could reap massive rewards. The global blood testing market is expected to reach $63 billion by 2024, according to Grand View Research. At-home testing is a rapidly expanding business; the direct-to-consumer lab test market was worth $131 million in 2015, up from just $15 million in 2010.

There are also hybrid services sprouting. New preventative health platforms include Omada Health, which works with employers to provide a digital diabetes prevention program via coaching, a tailored dashboard, and apps to monitor and encourage healthy behavior. "Welcome to the start of a life-changing journey. Omada is a digital behavior change program that can help people lose weight, reduce your risk of chronic disease, and feel better than you have in years." Similarly, Noom is aimed at preventing obesity, prediabetes, and hypertension by promoting behavioral change—Samsung Ventures invested in Noom in December 2016.

Taken together, the bigger picture presents an increasing blur between the idea of traditional professional health care and what previously would have been lifestyle health categories. But it's a blur that is creating a health boom for Silicon Valley in the area of new consumer products.

Tech is also being wrapped into traditional hospitals with new partnerships between tech companies and institutions. IBM Watson Health, IBM's AI venture, has been working with hospitals from India to the U.S. on a variety of applications such as using data analysis to identify tailored cancer treatments faster, match patients with clinical trials, and accelerate drug discovery.

Early on, the McKinsey Global Institute estimated that applying AI and big-data strategies to better inform decision-making could generate up to $100 billion in value annually across the U.S. health-care system, "by optimizing innovation, improving the efficiency of research and clinical trials, and building new tools for physicians, consumers, insurers, and regulators to meet the promise of more individualized approaches."

In 2017, it wrote of AI's impact: "The private sector has long recognized the potential inherent in the new technologies. Self-learning software and cognitive systems can either already be found throughout the value chain or are on the verge of deployment: forecasting and pricing tools for purchasing and inventory management, chatbots for customer service, delivery drones for the last mile. AI applications can help companies to optimize services and lower costs, accelerate processes, and make better decisions.

"A similar development is taking place in the health-care sector, although exploration of the possibilities that artificial intelligence offers in the field of medical care and management is in its early stages.

"The most progress to date has been made with AI use cases around providers: medical centers are increasingly using early detection systems supported by algorithms or automated recognition of patterns in patient data.

"Less known are the opportunities that the use of smart technology enables for health insurers."

AI will inevitably be one of the key tools used by Bezos, Buffet, and Dimon in their new model health-care company.

Tech entrepreneur Naveen Jain is bullish on Silicon Valley's ability to transform health care. "We're going to bypass doctors. Hospitals. Just like what's happening in education too," he enthuses of Silicon Valley's new ventures to transform health and education and make them more efficient and accessible—and to create life-changing innovations that transform our relationship with illness entirely, thanks to biotech, AI, and life sciences research.

Jain is not known for understatement. He believes that businesses—frustrated by slow, outmoded systems—will collectively start to change health care by going straight to consumers with new alternatives. Just as Elon Musk did in sidestepping car dealerships to market his Tesla vehicles directly to consumers, so too will new industries move into health care, encroaching on the established guard.

He's also confident about Silicon Valley's abilities to transform the way we live. In the near future, he believes, health advances led by technology will have the ability to eradicate disease by diagnosing at early stages. Jain is an investor in Viome, for example, which uses at-home microbiome testing to offer hyper-specific diet regimes. (It's been shown that gut health is integral to not only maintaining general well-being, but also warding off chronic diseases.) Viome customers send a stool sample to Viome's laboratories; the sample is analyzed to assess gut health and metabolism and create a picture of the customer's body on a molecular level. This is then translated, using machine learning, into a diagnosis and diet recommendation.

Viome's website, much like its investor, is filled with fanfare. Dreamy images of people atop mountains are layered with messaging: "What if technology could expand humanity's healthy lifespan?" Meanwhile, it touts its scientific credentials including having an "exclusive license to technology first developed at the prestigious Los Alamos National Laboratory."

To Jain, the possibilities of tech to transform health are endless: "What happens to life insurance if people are not dying?" he asks. "What happens to life insurance when sickness becomes optional, or even aging becomes optional?" (This thanks to diagnostic technologies that can warn you in advance and allow you to correct the onset of chronic illnesses associated with aging.) "All the traditional industries are now at a point where they all could be disrupted. And the old guard is going to die, and when the old guards die, it's a freer game for every entrepreneur to go capture that market, because there's a brand-new technology and everybody has the same access to it."

Dismissing concerns about privacy, Jain believes that direct-to-consumer models of health services will actually better serve consumer interests. "Uber has had to change its policy in response to consumer wants," he says. In Jain's world, citizens of the future will be the ultimate regulators of health because health-care providers will now be consumer brands, no longer at the mercy of a complex layered health-care system immune to consumer pressure.

Silicon Valley is changing health in other less revolutionary ways, too. As with all the other services and sectors it has disrupted, it is positioning health services as "brands" with pithy language, an emphasis on easy-to-understand transparency, and lifestyle design cues. It's also using apps and social media in creative ways. HealthTap has created Dr. A.I., an interactive doctor skill on Amazon Echo that uses artificial and "emotional" intelligence to be a talking virtual doctor for customers in search of medical insights and advice. Zoom+ is a new-wave health clinic with visits on-demand (like the Uber of health), and has an app and chatbot for additional questions. Baidu, the Chinese tech company, has created an artificial-intelligence-powered chatbot character named Melody who can give health advice. Many of these have all the trappings of the most successful lifestyle brands. They are presented with bright colors and sleek design.

Dr. Molly Maloof, a San Francisco–based physician, technologist, and wellness expert who advises many Silicon Valley health startups, has acutely observed Silicon Valley's expansion into health. She is a well-being and health "influencer," frequently found posting on Instagram trying out hyperbaric oxygen therapy, cooking superfood recipes, and recommending yoga brands. "There's a lot of interest in early-stage biotech," she says. "People are moving past software and looking at science as a service; novel ways of doing drug development; decentralizing drug development. There's some really interesting stuff coming from a new perspective on synthetic biology, digitizing the process of creating synthetic biology.

"There's a really big push toward data collection and aggregation," she adds. The next step is artificial intelligence and companies making sense of the data. "The hope is that, as we learn more about disease and more about how to parse it out and understand what it's made of, perhaps we'll come up with an even better system than we have today." Maloof believes the next opportunity will be in understanding "optimal health states." "We need just as many systems for improving health as fixing disease. I see that as a big wide-open space."

Could Silicon Valley replace our current health-care systems? There are tremendous benefits to this idea, but also drawbacks, beyond sharing data and privacy which has—as mentioned in an earlier chapter—already spooked British residents who discovered National Health Service had been sharing patient information with Google-owned artificial-intelligence company DeepMind. There is the fact that Silicon Valley is not representative of all people. Already this has been shown in its late awakening in its technology products focusing on women's health, for one. Apple was famously late to add reproductive health to its HealthKit monitoring suite on the iPhone. They have generally overlooked women's health, fertility, and maternity tech as an opportunity, which seems dumb, apart from anything else because women represent 51 percent of the consumer electronics market, according to HBR.

Today, the landscape is changing, especially as brands recognize the opportunity. As female-founded tech startups slowly start to attract funding, it's giving way to some important new products. One example of this is Willow, a discreet breast pump that lets mothers express silently while still going about their day-to-day lives (it can be worn under regular clothing and comes in a chic shade of pale blue). Willow was launched at CES in 2017 and has since been named one of *Time* magazine's top 25 Best Inventions for 2017. The reason it was so successful was its empathetic approach to design. "In this space, normally everyone focuses on the baby. We're really focused on the mom," Willow president and CEO Naomi Kelman told us. "It's subtle but it's different. In particular we say, how can we make moms' lives easier and better?"

The response has been rapturous.

"Someone Finally Invented A Breast Pump That Isn't Completely Awful," wrote HuffPost senior reporter Emily Peck, describing it as huge step forward for womankind. "Finally, Silicon Valley has moved beyond funding yet another food-delivery or Uber-like app and is bringing something truly revolutionary and necessary to market: a breast pump that won't make you feel like a sad bovine attached to a medieval torture device."

There are countless other examples of this. Sweden-based Natural Cycles is the first app to be officially approved for use as a contraceptive. It detects a woman's ovulation and calculates her fertile days; it was developed by CERN scientist Elina Berglund Scherwitzl, who founded the company with her husband Raoul Scherwitzl. It has been certified in the EU as a recognized form of contraception. NextGen Jane is a U.S.-based feminine care brand that tracks key health metrics using menstrual blood, so women can track their reproductive health.

How many products have we missed because a company didn't get access to funding? Skewing predominantly male, Silicon Valley's understanding of female-centric and female-designed products will be inevitably limited. But it could be missing out on countless opportunities as a result. There's also the issue of Silicon Valley's algorithmic approach to everything. The understood biases in algorithms are now widely known, so what if men are programming everything? Including women's health services?

Technology and algorithms are making things faster, cheaper, more personalized, and more accurate, but could this also work against us? If you are overweight, should you pay for more insurance, or be given less access to credit? If 23andMe discovers you are a carrier of an inherited condition, will that affect whether you are granted fertility treatment? Beyond health as a category of its own, there is also potential for data to be connected to the vast swath of other services that Silicon Valley already plays in, from finance to loans to employment. What are the implications of these private, commercial companies—which now offer credit, payment plans, and financing—knowing if you are HIV positive or have a history of health problems? It's a dangerous entanglement of private information that could be used against anyone.

In throwing vast amounts of money at various causes, Silicon Valley's biases and interests will have a magnified and distorting effect. In response to the wider privatization of science, or "science philanthropy," concern has already been voiced in some journals that having powerful individuals or private companies fund research may skew its focus (philanthropy experts say much the same about their area) or perhaps orient its direction.

In terms of research, this might have a socioeconomic or racial slant (in other words, illnesses and issues most prevalent in poor communities of color may get tackled last or ignored). Already, Amazon has come under fire for only introducing Amazon Prime to zip codes with more affluent residents, overlooking neighborhoods with lower-income consumers. What happens when it's only certain areas of health being addressed? Or when only certain populations are receiving the lion's share of health care and attention?

Most of Silicon Valley's innovations are, naturally, tech-solutionist in outlook, but tech advisor Maloof points out that (as with everything) their high-volume hype, glossy websites, and soaring rhetoric promising empowerment and "optional" disease doesn't always mean their outcomes will be as transformative as expected.

"There is a prevailing belief in Silicon Valley that they can solve all problems with technology," says Maloof. "I'm seeing companies trying to tackle gigantic problems that are far more complicated than they realize. People are seeing big diseases and the experience of health care in America as being fairly horrible, and finding ways to decentralize health care and give more patients a sense of autonomy—give them more information about their health, give them more access to their medical records, and give them more opportunity to track their health over time. But it hasn't blown anybody away yet. I don't think we've seen any studies that show that these offer a superior alternative to the analog version of what they do."

There's an element of risk in having Silicon Valley's unicorn-lusting, scale-quickly approach to health too—health is by its very nature not as predictable as algorithms. Humans are humans, after all. In other words, the dubious prospect of combining the Silicon Valley model (venture-capital cash, fast scaling, and big headlines) with the messy world of health. "The thing about health care is that you can't go around the rules of the game," says Maloof. "You can't play the game the same way you might play with a hardware startup, because the regulations are real. You can't ignore them. And doctors and health-care policy makers demand research. If you really want to disrupt health care, you have to think long-term."

One interesting thread to consider in relation to Silicon Valley's move into health is what its technologies, in the macro sense, are doing to our health generally. Tech may be stepping in to help us monitor aspects of our health, but many of its technologies are cumulatively creating health adverse conditions—making us more sedentary, changing our habits, and even affecting our minds. According to Nielsen Company, adults now spend over ten hours a day on screen time. Aside from the well-known side effects of using virtual reality, VR experts like Jacquelyn Ford Morie have pointed to rising questions about VR's impact on developing balance and children's relationship to memory (VR is so immersive, it has the potential to distort children's abilities to distinguish between real and virtual memories). "Nobody wants to do the research because it might show that maybe we shouldn't be doing it," says Morie. "That to me is the biggest gap. We don't have control groups."

Then there's also the burgeoning mental health crisis driven by excessive use of social media and smartphones, particularly among today's teenagers who have grown up with them attached to their hands. According to a headline-generating feature article published in *The Atlantic*, teenagers are more likely to commit suicide and experience depression than millennials, and their digital habits have been blamed for creating a sense of isolation from the real world. In "Have Smartphones Destroyed a Generation?" Dr. Jean Twenge writes: "It's not an exaggeration to describe iGen as being on the brink of the worst mental-health crisis in decades. Much of this deterioration can be traced to their phones." As we all, collectively, interact with technology every day, it's starting to affect our minds, with unknown or not yet known consequences.

Yet Silicon Valley is already stepping into meatier spaces like education with new theories and business models. If we don't even know what a lifetime of smartphone use does to our minds, what will it look like when Big Tech is baked into our schools and the way we learn?

7

"Fixing" Education

Education needs are evolving faster than governments can keep up. Generations have graduated in record-breaking university debt. The job market is demanding new skills, every few years. Self-employment is on the rise. Technology is changing rapidly. New jobs arise while others become redundant or obsolete. (See: automation; among its biggest casualties are workers in the retail sector. In the UK, 62,000 retail jobs were lost in 2016 because of growth in online shopping and automated cashiers. According to the British Retail Consortium, another 900,000 retail jobs will disappear in the next decade. In the U.S., between 6 and 7.5 million retail jobs are estimated at "high risk of computerization" in the next ten years, according to a 2017 study by Cornerstone Capital Group.) The school system isn't equipping people for jobs of the future. And the debate about state versus private responsibility for education continues. The future of education in this rapidly evolving world is a complicated and difficult puzzle. Increasingly, Silicon Valley thinks it has the answer.

Historically, governments have addressed dislocation brought on by great change by radically reimagining education. During the Industrial Revolution, or any major shift in the way wealth was generated, school systems and curriculums were overhauled to equip nations with trained people for these new centers of wealth creation. The same happened with the explosion of manufacturing in the post–World War II era. But this time, for some reason, governments have not acknowledged the seismic changes created by the vast digitization of our existence, much less made the dramatic changes needed to prepare populations for what comes next. Perhaps it's the speed of change. The speed of disruption. Or the pace at which gigantic sectors are being supplanted by platforms powered by five team members and an algorithm. Perhaps it's impossible to mitigate against this entirely. Regardless, the way we learn, and what we learn, is in desperate need of more attention.

"If you look at the first Industrial Revolution," explains Thor Berger, "or perhaps more the second Industrial Revolution taking place in the late nineteenth century, early twentieth century, what you see are huge overhauls of the education system." Berger is a post-doctoral researcher in the department of economic history at Lund University and an associate fellow at Oxford University, studying technology and employment. He points out that the high school movement in the United States was a direct response by the government to prepare citizens for the new knowledge-based jobs created by a transitioning economy. "There was a consensus that to maintain employment in the future, you would need to invest a lot more in education and also really think about the kind of education you want to provide."

Ask him why government today is so slow to respond to massive changes in the workplace, and he observes: "Modern Western economies are good at identifying what's going on but political systems are not designed to tackle longer-term challenges. They're quite good at crisis management, over a two-year, three-year horizon, but here when you are talking about overhauling education and trying to tackle what we think will happen in the future, say in twenty years, today's political systems are not equipped to deal with those time horizons."

In lieu of this governmental inaction, Silicon Valley is confronting the issue of education head-on. The tech world is looking at "broken" education not just from a philanthropic perspective but as a scalable industry. A new market to disrupt. It's entering it at multiple stages, from primary and secondary education to adult self-improvement. As with all the sectors it's moving into, its messaging is that education needs to be rethought, retooled, and engineered to create the workers of the future. And guess what? Student learning benefits from some forms of technology.

Education is a major area where most tech philanthropists are focused, both in the U.S. and globally. In 2018 Apple announced investment in the Malala Fund, championing access to education for girls globally. The Chan Zuckerberg Initiative has launched the Primary School, a free private school in East Palo Alto for "underserved children" that offers education and health care. Oracle has launched the Design Tech High School on its campus in Redwood City, California, a public charter school. Access is via a lottery system. As well as an education, attendees will have mentorship from Oracle employees and receive classes on wearable tech. Salesforce has pledged $100 million to San Francisco public schools. According to CNBC, CEO Marc Benioff treats the fund like a VC when meeting with principals.

Silicon Valley leaders are increasingly exploring how education works.

The Bill & Melinda Gates Foundation's investments in education are well storied, as is its participation in the education reform movement. Mark Zuckerberg and Laurene Powell Jobs, widow of Steve Jobs, are both investing in new education projects, and in education theory. Zuckerberg's efforts started in 2010 with a $100 million gift to New Jersey to fix its failing schools. The endeavor is now widely seen as a failure, but it also saw early examples of Zuckerberg's ideas for how education could be transformed—more competitive salaries to attract better talent being just one. More recently, like many tech leaders, he has started talking about individualized curriculum as a better way to learn. The common solution, according to the main Silicon Valley educational players, is that personalized learning is more effective than standardized tests. Here, technology is a means of lowering costs, or "scaling," and of broadening curriculums. (More on this later.)

Powell Jobs announced a $100 million investment in American high schools through a contest she helped design, titled the XQ: Super School Project, which awards funding to applicant high schools that are trying to find new and better models for learning. "People actually get excited about solving problems," she told *New York* magazine. "I feel very strongly that the problems we get to solve are really hard, otherwise they would have been solved already. Now it's our turn. We're going to bring in people from all different disciplines who think about things a little differently. Sometimes they take it to the extreme so, if we were to do this—which is not plausible— but, if we were to colonize Mars, what would be our first step? And so you backwards map. After a couple of decades of living there you think 'well, this shouldn't be insurmountable.' It's a lot harder to have an early detection of all cancers than it is to give an excellent education to every kid in our country," she said.

There's also a bigger-picture cultural angle to recognize when it comes to Silicon Valley and education. When it comes to higher education at least, they have criticized a person's need for a university education to be successful. They even doubt the need to take part in traditional systems generally. Why work for an employer when you can be a founder? Why be beholden to government regulation at all?

Peter Thiel's criticism of universities continues. He claims they are elite and not equipping people for the future. He set up the Thiel Fellowship in 2011, offering budding entrepreneurs $100,000 to quit the classroom and turn to "building new things." His criticism was less about education itself and more about the outmoded university institutions and their way of teaching. The feeling is amplified by the fact that Silicon Valley's most successful leaders, from Mark Zuckerberg to Bill Gates to Steve Jobs, dropped out of college, while Sergey Brin left his PhD unfinished. It's interesting that all were accepted into prestigious colleges (Harvard, Reed, Stanford) and then chose to leave—they didn't shun the system altogether. Almost as if getting in was the proof point of their prowess and jumping ship straightaway carried some bragging rights.

Is education broken? Silicon Valley may not be not entirely wrong.

Despite living in an affluent economy, U.S. students are far behind other advanced nations in their abilities, according to research by Pew. The Programme for International Student Assessment put the U.S. thirty-eighth among seventy-one countries. Access to quality education varies by state (and family income). Which is why, perhaps, e-learning has been touted to nearly double in value as a market. (In 2015 it was valued at $165 billion, but by 2022 it's expected to reach $275 billion, according to Orbis Research.) Then there's what we are learning itself, and how. Megan J. Smith, the former CTO under Barack Obama, launched many programs to make tech literacy and coding accessible to lower-income citizens.

The Pew Research Center has published reports of a national shortage of software engineers, and also shows that U.S. students fall far behind other countries in STEM achievement. The World Economic Forum's Future of

Jobs report outlines the new skills needed to be successful. In 2015, they were complex problem solving, coordinating with others, people management, critical thinking, negotiation, quality control, service orientation, judgment and decision making, active listening, and creativity. Fast-forward to 2020 and they predicted two significant new additions: emotional intelligence and cognitive flexibility. Is any of this featured in current curricula?

"The Fourth Industrial Revolution is interacting with other socioeconomic and demographic factors to create a perfect storm of business model change in all industries, resulting in major disruptions to labor markets," the report said. "New categories of jobs will emerge, partly or wholly displacing others. The skill sets required in both old and new occupations will change in most industries and transform how and where people work. It may also affect female and male workers differently and transform the dynamics of the industry gender gap."

Amazon has created a few initiatives to address changing skill needs in its workforce. It hired Candace Thille, an expert in learning science and open education at Stanford University, to be Director of Learning Science and Engineering. Her role is to "scale and innovate workplace learning at Amazon." As with Amazon's moves into health care and shipping, it starts out with self-interest, perhaps (needing to keep a large global workforce up to date in its skillsets; offering affordable health care to a massive employee-base also makes them more effective and functions as a de facto pay increase). But it could have commercial implications. The corporate learning market is estimated to be worth $130 billion. That grows larger if technology further accelerates the pace of change in the way we work and the number of careers we might have as a result. (Amazon has also been making commercial inroads into online education platforms and tools for children.)

But will Silicon Valley actually make a difference? There is a reasonable argument for using technology to offer high-quality education more accessibly thanks to efficiencies of automation, and that education is a great equalizer. There is also a big argument for learning new things—such as problem-solving skills and critical thinking that can adapt to any new wave of demands and careers, not simply learning historical facts verbatim. There is also a good argument for prioritizing tech literacy as a core element of the curriculum.

But there is the nagging idea that private companies would get more significant access to young people in their formative years, which could have lasting impacts. And, when it comes to the rise of charter schools in the U.S. (privately run and funded schools, more and more backed by tech), questions remain about transparency and accountability. Charter schools are a subject of hot debate. Once presented as a private alternative to the public education system, they've been criticized for high faculty turnovers, high student attrition, and cynical commercial behavior. They also receive government funding, which is, critics argue, eroding resources to existing public schools and putting further pressure on them. Yet charters do not face the same regulatory requirements. They've also been accused of racial and economic discrimination in their enrollment policies, driven by the need to maintain publicly high academic success rates.

Tech's mantra is that education is broken, but perhaps it isn't, counters Megan Tompkins-Stange, assistant professor of public policy at the University of Michigan and author of *Policy Patrons: Philanthropy, Education Reform, and the Politics of Influence.* "That's a nice clean narrative and it's one that's marshaled a lot of energy around education for the last fifty years," she says, "but in reality things are getting better in the United States, slowly but surely. People look at the international rankings and go, 'Oh, we're number forty!' but in terms of where American education started and where it's come to, and the achievement gaps within racial groups, for example, which are closing, people are doing better. There's a higher graduation rate. Generations of well-meaning philanthropists, who probably did not have a lot of exposure to public schools when they were growing up, see a problem from the outside. They say, 'Let's fix it, I have the expertise, I've been successful in business, I will bring that to the floor in terms of working for education'— and it doesn't work because it's a totally different system. There's no silver bullet because it's a twenty-year process to change education. Philanthropists don't like that; they want results next year."

This is part of a widely held tech solutionist outlook, says Debra Cleaver, founder and CEO of Vote.org and Bay Area native. "In Silicon Valley they'll often say the solution to education is technology. And it's like, 'No, the solution to education is paying teachers more money and then giving them more resources.' It's really comical the belief that only technology solves problems. No, money solves problems. Resources solve problems. If we gave public schools the same amount of money as we give these education tech startups, we would see better results."

"The longer I stay in education, the more nuanced my views become," says Dale J. Stephens, founder of UnCollege, a gap-year startup in the Bay Area. "If you look at the stats, half of college students are dropping out—a full 50 percent of students. When you look at the people who are actually graduating on time, which is not most of them, and the fact that they're racking up tens of thousands of dollars, if not hundreds, in debt, and they're not necessarily being able to use [their education] effectively, you definitely have to start questioning whether it's the right system."

Stephens also points to the wider culture of reverence toward traditional institutions. "We have stigmatized paths to apprenticeship, to trade schools, those kinds of things, whereas a lot of European models have multiple options after high school.

"It can be hard to change people's views when they're very set in their ways. I think the elephant in the room here is that a lot of colleges are closer to the brink than they want to admit, and a lot of that is because they took out the loans in the early 2000s to build student centers and gyms."

That debt is being passed down to students. In October 2016, the *California Aggie*, the University of California, Davis's student newspaper, reported a Board of Regents meeting discussing the management of the university's $17.2 billion debt. Between 2002 and 2010, the total debt liabilities of public research universities increased by more than 50 percent, according to a study published in the Scholars Strategy Network.

Of Peter Thiel's famously scathing comments about universities, Stephens says, "The biggest thing the Thiel Fellowship did was to cause people to ask the return-on-investment question around college."

Generation Z, the upcoming twelve- to nineteen-year-olds, might be at the forefront of seed change in this respect, too. The president of Northeastern University, Joseph E. Aoun, summed up Generation Z in a J. Walter Thompson study on the group: "A new generation of Americans is on the rise: highly entrepreneurial, pluralistic, and determined to take charge of their own futures. Those of us in higher education must listen to this next generation and enable them to chart their own paths, gain valuable experience, and become the leaders of tomorrow."

What's clear is that, with mounting economic pressures, changing educational needs, and spiraling student debts, people are looking to alternative ways to make themselves employable. And that's being met with a wave of new ventures from Silicon Valley. Udacity, Minerva, UnCollege, and AltSchool are among the many sexy new-model commercial initiatives coming out of the Bay Area backed by venture capitalists that are creating new approaches to education at every level. As with all Silicon Valley brands, their promises are rich and their rhetoric exaggerated. The familiar tropes abound.

Should Harvard be scared?

Netflix of Education

A number of new concepts are offering alternatives to traditional education for all ages, as well as business development and personal and vocational training. The prevailing thread among these is the message that the current education system is not equipping people with enough future skills. The further message is that education should be personalized and active, not standardized, broadcast, and passive. Most of the new systems naturally make tech literacy a focus. They are leaner than traditional learning institutes, often moving beyond the idea of a campus to incorporate travel and online tutorials.

Udacity, founded by former Google vice president Sebastian Thrun and backed by venture-capital firm Andreessen Horowitz, is aimed at adult professional education. Among other such organizations, Minerva is a new "active" learning institution and alternative to a traditional university; it pitches itself as the lean and superior alternative to Harvard. UnCollege, an alternative gap-year course in building core life skills, markets its offer as—apart from anything else—a way to focus students on their long-term career goals and find the right academic path, as well as build professional skills. There's AltSchool, for children pre-K through eighth grade, founded by Max Ventilla, formerly of Google. AltSchool's focus is on personalized learning as a more effective alternative to standardized education (this is rapidly becoming a mantra in Silicon Valley). AltSchool launched in 2014 and runs several small private schools in San Francisco, Palo Alto, Brooklyn, Manhattan, and Chicago. The company is planning to license its techniques.

Beyond altruism and a bold mission, these businesses have all recognized that education is a lucrative segment to disrupt. The global education market is worth $4.4 trillion, according to investment bank IBIS Capital, and the fastest-growing sector is e-learning. In 2015 McKinsey valued the U.S. education market at $1.5 trillion, growing at 5 percent annually. EdTechXGlobal and IBIS Capital further say the education tech market will grow to $252 billion by 2020.

It's an autumn afternoon in Palo Alto. On University Avenue, the main drag, a historic 1930s movie-palace-turned-bookstore has been reborn as HanaHaus, a coworking hotspot with a café courtesy of Blue Bottle Coffee. The interior is a blend of exposed industrial beams, white walls, and the Mission Revival–style building's carefully preserved features. A nest of grey armchairs stands next to a wall emblazoned with "Creativity comes from conflict of ideas."

HanaHaus is packed. And full of the sartorial choices you'd expect. There's an ocean of Patagonia, khakis, and Facebook-emblazoned backpacks. Step out into the open courtyard and meetings are happening at most tables. Shernaz Daver, the CMO of Udacity, arrives. Udacity is an adult online education platform with affordable, skill-based "nanodegrees" (short-term courses that focus on learning a specific tech skill). It teaches the programming skills in line with evolving industry employer needs, while offering credentials that the companies recognize and endorse (or even fund). It is one of a growing group of companies from the Valley rethinking traditional education, or coming up with new segments and submarkets.

Udacity's focus is a little different in that it positions itself outside the school curriculum. It's aiming at adults (college-educated or otherwise). It offers its nanodegrees or certificates in subjects such as Android basics (a course showing people with no programming experience how to develop apps for Android smartphones), predictive analytics for business, the basics of AR app development, virtual reality development, artificial intelligence, and software for self-driving cars. It does so at a fraction of the cost and time of traditional schools. Courses are taken online, supported virtually by coaches and other students. People learn through working on hands-on projects, which are then evaluated.

"We have this archaic packaging where people go to school for four or more years to get a degree," says Sebastian Thrun in an introductory video. "We at Udacity give our graduates the absolute latest skills that are in demand here in Silicon Valley."

Udacity's partners include Amazon, Google, IBM, and Mercedes-Benz. Its offer feels much like a consumer-facing shop—like a virtual supermarket or cool technology store selling off-the-shelf classes, rather than the more bookish presentation of traditional academic institutions featuring people at desks and smiling in class. The Android program is in partnership with Google and has an associate Android developer certification at the end. It costs $750, which includes three months of access, three courses, three projects, and the Google certification exam.

There are even customer ratings and holiday specials—and subscription models for $199 a month. Many courses come with a guarantee of employment within six months or your money back. Graduate within twelve months and you get 50 percent of the tuition fees back.

Every course at Udacity is focused on employment—becoming equipped to work in new areas of tech and being job-ready at the end. "Virtual reality is the future of creative content," promises Udacity in its sales copy for the VR course. "There is massive growth in the space, and job opportunities are skyrocketing, making this the perfect time to launch your VR career!"

It's almost like a modern-day apprenticeship company. Like Amazon, Udacity has clearly spotted an opportunity: employment increasingly requires our skill sets to be fluid and constantly adapting. And it's one with massive potential longevity if workers consistently need to learn new skills.

"Jobs are changing," says Daver. "The U.S. labor organization says people change jobs seven times in their career. The average tenure of a job in the Valley is eighteen months. Everybody has to learn new skills. Suddenly you enter this new area called lifelong learning; that's where we play. We're dealing with an area that says, 'education doesn't stop when you're twenty-two.'

That's our belief." But Udacity is not just selling to people in the Valley. All courses are done online so they can be taken remotely and are, in theory, open to anyone.

Udacity's relationship with partner brands and employers is also novel—and maximized to connect students to new career opportunities.

"We call the nanodegree a credential. It allows you to get the skills you want in an average of three to six months. So it's not a degree. It's not a bachelor's, it's not a master's, it's not something that's backed by a college. We have companies come in and they help create content with us. Google is a content partner; Facebook is a content partner. Say today you wanted to learn the latest in Android—it's pretty hard to learn it in college. And you're in the workforce and you're thirty-two years old. Where do you go? Do you quit and basically go back to college? You can't. So you can come to Udacity and we give you the latest skills because we're doing it with Google." (Google is, after all, the company updating this technology.)

Daver tells me that they have a broad audience that includes everyone from Silicon Valley engineers to ex-cleaners and immigrants. "We have a student out of San Diego; he used to work in McDonald's and he wanted to get a new job. He took a front-end developer nanodegree (a credential for website building). He got 50 percent back on his tuition, so instead of spending $2,400, he spent $1,200. He got a job at a tech company in San Diego and now earns three times his original salary. That's a large part of our business overall." Udacity is also used by developers who need to update skills, taking advantage of the fact that they can study toward their credential when they want. "You can do it in your own time," says Daver. "You can do it at night; whenever you want to. And that's how we work it."

There are big scaling ambitions for Udacity. Daver says that it aims to become the international go-to place for job skills, so "wherever you are in the world, you immediately think Udacity. Just like today, if I say search, you immediately think Google." She adds that already many Udacity students come from China and India.

In an atmosphere of anxiety about great swaths of people not having the necessary skillset to ride out the current industrial, automation, and tech booms, targeted individual education is an exciting prospect. It's one the government should be actively supporting, as driverless cars, automated kitchen equipment, and automated trucks become imminent, to enhance training and equip citizens for some of the highest-paying jobs in a fast-growing sector. Udacity should surely be focusing on America's Rust Belt. Of all the places being left behind by tech's fast pace of evolution, it's here, with declining industries and aging factories, propelled by the withering of coal and steel. These areas have, arguably, not been addressed by educational policy change either. And therefore their citizens are not enjoying the spoils of Silicon Valley. And if the government is not assisting the reeducation of this population, surely the Rust Belt and lower-income citizens left out from progress should represent a philanthropic focus for tech leaders and ventures. But, as is usual with tech, there's a socioeconomic bias. Yes, people from India and China can study nanodegrees. It's because they have agency and there's also a widely established practice of bringing affordable developers from these countries to Silicon Valley. Rust Belt workers are a less glamorous group; they certainly fall out of the desirable marketing demographic many Silicon Valley companies aspire to align with. They might have built the Hoover Dam during the Depression, but today they're facing an uncertain future.

"We talk to a ton of government people," says Daver, adding that Hillary Clinton had previously talked about nanodegrees in her education manifesto.

Shouldn't traditional universities be doing this? "Universities have a very different focus. Can you upend 200 years of the way colleges are?" Not in the short term, and the appeal of these alternatives is undeniable. But Silicon Valley is entering a landscape of entrenched university branding and entrenched regard for traditional qualifications, Oxford and Harvard degrees among them. "The biggest challenge is people accepting these credentials," admits Daver. Having launched in 2014, the nanodegrees are now being purchased in markets including Germany, Brazil, India, and China, and starting to be recognized in a more official way. The other big thing, says Daver, is trust; students need to trust what they learn at Udacity, and trust that it will lead to job opportunities, while employers need to trust Udacity credentials among potential staff.

From a student point of view, there's also a financial imperative involved here. American student debt is at $1.3 trillion, affecting 43 million people.

Couple that with rising cost of living and stagnant salaries, and alternatives to the traditional, expensive, lengthy degrees might become a more economical but successful option for the new world we live and work in.

Skype Harvard

Based some distance from Udacity in central San Francisco, a company called Minerva is pitching itself as an alternative to the usual liberal arts degree. But there are many of the trappings of Silicon Valley's educational outlook here, too. Rather than sit-in lectures, students engage in "active learning" and are taught to problem-solve and pick apart complex systems so as to understand them. They engage in intensive seminars via their laptops, where they debate, vote, discuss, take tests, and are graded by a tutor. There is also no library, no college newspaper. The city is the campus. Students travel each semester to Minerva's locations in seven cities across the world: Buenos Aires, Berlin, Hyderabad, London, San Francisco, Seoul, and Taipei, and stay in dorms dotted around each city, completing coursework supplemented by programs reflecting the given location. This costs less than a traditional degree (about $29,450 per year including dorm accommodation—traditional degrees vary wildly but on average run $18,000 to $44,820 per year in 2017–18, according to the Carnegie Classification and College Board). However, Minerva isn't going up against the online university market, which is generally associated with affordability. In fact, it describes itself emphatically as *not* an online university. It's going head-to-head with Harvard. (An audacious boast. But Minerva's shtick is that it's harder to get into and will give you a better education.) Minerva claims to have created an entirely superior system of higher education, and tech is a key tool in making it so.

Broadly speaking, Minerva is split into three: Minerva Schools in partnership with Keck Graduate Institute (KGI) offers traditional undergraduate and graduate degrees in subjects such as arts and humanities and applied analysis and decision making. The Minerva Project, backed by Benchmark Capital, TAL, Zhen Fund, and Learn Capital, is a VC fund for new-wave learning companies. The final part is the Minerva Institute, the nonprofit arm chaired by former senator Bob Kerrey, which offers financial aid to deserving applicants taking part in Minerva School degrees.

Visit the Minerva headquarters in central San Francisco, and Ben Nelson, founder, chairman, and chief executive, passionately explains Minerva's mission to reengineer the future of education as we know it, as well as the problems endemic to the current system. "A university today is first and foremost beholden to its faculty, then beholden to its donors. So that means that it has to increase costs while obliterating standards," he says. "Today, students spend 20 percent less time on their studies than they did when I was an undergraduate. At the same time, grade inflation is rampant."

Nelson says universities, even the best ones, are "running the world into the ground. And these are people who are inherently very intelligent." They are doing so, he thinks, with outmoded ways of teaching, bloated, expensive campuses, and a curriculum filled with the wrong skills that produces mediocre candidates who cannot think critically. They are focused on learning things by heart, not learning a way to think. And, by being so nepotistic and wealth-focused, are creating a closing loop of increasingly mediocre talent. His answer? Universities should be elitist, he says, but in a way different from our current hallowed institutions that focus on privilege and connections. They should be about finding individuals who are special for the way they think, learn, and lead. "You only need to go back in history to see example after example after example of the same kinds of things. It's individuals who move things forward." But, he says, it's rare that these individuals emerge from a legacy of multiple generations. They are anomalies. But it's often wealthy elites, and their children, that attend the most prevalent universities. In this respect, Minerva aims to be an egalitarian, modern alternative to universities with a relentless focus on excellence, regardless of background.

So far, so great, in theory. But concepts such as critical thinking and problem solving (which may be instinctive along the full spectrum of socioeconomic structures) are not understood universally, or easily articulated by those who do not have access to quality education, or who might not even have the wherewithal to stumble onto Minerva's website. Traveling to Seoul, Istanbul, and beyond sounds fantastic and mind-expanding. But also quite rarefied.

Although Minerva is backed by venture capital, Nelson says emphatically that it is not a typical Silicon Valley venture. Minerva is in the tradition of the universities once set up by Benjamin Franklin and Thomas Jefferson. Their aim was to "take the best raw material of society and train it to make decisions of consequence. Train it to create and lead the major segments of society. It was never about the dissemination of information."

How does Minerva return to this original purpose? Nelson talks about developing a scaffold on which students build their education and also understand the world around them. At Minerva students learn the common curriculum in their first year before moving into formal analysis, formal systems (such as logic and reasoning and advanced use of statistics), critical thinking, and components. They learn empirical systems (systems where you take ill-structured data—the world around you—and figure it out) and how to create and test hypotheses, how to evaluate conclusions, how to solve problems creatively, and so on. And lastly they learn about rhetorical systems—or how to communicate effectively. "We want to teach students to think critically," he says.

Students are expected to arrive at Minerva with an advanced understanding of subjects (by reading up on their agenda) before they are asked to engage in these skill-building classes. The classes are about combining that knowledge with analysis, problem solving, and discussion. Tutorial sessions are one unique thing at Minerva that Nelson is most proud of. By virtue of being in online video chat format rather than around a table, every student's response and engagement is instantly intelligible, and they can be put on the spot at any moment. He rails against the fact that because students are online, many people dismiss Minerva as simply an e-university. "Nothing like this has ever been done," Nelson insists.

He adds: "This is the thing about Minerva. We use technology because it's superior to not using technology."

The best part? It's much, much cheaper to run than a traditional university. Professors can work from anywhere. There are no classrooms. "If you look at the crushing layers of costs associated with building a campus, maintaining it, beautifying it, they're all gone," says Nelson. "And if you compare our students' campus to the best campuses in the world . . . Show me a better university museum than the San Francisco MoMA, or the British Museum which students visit when they go to London."

It's important to point out that, still, given the chance and a few hundred grand to spare, most people would love the connections, facilities, clubs, and networking that an institution like Harvard offers. Soft power. And it has nothing to do with the quality of education. Or not everything at least.

But not every university is Harvard. And many graduates, saddled with debt and struggling to get jobs, are already reviewing their expensive branded educations with a starker eye. Plus, as employment shifts (as it is) toward more contract-based work, entrepreneurialism, and new industries, traditional university brands will arguably matter less and less. It will only matter to Wall Street and established law firms, if at all, that an applicant went to Princeton.

With the rising costs of universities and the rapidly changing labor market, people may think more carefully not only about taking a degree but also what sort of degree they take. They may also question the purpose of universities and assess what will best equip them for life and, more important, work—whether that means being able to write code, to think critically, to gain practical skills, or to judge what will make them the most well-rounded individual. And sometimes the best way to assess what kind of higher education one needs is to take a year off.

Gap Year

UnCollege, another San Francisco education startup, is one of a rising number of institutions that fit with this wider remit, focusing on intensive, skill-based courses to set students up for college or other endeavors. Essentially, UnCollege offers a supercharged nine-month gap year program that, it says, "helps students identify areas of interest, accelerate their learning, and be happy at the next stage in life." Students "take ownership of their education."

UnCollege was founded by Dale J. Stephens in San Francisco in 2011. The story goes that Stephens—homeschooled between the sixth and twelfth grades—joined liberal arts institute Hendrix College in Conway, Arkansas, and grew frustrated by the standard of education. He worried that college wasn't teaching him the right skills. So he took action. In January 2011 he created UnCollege.org, first as a learning community and then, in 2013, as a fully fledged gap year program. UnCollege is backed by two venture-capital firms, Learn Capital and the east coast firm Charles River Ventures, as well as by 1776, the incubator seed fund, and other organizations such as Women 2.0 and General Assembly.

The mission of UnCollege is to teach life skills to students before they start university: "The experience-based program we've created teaches young adults the practical skills they miss in most conventional classroom settings through a blended approach of self-directed learning, accountability training, mentorship, and deliberate practice. This method, called Supported Self-Directed Learning, equips participants with the essential cognitive skills, confidence, and professional aptitudes they can utilize in all future endeavors."

At UnCollege, class groups are "cohorts" and each group begins the gap year with a "Voyage," living, traveling, and volunteering in India, Indonesia, Mexico, or Tanzania. This is described as Immersive Service Learning and students are taught about social impact, empathy, community, independence, adaptability, and reflection.

"You go to some weird place that's not anything like home and you unlearn, basically," says Vaughn R., a bearded, plaid-shirted hipster in the promotional video (he's now an entrepreneur and aspiring filmmaker). "You unlearn your old routines and patterns. And your old self." He explains that you then come back to the college and join the "Launch" phase "with your slate wiped cleaner, a bit. You still know who you are. But you re-evaluate a lot of stuff about yourself. Like opinions that are not so necessary." He describes diving, dawn hikes up mountains, and seeing monkey forests. "I learned as much about myself as I did about other people." (I imagine today Vaughn R. is taking sonic baths in L.A. and has invested in a recreational marijuana startup. Or he's working in a bank.) But you get the point. They take people, probably fairly affluent kids, out of their comfort zone and send them on a multidisciplinary program of experiences designed to home in on their skills, learn some basic professional aptitude, and identify long-term career aspirations. If only UnCollege had been there before I squandered a directionless year on an experimental arts course, sneaking out early and creating unintelligible textile pieces before opting to study for a history degree.

In the Launch phase, students at UnCollege live with their peers in San

Francisco "while learning new skills, networking, and enjoying life in the most entrepreneurial city in the world." The workspace for learning is not a school but a mixed-use coworker startup space. There are workshops and discussions based on three pillars: curiosity, creation, and self-advocacy. Students are mentored by other professionals and industry leaders in UnCollege's network. The final phase is a three-month work internship at a company matched with the student's professional aspirations. The entire program costs $19,000, including national and international accommodation.

The core focus of UnCollege, says Stephens, is to equip students with personal and professional skills so that when they start university, they hit the ground running. So UnCollege is a primer, if you will. It is unique in its focus on helping individuals become well rounded, so they understand other cultures, empathize, gain self-reliance, and develop self-directed learning skills.

Stephens says: "I asked why there isn't an institution that directly teaches the skills that make you a better learner; like how you negotiate, communicate, set goals for yourself, give and get feedback. All of these are basic skills that, if you go through college and have the right background, you might pick up, but no one bothers to teach you. The basis of this program is 'Why can't we teach those things directly?'—our hunch being if we teach those things explicitly, and make the implicit explicit, we can accelerate learning."

Stephens says a lot of the work done in the nine-month program, in particular the mentorship component, is "really social and emotional in terms of reinforcing someone's self-confidence and self-awareness, in terms of how they give feedback and how they advocate for themselves—things that are really touchy-feely. When we see students come out of the program they have an understanding of who they are and a comfort in that."

This is not a substitute for higher education, he emphasizes. "There are certain students who use it as such, but we think of ourselves as a complement; 70 to 80 percent of our students go on to college after doing our program. They do so with direction and intention. They have a clear understanding of what they want to do."

Will this be a growing trend? "Right now, people mostly choose to do our program because of a philosophical alignment," says Stephens. "But we're getting to the point where we have parents say, 'I don't buy into the philosophy of this program, but I know that it took me six years to get through college, and paying $19,000 per year for you to figure yourself out is way cheaper than paying $40,000.' People are starting to make the decision to come to our program strictly on an economic basis, and as the cost of college continues to rise, I think what we'll start to see is people starting to piece together different programs."

UnCollege is one of a group of new skills-based programs, including General Assembly in New York, Galvanize in Denver, and Dev Bootcamp in Chicago, which target candidates of varying ages. Some focus on personal transformation. Some (aimed at companies) focus on teaching existing employees how to code. Others position themselves as short-term, skill-focused alternatives to taking a full degree. All are an effort to supplement or supplant traditional degrees with something more practical and applied. "I think there's a category that doesn't even exist yet, that we're starting to see inklings of, that is essentially onboarding to employment programs," says Stephens.

If Silicon Valley Built a School

It's a stunning day in San Francisco. For a fleeting moment the mists and damp fog typical of the city have disappeared. The gridded mansion-lined streets are bathed in sunshine. Trees are verdant, their leaves piercing green, and the sky is clear blue. (Days like this, my taxi driver tells me, are why people live in the Bay Area.)

AltSchool's headquarters is in the South of Market neighborhood better known as SoMa. The school's exterior looks like a shop front, complete with logo—'Alt' being a reference to the computer keyboard key, rendered in bright blue, even brighter today in the sun. Except the windows are misted. A class on ground level is in session. Visitors are signposted to a side door. Climb the stairs behind the classroom to the offices, and the open-plan office with its large mezzanine balcony has all the trappings of a startup, with exposed brick walls, industrial steel beams, and rows of stand-up desks populated by millennial staff. None of the staffers look over thirty-five.

But it's not a startup. Or at least, not a typical one. AltSchool's ambition, or, rather, the ambition of founder and CEO Max Ventilla, previously part of Google's founding team, is to rethink how education works. Backed by Silicon Valley venture capital including Andreessen Horowitz and Mark Zuckerberg, it has created a group of "lab schools" developing technology for streamlined personalized learning, which will be franchised to sell to other schools so the project can be "scaled" (always the Holy Grail). Unlike Minerva or Udacity, AltSchool has picked the tricky area of pre-kindergarten through to eighth grade, children up to the age of thirteen. Rather than working from a platform or app, it has built actual schools, which range in size from thirty-five to one hundred and twenty pupils. Look at the HQ "lab" classroom from above, and some of the children are reading in one corner. Elsewhere a group is sitting around a table, in discussion. Prerequisite drawings are on the walls, and there is a row of computers and models. It all looks both functional and human. And surprisingly low-tech—the only obvious presence is three iMacs and a monitor suspended from the ceiling. Like Minerva and UnCollege, its approach is "lean"—no libraries and expensive facilities. AltSchools take over spaces such as former stores and gyms.

What's different about AltSchool? Aside from personalized learning—a Silicon Valley mantra—it's the use of technology. Lessons are assigned on personalized "playlists." (Ventilla specialized in online personalization in his previous tech jobs.) Playlists, which have garnered AltSchool most of its publicity, are described as "a set of tools that enables educators to manage what each child does to meet his or her personalized learning goals and functions as a customized workspace for students to cultivate agency by managing their own work. Educators create, sequence, and remix curriculum units to curate playlists where students can view assignments, communicate with their teacher, and submit work generated on- and off-line. Education teams provide feedback and assessments that update students' portraits in real time."

Tech monitors progress via data and regular assessment. There's an attendance app that students use to check in and out of school; wearable devices to keep track of students off campus; AltVideo, a camera system in the classroom, recording sound and motion. (Ventilla has said that at some point this data could be used to replace testing.) Though of course, there have been criticisms about issues of privacy with this scale of data collection. If a child's behavior and development, or lack thereof, are all documented in granular detail by a private company and used in assessments for university, for instance. Or if facial recognition can monitor changes in your child's height, weight, and health. Or conversations, by children, recorded and sold as consumer insight.

New Yorker Max Ventilla quit Google to start AltSchool in the spring of 2013. He was trying to find a preschool for his daughter and grew exasperated with the experience. He opted to set up his own version, using technology to respond to children's interests—not out of altruism but as a credible new business that could eventually transform education. The technology and software will be where it makes its money. Ventilla has no experience as a teacher or an educational administrator, but wanted to create an "educational ecosystem" that would focus on skills children would need in the workplaces of the future, not on an education determined by historical antecedents. The first AltSchool "micro-school" opened in September 2013 in San Francisco and has continued to garner attention—from parents, the tech community, and the press.

AltSchool's education model is built around the idea of personalized learning, as opposed to standardized testing in the U.S. Common Core State Standards (a set of widely adopted educational metrics in English and mathematics between kindergarten and twelfth grade). One of its goals is to improve the assessment of student learning and teacher performance through data collection. At AltSchool, teachers monitor students' progress daily, if not hourly. Every task card on a student's playlist takes into account not just academic skills like math and literacy but also social and emotional skills.

AltSchool seems to share much with Minerva's approach, which focuses on developing problem solving and analysis capabilities, as well as more fact-based learning. The company employs more than 150 people: educators, technologists, and operations managers. Its fast growth has been funded by $110 million in venture capital since 2015, one of the largest investments ever made in education technology. AltSchool's capital comes from Silicon Valley investors including the Founders Fund, Andreessen Horowitz, and

John Doerr. Last year the philanthropic Silicon Valley Community Foundation invested $15 million through a fund financed by Mark Zuckerberg and Priscilla Chan. AltSchool also generates revenue by charging $20,000 annual tuition fees.

This is not Zuckerberg's first foray into funding education. His first was in 2010 when, in front of a cheering Oprah audience, he pledged $100 million to transform the underperforming schools of Newark, New Jersey. The plan was to make Newark "a symbol of educational excellence for the whole nation," in partnership with then mayor Cory Booker and governor Chris Christie. It was stymied by political mismanagement and, controversially, little was achieved while millions were spent on consultants. The initiative was also criticized because it was not done in consultation with educators or local communities. Since then, Zuckerberg—it's fair to say burned by the initiative—has focused on efforts closer to home. While Ventilla says his backers are not closely involved, there are distinct aspects of Zuckerberg's underlying philosophy in AltSchool: paying competitive salaries to get better talent; the accountability of that talent; and using technology.

Surprisingly, given the rapid expansion of AltSchools' physical schools, Ventilla says these will not be the focus going forward. Rather, they are test beds for the IP, software, and technology. "The schools that we run today are really there to codevelop our platform with the product engineering and design team that we have, and to provide a very high-quality education to the kids, while building the next version. And the next version of the platform will serve not just those schools but other schools as well."

Ventilla is quick to point out that AltSchool is not creating a new model of education, but rather using technology in a new way to make an existing methodology more effective. It's not an entirely new educational philosophy, he says: "There is a pretty established and pretty inspiring progressive education model that exists already, and a number of different curricular approaches within that progressive umbrella. If you take a step back, progressive versus traditional education requires a much greater degree of flexibility while you deal with the inevitable complexity of enabling and educating children. That's a place where digital technology can serve a real purpose ... We've been waiting for digital technology to come along and be sufficiently advanced, certainly not so it can replace people and relationship-driven learning, but so that it can enable students and teachers and parents and administrators to operate in the highly complex educational setting with greater flexibility."

One would imagine that the version of AltSchool's tech that eventually gets rolled out will have "using less teachers" as a selling point—in other words, quite different from the physical lab schools it currently runs. Less human interaction means connection with a human teacher could yet be even more of a status symbol and economic divider.

Ventilla describes tech at AltSchool as a "third layer" that makes existing functions easier. "The intent is to create, ultimately, an ease of effectively personalizing education that is far above what exists today," he says. "Today you'd find very few schools that would say they don't want to effectively personalize education—very few, bordering on none. But you'd also find very few schools that would say it's easy to do. We would like to see a future where a lot of people say 'it's not that hard.'"

A criticism sometimes leveled at AltSchool is that it is private and fee-charging, and therefore elitist. Ventilla believes—as many Silicon Valley leaders do—that economies of scale will eventually bring down the price of this tech-led, personalized approach, and thereby potentially offer a solution for every child. It's starting as an elite model, but only temporarily. "Our mission is to enable every child to achieve their full potential. The word 'every' is right there, and requires you to be part of a very different kind of experience at scale," he says. "And one that has a real network effect. The average education should be better than the best education was a generation ago. And today it's not better than the best education was a couple thousand years ago, right?"

There's an undeniable appeal in combining "social good" with making money, and it has become somewhat of a mantra among Silicon Valley. But is this altruistic? "None of our backers are approaching AltSchool as a primarily altruistic purpose," says Ventilla. "Some of them are very interested in the sector because of the kind of social impact that business success in the sector would have." In other words, it's viewed as a win-win. The profit potential is the driving force, but the opportunity to do good is a bonus.

There's also money to be made from the sheer number of children who need educating. "If your mission is to enable every child to achieve their potential, there's a lot of children out there and a huge amount of dollars, in the trillions, that are spent on educating children and aren't spent as well as they could be spent," says Ventilla. "There's a big market on a multi-decade timescale for products where it's very expensive to make the first platform for the first user, but then relatively inexpensive to make the next thousand and the next million and the next billion, and at some scale those businesses are very profitable to run."

Is education broken? In terms of preparing children for the future, Ventilla believes so. At the least, it's not moving with the times. "You have this irony that the industry which is probably farthest behind the present state should probably be the industry that is the most ahead of the present state," he says. "To prepare a child for the future, you not only have to be contemporary, you have to actually be prescient in some sense. I don't think that schools are getting worse; I think that schools are getting better."

Part of the problem, Ventilla says, is not a lack of awareness among educators, but a lack of investment in evolving methodology. Education policymakers are behind in understanding where wealth is generated, where skills are needed. "There isn't any R&D in education. The White House estimates that less than two-tenths of 1 percent of expenditures are on R&D. It's hard to improve your future performance if you invest so little in it."

As with Hyperloop, does it take an outsider approach to rethink the way things work? Does it take an entrepreneurial and tech-based approach to effect change? Is the government simply unable to do this?

In education, says Ventilla, "It does seem like there is a dearth of people who think about the future, who have been in industries that are going to play a more prominent role in the future. It's problematic." This isn't necessarily confined to entrepreneurs, he adds. "It's about diversity of perspectives, broadly, and bringing in more people from scientific and technology fields. Separately from that, I think digital technology in particular has this superpower which is to allow you to be very complex and very flexible at the same time."

Part of AltSchool's unique approach is the variety of disciplines and a decentralized structure, says Ventilla. Schools are run by the teachers, for example. There are about 165 people in the company, fifty of whom are "world-class engineers" and fifty "world-class educators, working together under one organizational roof." The staff roster is divided into equal thirds: engineers, educators, and operators. "There's an opportunity in the education space to take a hard technology approach, and what we mean by that is an approach where you do meaningful R&D prior to when you start scaling," says Ventilla. "I don't think it's too off to say that virtually all of ed tech to date has taken the easy technology route."

It could potentially be the first slow-burn unicorn. Unicorns in Silicon Valley have historically been defined by being an anomaly, a quick phenomenon that takes off sensationally. AltSchool might have a similar scale and impact, but because it's in the field of education, it cannot be rushed. AltSchool is taking a challenging route toward long-term, meaningful change in education, rather than merely creating an app. It is an ambitious goal and a complicated field to step into. But it could have big financial rewards if it is successful, especially as more schools get privatized.

Megan Tompkins-Stange highlights that, while meritocratic in narrative, models like these are still inherently skewed toward children with an affluent background, sophisticated communication skills, and self-confidence. Children who have the confidence to choose their learning approach, or find a creative way to solve a problem, are often enabled by upbringing and resources. "It's about self-confidence and self-advocacy," she comments. "I work with a lot of first-generation college students, and just being able to advocate for themselves, like ask the teacher for an extension on a paper if something bad has happened with their family, is almost unthinkable. A child from a privileged family, or from a middle-class background with parents who went to college—they don't hesitate to do that. In those small, socially nuanced ways, you have a lot more advantages when you've had access to institutions that are associated with higher class levels. And, of course, race is also highly correlated."

In other words, despite the affordable price tag, few low-income kids will be skyping to Minerva or taking part in semesters from Amsterdam.

Ventilla, like Nelson, gets frustrated by the blanket view that AltSchool is another form of iPad learning or school tech. "There are a few very common misnomers about AltSchool, and they're probably not going to go away for a generation," he says. "If you say technology, people immediately go to e-learning; if you say personalization, they immediately go to kids doing whatever they want; if you say alternative, they immediately go to special needs. There are these ruts that language provides."

Does AltSchool have ambitions to affect mainstream educational policy? "No. We're blessedly small," says Ventilla. "We operate within the ecosystem as it exists, and we're a long way off from actually influencing policy." Though, he adds: "We would like to have meaningful scale, and as you have meaningful scale you start to butt up against the bounds of the ecosystem. You start to express your vision of what the future could look like in a way that could start to be relevant not just for policy but also for culture."

Not now, in other words. But soon.

From Hyperloop One to Altschool, Silicon Valley is stepping up its efforts to reimagine more concretely large aspects of our lives, and increasingly this is leaping off the screen to physical environments, systems, and even cities. Like the Victorian Industrialists before them who built model villages outside cities, many Valley people combine benevolence, social agenda, and business. What will these worlds look like in living color? The veneer of all of it is innovation, openness, broadly egalitarian principles, and altruism. And in many ways it achieves this, even if it's aimed at white, middle-class, already-somewhat-educated people. But it's not holistic. And it's not purely altruistic either. Education is a massively lucrative market and one, as Udacity is proving, that could last for a lifetime, not simply be isolated to one degree (if you can afford that). If tech's private iterations of charter schools scale and become a national precedent, the same biases that radiate through their existing educational ventures could place more pressure on public schools.

It's also another instance where, once again, Silicon Valley becomes the expert and leader by controlling one of the most booming sectors around, displaying an outsized influence on what the future looks like. It disproportionately seems to focus on technology and tech skills when in reality this may well, in itself, become an automated sector. Developers are the new factory workers, for now. And while data is being used to decide everything and viewed as the ultimate empirical proof point informing business strategies, will tech be able to teach the emotional intelligence and judgment that the World Economic Forum places equal focus on as future skills? Chances are, probably not. In recent years, liberal arts degrees have been maligned or shunned in favor of degrees that offer more direct links to a long-term lucrative career such as business and technology. Understanding nuance, culture, tone, and society at large have always been the rounding counterpoint to economics, science, and STEM subjects. Will tech's new-model schools help us learn this? Either way, as a result of market forces and rising prices of education, they will become a rare area of focus, accessible for only the rich to study. But this would arguably be a travesty. Empathy is the famed missing component from Silicon Valley. For all its rhetoric, empathy's absence is prominent in many of its civic endeavors. What will this world look like when these skewed ideas and biases are increasingly three-dimensional, immersive, and etched on our lives in social structures and institutions? Or worse, our coworkers, who are great at solving problems and coding, but also act like tone-deaf cyborgs. But that's the thing. Silicon Valley ventures aren't remaining in our phones anymore. They're leaping right of the screen into real-world constructs, Disneyland kingdoms of Silicon Valley's design. What would it be like to live in Silicon Valley's model of the future? And what, exactly, would that model look like? Perhaps a whitewashed theme park called Airbnb Land.

8

Airbnb Land

S outh Broadway in downtown Los Angeles is a curious relic of a bygone era. In its golden age in the 1920s, the thoroughfare was the
hub of the city's economic boom. But with the post–World War II
suburban sprawl and the development of the freeways, the area dwindled
and became a center for L.A.'s homeless population.

There are signs of its former glory everywhere, not least the string of
pleasure palaces for movies and plays. These include the Tower Theater, the
United Artists Theater, a neo-gothic beauty, and the Orpheum, which at
its peak played host to Judy Garland, Ella Fitzgerald, and Duke Elling-
ton. Nearby the Los Angeles Theater, built in 1930, stands as a flamboyant
tribute to the baroque period with a glittering interior so lavish it could
have been used as the set for Norma Desmond's mansion in *Sunset Boule-
vard*. The original ticket booth is still out front. South Broadway's Eastern
Columbia Building, also constructed in 1930, is a jade-tiled art deco jewel
that was created to house the famed apparel trader the Eastern Outfitting
Company.

Today, on street level on South Broadway, there's a mix of cheap jewelry
stores, a Burlington Coat Factory, bridal stores, a KFC, and vacant properties. But look up at the columns, soaring windows, and decorative stucco
work, and you get a snapshot of the vibrant center that the area used to be.

Little wonder it has proved irresistible to L.A.'s hipsters—and then, pretty quickly, developers. The area is in the midst of a major transformation into a hot new neighborhood. The Ace Hotel in the former United Artists Theater is just a start; the neighborhood is taking on all the bells and whistles of havens such as Brooklyn in New York and Shoreditch in London.

Luxury condos are being developed (reportedly 102 projects were underway in 2016, and the projects continue to get more ambitious). Historic buildings are being renovated into apartments, and new complexes imagined with star-studded renderings. Hip boutiques are moving in, too. Luxury brand Acne Studios has a spot in the Eastern Columbia Building. Urban Outfitters has taken over the former Rialto Theater. Nearby warehouse districts have become hotspots for tech startups, among them Virgin Hyperloop One. Meanwhile, in the streets stride bearded hipsters—boys with exposed ankles and brogues. Girls wearing felt hats, flowing skirts, and biker jackets clutch take-out matcha lattes. Inside the Ace Hotel, an army of laptops is opened projecting blue light, orb-style, onto the faces of its tapping users.

Downtown Los Angeles is also, aptly, where Airbnb staged its third annual host jamboree, Airbnb Open, described by the company as "a community-powered festival of travel and hospitality that celebrates a city and its neighborhoods." After all, Airbnb is all about authentic travel. From its beginnings as a couch-surfing website launched in 2008 for backpacking students, Airbnb has emerged as a bastion of more than economical travel (it allows homeowners to rent out their rooms or entire properties to travelers at rates historically cheaper than hotels). Today it's something altogether bigger. More than Homeaway.com or other homeowner rental sites, it pitches itself as a gateway to true local immersion and authentic travel. Staying in someone's spare room isn't just a cheap bed, it's a view into another culture that traditional hotels simply can't offer. And mingling with your hosts is all part of the experience. It's this emphasis that has in recent years given Airbnb license to become an aspirational brand, along with prices that now can match or exceed that of hotels. Today, mansions, private islands, and penthouses are available on the site.

Airbnb's rise has coincided with a shift in consumer culture toward spending on experiences over "stuff." Experience culture started with millennials, who in the absence of funds to buy apartments (some would say) have prioritized spending on travel, festivals, food, and living in the moment. After all, if you're never going to be able to buy that apartment any-way, why *not* book a life-enhancing trip to Petra, Jordan?

But experience culture is now a bona fide consumer movement for all generations, and one that favors unique, unchartered, and "authentic" (there it is again) above all else. All the better if it can be Instagrammed. As a result, it's become a new, lucrative industry. On cue, luxury-goods groups like LVMH and Ralph Lauren have diversified from bags and clothing to resorts, restaurants, and experiences. Department stores are rapidly being superseded by foodie theme parks like Eataly, packed to the gills with consumers on weekends. Or they've started adding yoga, spa treatments, and more to attract customers through their doors. And tickets to Burning Man have become hotter (and more desirable) than a designer handbag.

As a forecaster, I have found it fascinating to watch. The rise in global travel, intertwined with the explosion of visual media from Instagram to Snapchat, has accelerated the speed of travel and food trends and shortened the life of any hot destination, ingredient, or restaurant exponentially (and thus, its bragging rights). Cuba, so over! Ditto for cauliflower. Experiencing novel and arresting things in travel has become integral to people's projected social media identity and personal brand. And it has all put Airbnb—with its promises of raw authenticity, localism, and connections—in prime position to lead.

Airbnb has grown in sync with millennials becoming the most influential consumers to the travel industry, prompting major hotel chains and airlines to hurriedly switch up their offerings to cater to their tastes, from hipster stylings to global cuisines to free wi-fi in an attempt to claw back market share from its coral-hued new competitor.

Much like its founders, who are now in their mid-thirties, Airbnb is growing up, trying to pitch itself as the ultimate experience brand for people seeking original and life-transforming travel, for work and play. Today it's expanded beyond property rentals to Trips; it's platform that lets hosts sell guided local experiences. It's partnered with Delta Airlines so Airbnb guests earn Delta SkyMiles on bookings. It's paired up with booking app Resy to offer restaurant reservations. In October 2017, it took this a step further, announcing it was planning to launch its own branded apartments. Its first property in Kissimmee, Florida, will feature 300 units, according to the

Financial Times. Its purported aim, and the theme of its new festival, is to allow people to "Belong Anywhere." In May 2017, the company was valued at $31 billion.

Airbnb Open DTLA is one of the latest examples of its expanding ambition. The event is part of a new trend in consumer events—part festival for members, part educational platform, part rally, part entertainment, and part gala, in some instances brand extensions—that blend thought leadership with self-improvement and celebrity culture. (At Airbnb Open, Gwyneth Paltrow, Brian Grazer, and Ashton Kutcher are speakers on the lineup of talks staged in the district's historic theaters.) They have become attractions people will travel to; they are akin to concerts but present branded content in experience form. They have also become a cash cow and prime platform for other brands to participate and market toward audiences. Airbnb Open 2016 cost $345 to attend, plus $60 for the Bélo Awards celebrating the best hosts, and it accommodated 6,000 attendees. In 2016, Salesforce's Dreamforce tickets cost nearly $2,000. Women's media brand Refinery29 has launched 29Rooms, an interactive exhibit of twenty-nine immersive, highly Instagrammable installations—tickets were sold out the entire weekend at its 2017 events in New York and Los Angeles. *Teen Vogue* staged a ticketed Summit in L.A. in December 2017, with single-day entrance starting at $399 and guests including Hillary Clinton and teen influencer Amandla Stenberg (the lineup was a testament to *Teen Vogue*'s new "wokeness," but only for those who could afford it). Goop's sold-out well-being bonanza weekends In Goop Health started at $500 a ticket. Vaginal steaming, presumably, not included.

Salesforce's annual Dreamforce extravaganza, staged in San Francisco, is for businesses or entrepreneurs that use, or may want to use, Salesforce's cloud computing or CRM (customer relationship management) tools. "At Dreamforce, you'll learn, connect, and grow. You'll mingle with thought leaders, industry pioneers, and thousands of your peers, and you'll walk away with knowledge, connections, and memories that last a lifetime. Best of all, you'll have the time of your life," promises the company. It's attended by 130,000 people—which makes getting a hotel room in San Francisco at this time akin to a challenge from *The Hunger Games.*

As events go, Airbnb Open is a master class in brand immersion. From enthusiastic slogans to banded merchandise to talks and appearances, it simultaneously entertains while making Airbnb the educator and champion of its entrepreneur community. As a 3-D, three-day experience, it's also like stepping into an Airbnb-branded town, with all its rainbow-hued optimism, but also its failings. After three days, the placards are taken down, and the speakers wheeled away, but what if we were forced to live in Airbnb Land forever? Many of the tropes and the disconnects at Airbnb Open are universal to Silicon Valley. And attending, in some ways, gave a glimpse into the future of what a Silicon Valley world might look like.

The Truman Show

It's lunchtime on registration day at Airbnb Open and already the music is blasting. It's sunny, and as part of the three-day affair, downtown L.A. has essentially turned into an Airbnb-branded village. People are carrying branded totes everywhere, like a mini army. Free coffee, snacks, and bottled water are abundant. Airbnb merchandise, from bags to mugs emblazoned with the famous "Bélo," is sold at stands. Bands are playing in communal areas. The car park is a hotspot for wi-fi and taking selfies next to a giant sculpture of the Airbnb Bélo logo. People run through a white suspended installation behind, which is lit up at night.

Elsewhere there are lounges dedicated to Airbnb's brand partnerships with American Express and Delta. The historic theaters are venues for talks featuring Airbnb founders Joe Gebbia, Brian Chesky, and Nathan Blecharczyk, as well as senior staff such as then marketing chief Jonathan Mildenhall. Neighborhood stores are settings for seminars on entrepreneurship, interior design, and how to be a better host. There are installations exploring notions of belonging and authentic travel. The brand announces the unveiling of a new, beautifully designed community center in the mountains of Yoshino in Japan, a World Heritage Site where, because young people are increasingly fleeing villages to work in cities, traditional life and homes are dwindling.

As for the experience itself, it's like a cross between a cult gathering and the audience of a children's TV show. TED-style microphones abound and speeches are delivered slowly, with dramatic flair, to incite cheers and adoration, announcing new services on the platform, offering tips on hosting, and telling inspirational stories about the Airbnb community.

And incredibly, people buy it. There is a genuine sense of hysteria at some events. Especially when, after announcing the launch of *Airbnb Magazine*, Hearst Chief Content Officer Joanna Coles exclaims, with true Oprah Winfrey drama, that there is magically a copy of the first issue under every seat. On cue, everyone in the audience rushes to yank the magazine out, flipping through, with collective gusto, what amounts to be a fairly thin glossy branded title. (Each copy is taped to the bottom of the seats. Who knows what damage was inflicted by an audience of hundreds yanking the publication from the bottom of withered theater seats.)

Attendees vary, from ardent Airbnb hosts who now use the platform as an income stream, to curious punters in search of contact with celebrity. There is laughter when Gwyneth Paltrow announces her latest travel-tips app G Spotting with a wink. There are tears as a cancer survivor talks about a transformative trip to Paris with a host, as part of the Make-A-Wish Foundation partnership (the talk's title is "Building Empathy Through Community"). There are boos when a woman goes onstage to protest against Airbnb in Palestine. This is during Ashton Kutcher's fireside chat with Brian Chesky in a session called "The Game Plan: Strategies for Entrepreneurs" (Kutcher is an investor in Airbnb). The protestor is promptly taken off stage by security as the crowd jeers. Kutcher seizes the moment to embark on a rousing speech about a world without borders and his belief in Chesky. An audience of smartphones records it.

Then there are the "experiences"—which are actually an Airbnb specialty. From the London Design Festival to Milan Design Week, Airbnb has used pop-up immersive "experiences" as a way to generate PR, communicate sophistication, and connect with artist communities in many cities.

One, in a South Broadway BNKR store, is a walk-through installation exploring different words associated with the concept of home. For *hygge* (the Danish term for mindful comfort and indulgence), visitors can have personalized tea bags made and sit in comfy armchairs. There are strange, cardboard bamboo-ish pods set up in another corner for *fernweh*, a German term for wanderlust. Here, visitors are encouraged to contribute their visions of faraway places in hand-painted journals. "Share your curiosities, your fantasies, or the adventures you envision ahead of you," they are exhorted.

Suffice it to say, irony and humor, much less self-awareness, is in short supply. It's all incredibly earnest. Why wouldn't you want to sit in a tent, indoors, and journal with a crayon about that time you had a cup of tea near Ayers Rock?

The centerpiece of the event, from a press perspective, is the launch of Airbnb Trips, a move into branded travel experiences. It is a platform for bookable tours; the ability to make restaurant bookings is in the pipeline. Experiences for sale include stargazing, truffle hunting, social-good and charity projects, and cookery classes. They are led by Airbnb expert members and packaged with sleek, inspirational photography. Given the brand's challenges with local legislators in numerous countries, it's also a canny extension from home sharing into a less regulated arena. In addition, there are online lifestyle guides created entirely by community members to offer authentic local content. This is all part of a bigger move into 360-degree travel booking in the hopes that Airbnb can inch bigger ground away from traditional travel companies.

Another new app feature is curated travel content, described as Places. This includes travel guides penned by Airbnb members about local hotspots and audio walking tours. There are local "meet-ups" on offer, connecting travelers to events that are running when they are visiting.

In addition, Airbnb is enhancing the service aspect of its offer—in the future its Homes section will allow people to pre-order groceries and book rental cars, not just reserve accommodations. It is all part of Airbnb's grand plan to make itself a one-stop, authentic travel shop for social media–savvy, upwardly mobile young people.

The event culminates in the Bélo Awards ceremony, compèred by TV host and comic James Corden. It celebrates the "brightest and best of the Airbnb community" by championing "their stories of playful creativity, limitless care, and unexpected heroism." After this there's a concert headlined by Maroon 5.

Sermons of Authenticity

There's a religious feel to Airbnb Open 2016. Key words such as ʻ
nity" and "authenticity" are peppered through every talk. Upbe
pumps everywhere like audio Prozac.

There is also an underlying tone that the traditional hotel ind
prosaic, sterile, and only out to turn a profit. The implication is that
who doesn't want a more "personal" experience is somehow lacking ar
never truly experience cities, that staying in a traditional hotel can in n
give guests the kind of immersion into a place that staying with som
local does. And it's all about authentic experiences, of course. Why w
you want to stay in the boxy room of a faceless hotel, not getting to k
the area or the culture? What compares to getting to know your host,
ing on journeys, eating with his family? Pity the fool for whom the gu
antee of clean sheets, mini-bar, and clean carpet is appealing, or the ic
who'd prefer to passively consume an episode of *The Bachelor* and order ro
service than talk to a stranger. In Airbnb world, we should be constan
experiencing, connecting, and living authentically. It's an incredibly clev
form of messaging, even if it does belie a reality that not everyone war
true immersion when they travel. And many of the experiences at Airbn
thanks to professional Airbnb-ers and their now massive membershi
aren't that different from a hotel or traditional home-rental platform—th
are whole-property rentals so there's no fireside chats with owners occu
ring. And it's not even that affordable anymore in many cities. It's not s
special, for all the spin.

The Kutcher protest scene isn't the only area of unrest. During the even
labor union members and affordable-housing advocates stage a rally callin
for tougher regulations for short-term rentals. They contend that owners are
repurposing affordable housing units, listing them on Airbnb and other such
sites, shrinking the housing supply and distorting rents. (New York and San
Francisco are among cities starting to clamp down on Airbnb for this reason.
Airbnb has recently agreed to collect taxes from tenants in Los Angeles and
pay these to the city.)

There's also a small, ragtag troop—presumably unrelated—marching and shouting about Donald Trump and his attitude toward immigrants. They march around the Airbnb blocks with drums and horns, chanting. It all contributes to a slight air of tension as the event progresses.

The politics don't end there. One of the items on the agenda is championing Airbnb's position in policy. Airbnb, like many growing tech companies who encounter restrictive legislation, has hired a head of policy, in this case Chris Lehane, formerly a White House spokesperson during the Clinton/Gore administration. During his talk, "The Making of a Movement for Home Sharing," he discusses how the sharing economy is not only good for the community but also a sustainable way to travel. "A year ago, I was in Paris and together we formally launched a movement, a home-sharing project," says Lehane. "And today as I stand here I can say that the state of the movement is strong and is getting stronger. And that this really attributes to you—you are the heart and soul of what makes us strong."

If Airbnb cofounder Gebbia, clad in a fitted T-shirt and jeans, is the rock star of the event, Lehane is the pastor. Lehane's speech positions Airbnb for the future, arguing that major consumer trends mean it will only become more popular. Airbnb has "democratized travel," opened up new areas to tourism, and is—now, finally—providing tax revenue to governments.

However, this isn't entirely true. As the *Guardian* noted in December 2016, Airbnb Payments UK Ltd handles the company's rental payments from everywhere in the world other than the U.S., China, and India. The commissions on these payments pass through Ireland, which allows Airbnb to benefit from friendlier corporation tax. The *Guardian* said Airbnb paid UK tax of just £317,000 in the eleven months to December 2015, despite handling hundreds of millions of pounds in global rent payments that generated commissions for its Irish operations.

Lehane argues that Airbnb also helps the environment, because it's a more sustainable way to travel. "Millennials care more about sustainability issues and climate change than baby boomers, and that manifests itself in how they live their daily lives," he says. "You see shared bikes, shared gardens, shared tools, shared everything on energy distribution. We even have shared pets in some places. Think about it from the perspective of home sharers. Right now, in the United States alone, there are over 13 million empty homes and over 33 million empty bedrooms."

The services of Airbnb will also save the ailing middle class as its incomes shrink: "A typical middle-class family has fallen behind by about $7,000 from where they would have been otherwise," Lehane says.

This positions the democratization of travel and the sharing economy as an engine for economic growth. "When you look at tourism and travel, it's almost 10 percent of the global GDP. That's an enormous figure. And you've got Chinese travel coming behind us, and that will continue to accelerate that growth." The sharing economy, Lehane says, is "about a $15 billion-a-year business but is projected to grow to $335 billion over the next ten years or so. There's a really simple reason why this growth is taking place. People really, really, really like it. It's easy, it's affordable, it connects them, and it's very consistent with their sustainability beliefs and values."

Despite claims of being more sustainable, this increased travel demand, even if users are staying in other people's apartments, inevitably increases usage of cars, planes, and trains.

Nevertheless, Airbnb is already mobilizing its membership to push its agenda. It's launched Airbnb Citizen, a separate website "advancing home sharing as a solution" as well as being a global movement with news on policy updates. "As our community grows," the company proclaims on its website, "we appreciate the opportunity to work with local governments to craft progressive, fair rules for home sharing. With this in mind, we are releasing the Airbnb Policy Tool Chest, a resource for governments to consider as they draft or amend these rules." The company has also announced approval of Airbnb clubs, support groups, and focal points for local hosts to gather. Described by Airbnb as independent, these branded, sharing organizations now number one hundred globally.

Lehane frames sharing economy hosts as a new employment group, a new digital iteration to previous centuries' craftsmen and artisans who came together and created guilds, and who the government has simply been behind in recognizing. "In the Industrial Age, working men and women organized themselves into trade unions, and I fundamentally believe that as we enter this age of a sharing economy, clubs are the next iteration of people organizing themselves, to represent themselves, advocate for themselves."

"Building Empathy"

All things considered, while bizarre in places, Airbnb Open is a masterpiece in immersion and onboarding (a term that means familiarizing potential customers with the brand). One of its key methods is in controlling the dialogue and messaging. Everything is tightly focused and planned. But for anyone with an ounce of cynicism, holes quickly appear. That's the fallacy in having a branded rather than an editorially led conference, similar to those staged by the *Economist*, *New York Times*, and *Financial Times*, which are largely brand agnostic. Brands sponsor newspaper conferences too, but journalists and moderators are relatively free to grill, challenge, and discuss topics with guests. The audience is made up of informed critics, rather than middle-America evangelicals looking at ways to supplement their incomes. Airbnb Open is not a dialogue; everyone is singing in unison. One by one, all the criticisms of Airbnb's platform are addressed with soaring speeches, keynotes, and data—it's a one-way broadcast rather than a discussion. Panels such as "Working Together with the Travel Industry" and "Building Relationships with Landlords and Neighbors" address hot-button issues only on its terms, but everything is extremely and disconcertingly cordial—a world away from the reality of actual debates on these important topics, in which an entire industry is being disrupted by a platform that is distorting rents. In the minds of the audience, however, when they exit the matter is resolved, which is potentially dangerous as Airbnb blasts similar messaging to its several million users. Attendees at In Goop Health would likely experience the same evangelism about well-being (without those grumpy doctors who have criticized some of its more wacky recommendations). But the difference is that Goop is selling jade eggs and face cream, not encouraging people to flout legislation by renting properties illegally.

In many ways Airbnb Open reflects the dissonances in the impact of Silicon Valley's ongoing rise. Not least is the location choice. Staging the event in one of L.A.'s hottest new neighborhoods seems apposite but takes

little account of the fact that this is the heart of the city's homeless population, who may face being uprooted as the new wave of more affluent residents
move in. Gwyneth Paltrow references authentic downtown L.A. eateries.
Yet, step outside the actual theater, and the area is a portrait of the economic disparity so prevalent in the U.S. The neighborhood is in transition,
becoming a gentrified millennial enclave. Half the jewelry shops and textile
warehouses won't be here in five years. In the same way that the West Village in New York was adored for its small boutiques and antique shops and
cafés, the influx of wealth has put rents way above affordability and forced
most tenants to depart. Now the stores are empty. Ironically, what makes
Downtown L.A. so seductively authentic and interesting might vanish with
its ascent.

The talks about Airbnb creating empathy, while laden in Goop-ish sunshine, stand in uncomfortable contrast to the security guards on a number
of corners to marshal local homeless people. (If Pishevar wants to flatten the
cities and terraform them, Airbnb wants to paste a Polaroid filter over the
best parts, keep the local taco stands, and sweep out the undesirables.)

In 2016, Airbnb donated $100,000 to a project working on the home-
less issue in L.A., which seems relatively meager for a company valued at
$30 billion. In 2017, it also launched Open Homes, a platform allowing
anyone to register vacant spaces for people in need such as displaced citizens
or those forced to move due to natural disasters. It contributes to the feeling
that while dwindling communities in cherry blossom–bedecked Yoshino in
Japan are picture-book problems to solve, issues of rising homelessness in
states such as California are not. And therefore, they are not part of Airbnb's
marketing platform.

One block from the main thoroughfare of theaters where Airbnb Open
speeches are held, the dense smell of urine is overwhelming. Despite the
international emphasis of the event—seeing new cultures in far-off lands,
democratizing travel—it is attended almost exclusively by white, middle-
income Americans. They no doubt see it as a lifeline, or a lucrative income
stream, but overall the demographic of the audience feels quite narrow. Like
a convention of small businesses that wouldn't look out of place in a conference room in Las Vegas.

In its broadcast nature, Airbnb Open is also emblematic of Silicon Valley's approach to critique. Much is made of the journalistic interview on the final day of the event, in which Airbnb's founders face "tough questions," which are all pre-planned, presumably pre-approved, and without recourse and interrogation. (*"He says he didn't do it." "OK, great!"*)

Airbnb, as a bastion of the Sharing Economy, is also positioned as the symbol of future and progress. Governments trying to hold it back are backward and are stopping people from traveling affordably or earning a little money during challenging times. Some of that might be true, but Airbnb lauding itself as a civic leader and champion of the people certainly isn't. It's a company.

Airbnb adopts a very worldly, internationalist rhetoric, and this is a message throughout. Audiences are presented as travel-hungry, intrepid explorers of the world, collecting life-changing memories while enriching their lives. But there is a disconnect here, too. It's a worldliness in the context of the exoticism of travel for affluent millennials visiting new places for leisure. It's not about true diversity, at least not at home where its audience is mainly white. And certainly not within its own company.

The uncomfortable truth is that often, in reality, its audience is not diverse, as evidenced in news reports of host racism. This is backed by a recent Harvard Business School study, "Racial Discrimination in the Sharing Economy: Evidence from a Field Experiment." Released in September 2016, the paper found significant bias occurring in booking requests from certain potential renters. It opens with the following abstract: "In a field experiment on Airbnb, we find that applications from guests with distinctively African American names are 16 percent less likely to be accepted relative to identical guests with distinctively white names. Discrimination occurs among landlords of all sizes, including small landlords sharing the property and larger landlords with multiple properties. Discrimination is most pronounced among hosts who have never had an African American guest, suggesting only a subset of hosts discriminate. While rental markets have achieved significant reductions in discrimination in recent decades, our results suggest that Airbnb's current design choices facilitate discrimination and raise the possibility of erasing some of these civil rights gains."

Airbnb has many progressive initiatives in place, including platforms for hosts to house refugees from Kenya to Rwanda and other areas embroiled in the global refugee crisis. It has taken reports of racism among its hosts seriously, instituting polices that will punish hosts for discrimination based on race, sexual orientation, or gender identity. Each time they are criticized, its founders respond thoughtfully and with more authenticity than neighboring Silicon Valley giants. "I think they've actually done a really phenomenal job. Every time there is an issue, they use that to make the company better," says Margit Wennmachers, pointing to research and to the philanthropic efforts of the company.

With housing shortages in many parts of the world, Airbnb is reacting to pressure over controlling the lengths of stays. In response to criticism about the removal of properties from the traditional rental market so that they can be listed on Airbnb, it recently announced it would help enforce a ninety-day rule, which prohibits short-term lettings of entire properties for more than ninety days in a calendar year.

In response to the Muslim travel ban by President Trump, its founders have been vociferous about inclusivity being at the core of its values. It offered housing to anyone impacted by the ban and launched the ad campaign #WeAccept, touting its principles of accepting people of different ethnicities, sexual orientations, and backgrounds. It revived this in the wake of Trump's statements about "shithole" countries, referring to immigrants coming from African nations, with a digital ad campaign promoting listings in the same countries and with the same hashtag. But that could be seen as much as a smart way to connect with its millennial audience (which statistically skews more liberal) as much as altruism.

Still, much of this is all too revealing. Like Google's infamous company mantra "Don't Be Evil" (since dropped), none of this is mal-intended, but some of the limitations in Silicon Valley's approaches and endeavors are indelibly linked to the rarified enclave in which they perch and the socioeconomic pools from which their team members are drawn.

Despite its global stance, Airbnb, like many Silicon Valley companies, is predominantly white and affluent. The company's 2016 diversity report records a 57 percent white workforce (in 2015 this was 63 percent white); it has a 43 percent female workforce—down 3 percent from last year. Airbnb's workforce is 6.5 percent Hispanic and 2.9 percent black. The company's 2017 goal was to increase its overall percentage of employees from underrepresented minority groups from 10 to 11 percent.

It's a similar story when it comes to its hosts. According to a 2017 study by Inside Airbnb, an independent research platform examining the impact of Airbnb on communities, there are already distortions occurring within key Airbnb markets thanks to its disproportionately white host makeup. The study, "The Face of Airbnb, New York City. Airbnb as a Racial Gentrification Tool," states, "across all seventy-two predominantly black New York city neighborhoods, Airbnb hosts are five times more likely to be white. In those neighborhoods, the Airbnb host population is 74 percent white, while the white resident population is only 13.9 percent.

"When we look at economic disparities, we see that in black neighborhoods, not only do whites make up the majority of Airbnb hosts, but we also see that white hosts benefit the most economically," it says. "White Airbnb hosts in black neighborhoods earned in total an estimated $159.7 million accumulating with a group representing only 13.9 percent of the population is a 530 percent economic disparity."

Prejudices among the Airbnb host community have also manifested in the counterpoint hashtag #AirBnBWhileBlack, highlighting instances of host discrimination. Reports have also surfaced about Asian and trans guests being denied bookings.

In 2018, Airbnb announced the appointment of prominent African American businessman (and outgoing CEO of American Express) Ken Chenault as a board member. Next, it says, it is looking to add a woman to its board.

And Airbnb's lack of internal diversity is not unique to the company, particularly. It's a similar case at many Silicon Valley companies—and indeed, industries, including mine. Its founders' messaging is doubtlessly progressive, and outspoken on political issues. But it's still, ultimately, emanating through the lens of a privileged, often neoliberal, twenty-something. It's an elite form of progressivism, too. What rarely gets mentioned about Big Tech companies, beyond their lack of racial and gender diversity, is the skew toward economically privileged and educated staff.

"We still live in a world today where a vast majority of programmers and engineers working inside Silicon Valley companies are white males of a certain age bracket. This inevitably leads to algorithmic bias embedded across the systems that are seamlessly taking over some of our most intimate activities: communication, discovery, security," says Puneet Kaur Ahira. "I think we grossly underestimate just how pervasive this algorithmic bias extends— it's hard because every day you lose more yardage."

"It is an argument for diversity in the workforce; not just race or gender, but background experience, economic experience," says Macon Phillips. "You're seeing a big pipeline of students that go from Stanford into Silicon Valley and have a sort of crazy sense of entitlement. It affects their approach to innovation . . . Silicon Valley companies are focused on problems that they think that they can solve. They think these are problems they can solve more easily than government can, which is probably true. But while they've been solving their problems about how they can get their dry-cleaning done, people are being displaced from houses in San Francisco because it's not affordable; the schools continue to get worse in the public school system; and there's an inequality. It's happening right in that city and no one in Silicon Valley seems that preoccupied by it. So it's an unequal approach to innovation."

But the biases are important to address, especially as this group expands. Airbnb Open of course was not openly biased, but there were scant black attendees. Doubtless the founders would hate to think of themselves as anything but champions of freedom (complete with Maroon 5 soundtracks). And with noble ambitions to boot. They are champions of empathy, after all (even as they are stepping past the large homeless population of downtown Los Angeles). All of this gets caught up in the murky area of tone and invisible barriers, though, and subtle choices that radiate through decisions in policy, product, designs, and systems if not addressed.

It's telling, for example, that Airbnb's founders didn't do something more meaningful in relation to the homeless issue of the downtown L.A. situ they were co-opting for a week. Their focus is on philanthropy that is desirable, which is also part of a wider trend in how Silicon Valley companies focus their attentions, particularly when it comes to problem solving.

It would have been less glamorous to help local homeless, and less PR-worthy than the blossom-bedecked community center in Yoshino, for sure. But it would alleviate a real problem on their doorsteps, and one that

Airbnb and other Silicon Valley companies are both driving and ignoring. But this is another example of the chasmic gap between Silicon Valley's messaging and hard-nosed reality. And one in which the problems it tackles are driven by PR and marketing, and therefore inherently skewed toward the concerns of its affluent audience and aspirational causes. And they are PR platforms alone, they are not oriented toward real change, or real progress. Its refugee housing platform is just that, a platform, reliant on others' participation.

The struggles of Silicon Valley don't stop with racial diversity in its businesses and practices, either. There is another growing chasm, and it's a problem that's going to get much louder as the apparent forces that ignited the #MeToo movement sweep through all male-dominated industries, exposing sexual harassment and more, and move on to its most powerful, most male industry ever: Big Tech.

Silicon Valley has a woman problem.

9

Women and Silicon Valley

The cover profiles of technology magazines (actually, let's just make that magazines generally) are illustrative of the bias. When it comes to the rapid rise of technology, and its subsequent mass festishization and global cultural influence, women have largely remained absent from the popular narrative and heroism associated with its success. Oh, OK, Whitney Wolfe, founder of Bumble, the feminist dating app, has been featured on the cover of *Wired UK* (she's also model-pretty, blond, and thin, which may not be a coincidence). For every ten, twenty, thirty, forty cover features venerating male tech heroes, there are scant equivalents celebrating women. Megan J. Smith, the first female CTO to the president of the United States, made it to the cover of *Wired*. Sheryl Sandberg has made the cover of *Time* magazine. But taken amid the torrent of press featuring male leaders, it's like a bucket of water in a tsunami. Consider such infamous examples as *Newsweek*'s clanger of a special issue dubbed "The Founding Fathers of Silicon Valley: Exploring 60 Years of Innovation." Or Walter Isaacson's book *The Innovators: How a Group of Hackers, Geniuses, and Geeks Created the Digital Revolution*, which is dominated by men. There is a sea of other examples. Tech giants have become part of a huge narrative of success and leadership, and women are largely missing from the story.

The sad thing is that this dearth of press kind of reflects reality. Or, at least, reality now. Historically, women—not that you'd know it—were a key part of Silicon Valley. Integral to Apple's growth. Integral to technological ingenuity at NASA. And have been pioneers behind a string of firsts in technological advancements.

Smith, when she took the government role in 2014, made unearthing these invisible stories a key mission. She's spoken frequently about Ada Lovelace, the English woman born in 1812 who was the first computer programmer, or Katherine G. Johnson, the African American woman featured in the Oscar-nominated film *Hidden Figures* who helped put NASA astronauts on the moon and was awarded the Presidential Medal of Freedom in 2015. She's also highlighted Grace Hopper, who invented coding itself.

In fact, look back even fifteen years and a considerable number of women were involved in Silicon Valley's ascent. Judy Estrin, part of a research group, is credited with developing the internet in the 1970s. Sandra Kurtzig sold her software to Hewlett-Packard in the 1970s and became the first software multimillionaire. Donna Dubinsky was the founding CEO of PalmPilot, the precursor to the BlackBerry. The list goes on.

Prior to Big Tech's explosion, Silicon Valley generally seemed to have been more gender friendly. "Myspace was really diverse in terms of gender and race," says Debra Cleaver, founder and CEO of Vote.org. "I don't know if this is just a Silicon Valley thing but straight white men are overrepresented up here now. Myspace was not like that. If you saw a woman at Myspace on the tech side of the building, there was a really good chance she was in charge of her team. We all knew this. Most of the best people in engineering are women." She adds: "Silicon Valley has diversity problems, but the problems are that they create a hostile work environment for people who aren't white and people who aren't male, generally. I tell people that it's like men have found a way to automatically be on top and have the best-paid jobs."

There have been high-profile female leaders such as Marissa Mayer, former Google then Yahoo executive (news coverage of her has largely been highly gendered, centering on her role as leader and mom, with controversy over her short maternity leave). And of course Sandberg, whose book *Lean In*, about women taking a seat at the table in leadership, was hugely influential on a global scale (but which has been criticized for elitism and what has been dubbed "Trickle Down" feminism). Sandberg has collaborated with Getty Images to curate new pictures of women leaders. More recently, she has launched a new initiative, #MentorHer, in the wake of the #MeToo movement and a survey commissioned by Sandberg's LeanIn.Org that found half of male managers are now uncomfortable participating in work activities with women.

#MentorHer, as reports go, has the backing of more than thirty-eight prominent leaders and CEOs, including Disney's Bob Iger, General Motors' Mary Barra, and Netflix's Reed Hastings, who are all committed to mentoring women at their own companies.

The public figureheads are one thing, but it feels like a high-profile excuse for a reality that, despite overtures to correcting its lack of diversity, shows women and minorities still barely represented. Facebook's 2017 diversity numbers reveal that female employees make up 35 percent of their workforce. Overall, women hold 19 percent of tech jobs, and 27 percent of new-graduate hires are now women. Twenty-eight percent of leadership roles are held by women. Google said in 2017 that 69 percent of its employees are men, while 31 percent are women; 20 percent of Google's technical roles are held by women. Women hold 25 percent of leadership positions in the company, up from 24 percent the previous year. Such numbers are replicated pretty much throughout the publicly issued status reports of these companies. In Airbnb's 2017 diversity report, it was found to have a 49.8 percent white workforce (in 2016 this was 56.6 percent white). It has a 41 percent female workforce; 30 percent of its leaders, as of 2017, are female.

Interestingly, the advertising industry may—by necessity—be moving faster on this. General Mills and Hewlett-Packard are among the major companies insisting that their advertising agencies meet diversity quotas. (Which is ironic given their own makeup.) As such, advertising agencies, including my own, are putting diversity—not just of gender and ethnicity, but also of background—at the core of future strategies. The Brexit referendum and the 2016 U.S. presidential election have also created a major shake-up in the normally affluent, liberal, creative confines of advertising agencies, which are recognizing a disconnect with a growing consumer segment.

There are other efforts to change. Tech, ever the lover of buzzwords, has started to embrace the emerging popular term "intersectionality." In 2017, Twitter hired Candi Castleberry Singleton as vice president of intersectionality, culture, and diversity. Lawyer and feminist Kimberlé Crenshaw coined the term "intersectionality" in the late 1980s to capture the premise that when it comes to identity, the overlap of race, gender, sexuality, and class can contribute to a specific type of experience in the world—and create unique overlaps in discrimination or bias. Now, as dialogue around the importance of diversity reaches a fever pitch, intersectionality is resurging in popular discourse, conference panels, and think pieces, embraced by diversity chiefs. It's also extending to consideration of neurodiversity and disability inclusion.

There have been very public new hires. Uber has hired two senior women following a series of controversies about its misogynist culture, management practices, and scandals. They have appointed marketing executive Bozoma Saint John as head of brand. Saint John is a prominent African American leader from Apple (and a single mother). They have also hired Harvard Business School professor Frances Frei as senior vice president for leadership and strategy.

But it's all flying in the face of a bigger picture in which the women of Silicon Valley struggle to get funding, endure sexism, and face an entirely different experience from their male counterparts. These recent hires are generally reactionary, responding to public shaming rather than being part of a concerted, proactive attempt to create a fair, inclusive, and empowering industry culture. Many of the much-purported diversity chiefs feel like conference panel talking heads rather than people focused on decisive change.

Diversity chiefs have been one tool in Silicon Valley's PR battle, but the numbers only shift at a glacial pace from year to year. And some of the chiefs themselves have shown a staggering lack of self-awareness. Apple's diversity chief Denise Young Smith, herself an African American, was forced to step down after only six months after making controversial comments at a summit in Bogotá, Colombia. "There can be twelve white, blue-eyed, blond men in a room and they're going to be diverse too because they're going to bring a different life experience and life perspective to the conversation," she is reported to have said at the summit. "Diversity is the human experience. I get a little bit frustrated when diversity or the term diversity is tagged to the people of color, or the women, or the LGBT." She was slammed for appearing to defend Apple's overwhelmingly white and male leadership at a time when the company's makeup is so markedly uneven.

"There are huge issues with the power structure," says VR pioneer Jacquelyn Ford Morie. "Certainly, as a woman, I have not been able to get funding for any of my companies, while my male colleagues are being thrown millions of dollars. The second thing, that's even worse, is ageism. As an older woman, the chances of my getting money are 2 percent. The chances of my colleagues who are men, who haven't done half as much as I have, of getting $500 million in the next six months are about 90 percent."

She's right, of course. According to PitchBook, in 2017, 2.2 percent of all venture capital in the U.S. went to companies founded solely by women. When it comes to deal count, roughly 4.4 percent of venture-capital transactions last year were for women-founded companies. Just 11 percent of partners at VC firms are female. This despite numerous studies by *Harvard Business Review* and First Round Capital showing that women-founded companies often outperform men's. (In 2015, First Round measured the outperformance at 63 percent.)

"It's a boys' club, and it's not just a boys' club that's making things—it's the boys' club financing the things to be made. We need to add seats to the room, in every kind of room where catalytic decisions are being made," says Puneet Kaur Ahira.

People are quick to point out, rightly, that this is not just a Silicon Valley issue, but a wider problem endemic to Hollywood, government, and all our power structures today. There are "too many instances where women are underrepresented," says Margit Wennmachers.

There are some hopeful signs. For the first time, computer science is the most popular major for female students at Stanford University. "Maria Klawe at Harvey Mudd College in Southern California has done outstanding work getting women into coding, and it's just how she changed the initial process to get women into coding," says Wennmachers. "I don't want to say the pipeline is an acceptable excuse at all, but I think it's true for every industry. That doesn't mean we get a pass, none of us should get a pass." (The macro picture, far from the confines of Silicon Valley training ground Stanford University, shows slower progress. According to a 2018 study, while numbers are growing, only 27 percent of all students taking the

AP computer science exam in the United States are girls, and just 18 percent of American computer science college degrees go to women.)

Wennmachers also concedes that "with clients you're often the only female in the room, and there have been thousands of times where I say something and, three men later, it gets repeated, and all of a sudden, it's a thing. It's beyond infuriating. I think it's good that tech gets beaten up, just as I think that it's good that every industry that deserves to get beaten up does get beaten up."

She also tells me: "I think the conversation around getting a female board member is a little bit annoying—to me, it's a nasty bit of tokenism, because it's like, 'Oh yeah, we have a woman on the board, so now, our problem is solved.' The woman on the board doesn't actually hire people or create careers. The woman who is the VP of sales can mentor a lot of women and can actually make several careers. It's not just about the board."

Talk to women startup founders, and familiar themes and frustrations emerge. These include funding and implicit bias in the venture-capital world. "If I were a guy, people would shower me with money," says Cleaver. "I have raised money, but men in my space, who were nowhere near as good as I am, have raised way more. I'm better than most other people in my field but meanwhile there are really young white guys with no experience who are getting all the funding."

Cleaver says the biases, gender politics, and social dynamics that affect women in all industries' senior positions are highly prevalent in Silicon Valley. "I had someone say to me once: 'It's clear that you're really confident.' I just looked at him because in my head I had to count to ten before I could answer. When I finally answered him, I said: 'I'm pretty confident that the past thirteen years of success that I've had are due to something other than luck.' Of course I'm fucking confident."

She adds: "He kept saying things like, 'That seems too ambitious.' I replied, 'Too ambitious? Anything less than that is inadequate.' He was an older white guy, probably sixty years old. If I were a young man he'd be thinking: 'I see myself in you.' But I'm not a young man, I'm a middle-aged lesbian."

For Cleaver a lot of it is about the subtleties of tone and language. "Lots of VCs will talk about founders when they are not in the room. If it's a woman, they say to each other, 'I don't know if she can pull this off. I don't know if she has the connections. If it's a man they say, 'We're gonna have to introduce him to A, B, and C and help him.'"

Amber Atherton is founder of Zyper, a new ad tech company (ad tech refers to making digital brand placement and advertising more impactful). Zyper's aim is to help brands connect with their most devoted fans on social platforms and incentivize them to share more with brand rewards. Atherton recently received additional backing from Y Combinator, relocating from London to Palo Alto to take part in its program. "We had traction and I had a track record," she says of getting funded (Atherton also created and sold an online fashion jewelry company in the UK). "So while I'm not going to say it was easy, it took us four months to close."

Atherton was drawn to the Valley for its atmosphere of ambition and optimism. "I came here because I wanted to look at things through a Silicon Valley hyper-growth perspective, which I don't think you have in the UK. There's not the ambition or blue sky thinking that they encourage in Silicon Valley."

Atherton thinks one reason for the funding disparity between male- and female-backed companies is the types of things they're typically pitching. "The majority of female entrepreneurs are coming up with consumer-led companies. Brands. There are very few female entrepreneurs coming up with ad tech, for example. Or software companies. Or AI. Which is what they [VCs] are used to."

Atherton, a highly ambitious entrepreneur, has experienced other biases, especially as a solo founder of a rapidly growing company. "I often get asked: 'Oh, so you're the only founder?' And I say, 'yes.' And then they say, 'Do you not want a cofounder?' and I say, 'No!' . . . They assume that I would need somebody."

What are we missing out on by not funding all these women-founded companies? After all, women are the dominant consumer base in most markets. When it comes to health, personal care, and more, men are creating, devising, and marketing the products aimed at women. The female perspective is often missing. And products being launched by women to fill the gaps often receive resistance to investing.

Eva Goicochea is the founder of Maude, a new direct-to-consumer condom and sexual-health brand, with ambitions to disrupt the global condom industry with sleek, beautifully designed products marketed to both women and men. Her brand, with understated packaging and pithy language, is in the same vein as Dollar Shave Club, Harry's, Everlane, and Warby Parker, which have disrupted shaving, clothing basics, and eyewear with hip, new alternatives. (Goicochea actually worked with Everlane, among brands including Herschel, Shinola, and Squarespace.)

Goicochea said she initially struggled to get backing, in part because VCs did not understand the insight into why she was launching—that women, and people in general, don't like shopping for condoms in stores. They're all marketed to men in black and gold packaging anyway, and are therefore highly outdated. And, while the category (like the shaving vertical, which was recently disrupted by Dollar Shave Club) was very successful before, that's not to say it didn't need rethinking. "The first thing was them recognizing that the culture around sex products needed to be changed. Then there were other people looking very much at it as an industry that is so monopolized that it's hard to change it," she says.

"Because my idea is not tech-based and because I didn't lead with the business model, I lead with the brand and the culture angle, I was also met with way more pushback. I think that many brands by men have been funded, and they're shitty brands, and the business model is not as strong as mine. I had all the numbers, I just didn't lead with that. They assume that men are business savvy and business minded. And they're more willing to listen to the other parts of the story."

Goicochea also highlighted lack of diversity in VC companies. "I pitched to white guys, Indian guys, or Asians. There's nobody else. There are no African Americans. And then when I pitched to women, they were way harder on me than men." (Suffice it to say, Maude has now been enthusiastically funded and launched in 2018.)

Naomi Kelman, CEO of Willow, the award-winning breast pump, faced less difficulty when Willow first started. "We were very fortunate in getting our funding for Willow. I think part of it was that we were clearly reinventing a category that had been sleepy and hadn't had a lot of significant innovation in a long time. And so what we were solving for was clear enough, and we got a lot of advocacy and support from the VC community."

She also says the narrative about VCs is not clean-cut. "There's been a lot of negative things written about some of the VCs and just as it's inappropriate to stereotype women or stereotype men, I think it's also equally inappropriate to stereotype VCs. I would say that the ones that I have interacted with I have found to be welcoming, understanding of women's health and women's issues, incredibly supportive of Willow and what we're trying to do."

The former CPG veteran (she worked at Johnson & Johnson for years as an executive) loves working in the Valley. "I love the very fast pace. Decision making is really quick. The organizations are super flat and I find people to be extremely collaborative, open, and very, very helpful. I quickly built a network of fellow CEOs and startups and we all try to help each other out . . . It's been very different to corporate culture where I think the positives of corporate is that you have a lot of resources, you have a lot of clout, you have a lot of great talent, but corporate tends to be slower on decision making. Sometimes great ideas need to start out as small ideas and be nurtured to become gigantic businesses, and corporate cultures can sometimes judge ideas in terms of size only. They can sometimes shut down what could become a giant business very quickly."

Kelman is excited about Silicon Valley's awakening (albeit belated) to the massive market in women-oriented personal care, health, and fertility technologies. "I think that women's health overall has been very underserved by companies and also by technology. It's why Willow has gotten a lot of recognition, which I think is great and exciting. It's also helping to open up the opportunities for women's health in general. You're seeing more interest in spaces like fertility monitoring and beauty. Health tech hasn't yet fully entered into women's health, and it's very exciting to see that starting to open up. Women are the primary purchasers in life. They're the primary decision makers if it relates to health care, and so to see companies recognizing the purchasing power and the need, the unique needs of women, is really exciting."

Does she experience any of Silicon Valley's sexist culture? No. But that in many ways comes down to the fact that Kelman is in charge and has supportive founders and VCs. When it comes to overhauling industries generally, as Wennmachers points out, it's being increasingly recognized that a board seat is just one thing. But real change will only come from women founders, CEOs, directors, and people with decision-making power behind the formation of a company.

"I'm the CEO of the company and so I can set the tone and the attitude toward gender, and clearly it's established that Willow is a very positive, warm, involving culture. So it's a very different circumstance. I am very committed to focusing on the nurturing and development of all kinds of talent, especially women. Because you hear the stories and you want to be part of the change, not part of the issue."

Goicochea believes women have an innate understanding of culture and brands, which helps them create companies with longevity—they know how to define and build brands we believe in and care about, thereby experiencing longer-term loyalty from their audiences. And it is continually ignored by Silicon Valley. This can be seen in the subtle nuances in how female-founded companies are designed, run, and communicate, she says. Women founders are able to spot gaps in markets for female audiences and create products that resonate more effectively. "Look at [online supplements brand] Ritual, for example. It's female founded and you can really see that in the product. You can tell they really care about their customer and they live and breathe the brand and connection with their customers." Which contrasts greatly, she says, to other more transactional equivalents led by men. "You have to find ways to be culturally relevant and it can't always be buy-my-product."

The execution of Willow is also evidence of this: "A female CEO certainly brings a different perspective to things," says Kelman. "But I would also say that one of the things that we do really well is touch base with moms and the consumer often. I think a big part of it is listening to your audience, as opposed to just designing in a vacuum and just taking technology for technology's sake. We talk about Willow as a personal-care product for women because it's something that a mom puts on her body."

Emotion and brand equity are interesting points when it comes to Silicon Valley, and an area in which women might ultimately have the upper hand when it comes to creating long-lasting products. Recent research by BrandZ, a consultancy and brand equity research platform, supports this. In 2018 BrandZ measured Silicon Valley's biggest brands by several axes. In a survey that asked people about Amazon, Facebook, Google, and Netflix, among others, tech brands had a lot of functional equity (in other words, we love them because they work), but all of them had comparatively low emotional resonance in the mind of consumers. This feels intuitive to the way we interact with these brands. After all, if there was a cheaper, faster shopping site, we'd probably switch away from Amazon. If there was a better version of Uber, we'd probably use it. Yet brands we really connect with become more embedded with the way we see ourselves. We shop at Adidas, or attend SoulCycle, or fly with Virgin Airlines not just because they're functional, but because they create a bigger emotive meaning in our minds. Maybe Maude will be one of the next waves. Either way, there's a disconnect between women's track records in running businesses and the support and backing they receive from Silicon Valley.

Canaries in the Code Mines

Silicon Valley's relationship with women is more complex than funding, products, and leadership. As a male-dominated industry with men at the top of every totem pole, it's little wonder that the #MeToo movement, which has shattered several industries, is now creeping into tech, too.

The experience of whistleblowers in Silicon Valley now versus just a few years ago is in many ways prophetic of what changes might lie ahead for Silicon Valley's women problem.

Ellen Pao, the former investment partner at legendary venture-capital firm Kleiner Perkins Caufield & Byers, sued the company in 2012 for sexual discrimination. She hit the headlines for claiming that she experienced sexual discrimination in the company's promotional and pay practices. She also alleged workplace harassment after an affair with a male partner ended, and subsequent retaliation when she was abruptly terminated after raising a complaint. The company argued she was fired for performance issues, which she disputed. She very publicly lost the lawsuit.

But that was only half of it. It came amid a very public discourse in which her character, professional capability, and standing were attacked by the media and KPCB. Writing several years later in 2017 for *New York* magazine (to coincide with the publication of her book *Reset: My Fight for*

Inclusion and Lasting Change), Pao described the experience as "a widely publicized case in which I was often cast as the villain—incompetent, greedy, aggressive, and cold. My husband and I were both dragged through the mud, our privacy destroyed."

Pao's reputation was smeared. She was described as a "poor performer."

Meanwhile, a *Vanity Fair* story took aim at the sexual history of her husband. The issue created a wide debate about the treatment of women in tech and exposed many of the subtleties (and not so subtleties) of sexual politics, harassment, and discrimination in the VC workplace. Pao was given a wringing in the media. In just five years, while the incidents that took place might have been the same, it's difficult to imagine she'd now receive the same response, both to her case and in the media.

Pao's since gone on to become investment partner at Kapor Capital, the chief diversity and inclusion officer at the Kapor Center for Social Impact, and cofounder of the diversity consulting nonprofit organization Project Include. While formerly vilified over her lawsuit, Pao now enjoys adulation as a precursor to a sea change that is starting to gain momentum in the tech world. Many now credit Pao as a canary in a coal mine, her case a precursor to a much-needed debate about the treatment of women in Silicon Valley.

"She got the short end of the stick, but she's on top of the world now . . . If she filed this lawsuit today, she would win. Everyone knows that," says Debra Cleaver. "Things are changing faster, too. I think the rate of social change is accelerating and that includes things like Silicon Valley. It is changing, but it's changing in the way that society is changing. All of these things are intertwined. It's like watching what is happening in Hollywood. All of this is going to have trickle effects to everything else."

Indeed. Fast-forward to 2018 and it's a different scenario, from the global Women's March to the #MeToo movement. And, hot on the heels of fourth-wave feminism making women's empowerment central to the popular zeitgeist, Silicon Valley's long history of how it treats women quickly discovers it has nowhere left to hide.

A series of highly public stories about Silicon Valley's misogynist culture has come to light over the past few years. There was the explosive blog post written by former Uber engineer Susan Fowler that exposed the company's culture of harassment and discrimination. Twitter erupted over Fowler's story, written in February 2017, which said: "As most of you know, I left Uber in December and joined Stripe in January. I've gotten a lot of questions over the past couple of months about why I left and what my time at Uber was like. It's a strange, fascinating, and slightly horrifying story that deserves to be told while it is still fresh in my mind, so here we go." She outlined instances of discrimination, having experienced both nuanced and explicit unfair treatment and unwanted sexual advances from Uber management. The sensational story prompted then CEO Travis Kalanick to call a company meeting to apologize for its cultural failings. Amid this and other speculation about leadership trouble at the company, shareholders ordered Kalanick to step down in summer 2017. More important, Fowler's blog post was followed by a tidal wave of additional complaints from others at Uber that were largely greeted with sympathy online, and Fowler experienced a flurry of support in powerful media outlets. Uber board member Arianna Huffington praised her, and the *Financial Times* named her its 2017 Person of the Year.

Instances like this followed, forcing Silicon Valley to address the issue. In July 2017, Dave McClure resigned as general partner of 500 Startups, an early-stage venture fund, in the wake of sexual harassment allegations. By way of apology, McClure wrote a lengthy confessional blog post on Medium: "I'm a creep. I'm sorry." Toward the end of 2017, VC Shervin Pishevar stepped down from Virgin Hyperloop One and his venture firm Sherpa Capital in the wake of allegations of sexual misconduct.

Silicon Valley's gender politics have been further exposed by Bloomberg reporter Emily Chang's 2018 book *Brotopia: Breaking Up the Boys' Club of Silicon Valley*. Chang's heavily publicized tome reveals Silicon Valley's culture of drug-fueled parties, orgies, and sexual favors (in return for professional advancement) with multiple accounts from bystanders, many so juicy the interviewees insisted on anonymity. She also describes how Silicon Valley's dominant type—late-blooming tech nerd—has propagated a culture in which women are mistreated in relationships and viewed as disposable. This has come amid a wider power shift in which Silicon Valley billionaires have become more desirable than Hollywood actors thanks to their extreme wealth. All this, she said, has inevitably permeated into the wider business culture, creating an unwelcoming and often hostile environment for women and their contributions.

With this heightened awareness of misogynistic culture and companies' poor regard for women in the workplace, is Silicon Valley male dominance finally running out of rope?

There are of course other complex gender issues driven by tech. Consider for example the technologies and business models that Silicon Valley puts forth. Human Resources departments at traditional firms may be rapidly brushing up on their employee education policies and bracing against further #MeToo cases, lawsuits, and more, but there are federal laws in place to protect against discrimination and harassment. This is in the world of traditional work, civic employee protections, and statutory rights. None of this exists in the gig economy, a Wild West for workers on multiple levels, and one with few rights for recourse, much less protections, against sexual harassment. The narrative of the gig economy is freedom, autonomy, self-determination, and flexibility. But for people dependent on it, mostly freelancers who sit outside the usual protections of traditional employment, it can be anything but. For women this is especially pronounced. And while current social movements may have enabled many to speak out about abuse, the gig economy's reliance on user reviews to even remain part of a network (such as Uber, or on-demand cleaning company Handy) puts women in a highly vulnerable situation. They are subjected, and evaluated, after all, by unmediated and often unregulated reviews. The star system rules all.

HoneyBook, a platform for self-employed creative-industry workers (designers, florists, photographers), released results from a sexual harassment survey in December 2017 that shed light on the issues faced by gig economy employment. In the survey of its members, it found that 54 percent of women freelance creatives had experienced sexual harassment, compared to 48 percent of women in the overall workforce. But this could be only the tip of the iceberg when it comes to self-employment overall. Honeybook's user base, one would assume, is more affluent, vocal, and empowered in industries that while dominated by freelancers are still to some degree formalized and public. Women at the sharp end of the gig economy, working in low-income, isolated, and transient positions, would likely have far worse stories to tell. But there are potentially universal findings in Honeybook's study. Of women who experienced sexual harassment, 77 percent said they'd experienced unprofessional comments on their appearance. Demeaning nicknames accounted for 76 percent of the harassment, and 60 percent had fallen victim to physical intimidation. The issue of reliance on reviews, recommendations, and good feedback was universal. Sixty-five percent of respondents in Honeybook's survey were sexually harassed by an attendee of an event they were working. Eighty-three percent did not report the sexual harassment to anyone. When it was reported to the authorities, the study found no action was taken 51 percent of the time. Fifty-eight percent of respondents said they did not have a sexual harassment clause in their contract. Staggeringly, 18 percent of victims have been harassed by the same person/people more than four times.

"Professionally, these creatives are faced with a choice: continue with the project and earn their desired rate at the risk of another instance of harassment, or report it and sacrifice the client and rate and possibly future business," said Honeybook.

Eighty-two percent of creatives who experienced sexual harassment chose to continue with a project in spite of the harassment. Of the 18 percent who reported an incident, less than half were paid for that project. Forty-one percent even kept working in similar environments. "Forfeiting business opportunities for their own safety, 34 percent of creatives did not work with the client again because of the experience of sexual harassment."

Again, the mind boggles at the scope of this when applied to the altogether more lax world of the on-demand gig economy.

Large institutions and corporations are experiencing a torrent of threats from the #MeToo groundswell and are being forced to address issues from abuse of power to sexual harassment to inappropriate behavior. Of course, it's not always quite so simple. Let's not forget the #MeToo backlash, the "Witch Hunt" outcries. And let's not forget that when it comes to financial resources, collective influence, structural power, and frankly the misogynist skew embedded in a lot of popular media discourse about abuse and rape culture, women continue to be in the firing line. The ability to do anything about abuse is deeply intertwined with class, agency, and income level. Not everyone—unlike Uma Thurman, Rose McGowan, and many others embroiled in sexual harassment and abuse claims—can reach a mass audience with social media or afford to blow up their life to expose injustice.

Pop culture is catching up to these layered issues. The 2018 Women's

March drew attention to the ethnic and economic divide when it comes to female empowerment (perhaps in response to popular criticism that the 2017 march skewed toward what was charged as being a white, exclusive form of feminism). In her headlining speech at the 2018 march, actress Viola Davis addressed the crowd: "I am speaking today, not just for the #MeToo's, because I was a #MeToo . . . But when I raise my hand I am aware of all the women who are still in silence. The women who are faceless. The women who don't have the money. And don't have the constitution. And who don't have the confidence. And who don't have the images in our media that give them a sense of self-worth. Enough to break the silence that's rooted in the shame of assault . . ." She concluded: "We've got to bring up everyone with us."

Will Silicon Valley bring everyone up with it? Will they buck their own trends and embrace inclusivity as tech moves into philanthropy at an unprecedented scale, with promises to save us from disease and more? If its efforts in correcting diversity issues in its own backyard are anything to go by, the results will likely be equally disappointing.

10

Hacking Philanthropy

I t started at industry networking events, as these things tend to. *Social good. Social good. Social good.* It became the whisper. "We're trying to 'bake in' social good to our business model" became the earnest refrain of skinny-jeaned startup founders on evening panels. "We're trying to solve problems, you know?" Tables at the back of warehouse spaces, draped in white paper with wilting grapes, stale crackers, and sweaty cheese. As crowds nodded reverently.

By 2015 this had reached critical mass, not just at every technology conference but every entrepreneurship conference in general. Millennials weren't just in search of money—no. They wanted meaning. All the better if it were possible to find both in one convenient package.

On cue, one of SXSW Interactive's core themes that year was social good enterprise with tie-ups between the United Nations and Google. A plethora of new business models has emerged, baking social good into their output. There's even a book, *Good Is the New Cool: Market Like You Give a Damn* by Afdhel Aziz and Bobby Jones.

The terminology has also evolved. Today, the buzzword is "purpose." The word was scattered through Mark Zuckerberg's Harvard address. It's become a social media meme—five million #purpose Instagram hashtags and counting (though that could also be because it was the name of Justin Bieber's tour). The power of "purpose" is being touted around tech conferences.

There's "a big focus on the triple bottom line: People, Profit, Planet," Elizabeth Gore, Dell's entrepreneur-in-residence at the time, told me as this was emerging. "It's being driven by a number of things. There's so much idealism among millennial entrepreneurs. It used to be that you made your money then you entered philanthropy. Millennials want to start doing good through their businesses right away and find new ways to give money while still being profitable."

Gore was in many ways articulating what has become a cultural movement among millennial startups, giving way to lifestyle brands pledging to donate underwear to women in Africa for every bottle of water sold, to send a new pair of shoes whenever one is sold here, or to donate glasses when you buy a pair for yourself online. Commerce driven by aspirational, demonstrable benevolence, in other words, though often tackling the more desirable and marketable problems as a result. But she was also describing a broader philosophy that has become endemic in modern business culture and an essential talent-acquisition tool for business—all new companies must incorporate social good in some form into their mission.

This has become emblematic of Silicon Valley's approach to philanthropy, which it's quickly embracing as it models itself on the great Industrial philanthropists of history. Except, as with everything this group does, it's on steroids, promising to "reinvent" everything, to fix old problems in new ways.

Call it Philanthropy 2.0. Silicon Valley is moving into philanthropy at a scale unseen since the Gilded Age, and it has moonshot goals in mind. Giving by individuals is now at a record high. Charitable donations reached an estimated $390 billion in 2017, according to a report by Giving USA. Individual giving accounted for a staggering $281 billion, and the study found that growth in giving is outpacing growth in America's GDP. Individual giving has increased almost five times since the 1950s, also according to Giving USA. But the giving is different. This group is using all the tools in their arsenal—data, technology, and science—to demonstrate tangible results and solve problems with a solution and maximum press exposure in the process.

Sean Parker, founder of Napster, has described the Valley's approach to giving as "Philanthropy for Hackers." With this approach they are applying many of the tools that made them big in business, setting up VC funds over traditional charities. In this new version of philanthropy, social good and profitability are not at odds. In fact, the combination makes the effort faster, leaner, and more effective. It's altruism with impact.

Organized philanthropy has historically been a third pillar to government and business in the U.S. It acts as a balance to capitalism and extreme wealth (which today is more extreme than ever), with funding doled out strategically by powerful individuals. It's another power center with a civic outlook and the potential to affect public policy.

Silicon Valley's philanthropic endeavors are worth examining for this reason. Whether it's setting up new social good enterprises, or growing (even more) its outsize philanthropic organizations, or funding charities in a narrow vertical, Silicon Valley's philanthropic activities are in line with its value systems and priorities, which could have big ramifications if it becomes the single biggest force in philanthropy in the future. (How many other wealth centers will compete? More railroad billionaires are surely unlikely . . .)

As ever, Silicon Valley's souped-up version is seductive and radically improved, with a disruptive veneer. But is it actually any better? Or a Trojan Unicorn?

Barely a day passes without a headline about another Silicon Valley donation. In 2017, Jeff Bezos gave $35 million to the Fred Hutchinson Cancer Research Center in Seattle—one of the largest single gifts in the institution's history. In early 2018, Bezos, now named the world's richest man with a net worth of $105 billion, created a $33 million college scholarship for Dreamers—undocumented immigrants who were brought to the U.S. as children—in tribute to his Cuban stepfather, a U.S. immigrant.

Mark Zuckerberg has emerged as a major philanthropist in recent years, pledging to donate 99 percent of his Facebook shares toward education and poverty, as well as health issues, including the goal of curing all disease. He has set up the Chan Zuckerberg Initiative with his wife, Priscilla Chan, and cohosted a 2016 summit with Stanford University and the White House on poverty and opportunity, looking at the role of technology and innovation in addressing poverty, inequality, and economic mobility. Zuckerberg's approach has been a combination of investing in research institutes, venture-capital-type investments in social enterprises, and policy.

Sean Parker launched the Parker Foundation, with $600 million dedicated to life sciences, global public health, and civic engagement. Apple CEO Tim Cook has pledged to give his entire fortune to charity. Salesforce founder and CEO Marc Benioff has donated $10 million to alleviate family home-lessness in San Francisco. LinkedIn cofounder Reid Hoffman has donated $20 million to fund the Chan Zuckerberg Initiative's Biohub.

In this new era, philanthropic double-downs have almost become oblig-atory to those joining the ultra-rich tech crowd. Bill Gates and Warren Buf-fet started the Giving Pledge in 2010, encouraging billionaires to donate the majority of their wealth to charity. Airbnb's Brian Chesky, thirty-four, Joe Gebbia, thirty-four, and Nathan Blecharczyk, thirty-two, and his wife, Elizabeth Blecharczyk, thirty-two, are among the newest (and youngest) members to join the group, which now has more than 150 members. Each Airbnb cofounder is said to be worth $3.3 billion. (Mark Zuckerberg, thirty-two, and Priscilla Chan, thirty-one, are also members.)

Bill Gates and his wife Melinda have given away a staggering $28 bil-lion since 2007, 48 percent of Gates's net worth, and the couple has helped to save millions of lives through the Bill & Melinda Gates Foundation, which aims to eradicate malaria from the world. Gates too has pledged to leave his $70 billion fortune to charity when he dies. Theirs is a more stately precursor to this trend, but many of its values are threading into these newer iterations.

"Philanthropy for Hackers," Sean Parker's 2015 op-ed piece in the *Wall Street Journal*, in many ways evokes the tone for Silicon Valley's new rad "hacker" view on traditional philanthropy—though it does vary by individ-ual and organization. "The techno-utopianism of hackers has already trans-formed our lives. But the greatest contribution that hackers make to society may be yet to come—if we are willing to retain the intellectual and creative spirit that got us this far," says Parker.

Parker writes that "a new global elite, led by pioneers in telecommunica-tions, personal computing, internet services, and mobile devices, has claimed an aggregate net worth of almost $800 billion of the $7 trillion in assets held by the wealthiest 1,000 people in the world. The barons of this new con-nected age are interchangeably referred to as technologists, engineers, and even geeks, but they all have one thing in common: they are hackers."

So, says Parker, it's no wonder they're applying a hacker's perspective to philanthropy. "This newly minted hacker elite is an aberration in the history of wealth creation. They are intensely idealistic, so as they begin to confront the world's most pressing humanitarian problems, they are still young, naïve, and perhaps arrogant enough to believe that they can solve them," he says. He takes aim at older philanthropic institutions, launched by early-twentieth-century industry barons as havens for tax-free funds, noting that "no one knows how much money is stored within these institutions, which are the tax-exempt vehicles of private foundations and endowments."

He is, presumably, missing the irony that Apple, Microsoft, Alphabet, Cisco, and Oracle now have $504 billion in offshore funds. If taxed at 40 percent, this would theoretically inject $200 billion back into the state, which would, one would hope, help citizen services.

Parker continues: "An additional $300 billion a year is given to private foundations and public charities, which offer little in the way of transparency or accountability. This is not entirely their fault. Philanthropy isn't subject to normal market forces. From an economic perspective, it may be the most distorted market in the world, the only one where the buyer of a good or service—the 'donor'—isn't the ultimate recipient of the value that good or service has to offer."

Like many tech philanthropists, Parker's biggest beef with these institutions is impact. And he believes philanthropy, like the government, is a dusty old model ripe for reframing. Parker recommends that, above all, hacker philanthropy should remain small and agile, not bloated and slow, "taking on the worst characteristics of government. Hacker philanthropists must resist the urge to institutionalize and must never stop making big bets."

While approaching it in new ways, Silicon Valley individuals are following a long tradition in American history among its industrial leaders by moving into philanthropy. Andrew Carnegie wrote the article "The Gospel of Wealth" in 1889 about the responsibility of philanthropy for those of self-made wealth, and John D. Rockefeller set up his foundation in 1913 "to promote the well-being of humanity throughout the world."

Social good enterprise and the idea of being good and profitable at the same time aren't totally new either. Many historic leaders simply saw keeping a town employed as a form of benevolence. Rockefeller, in his autobiography, said his biggest philanthropic achievement was providing employment, notes Ben Soskis, research associate at the Center on Nonprofits and Philanthropy at the Urban Institute, George Mason University. Though Silicon Valley's approach is more intertwined, he says. "The idea of marrying capitalism with philanthropic good work was there, but there were still boundaries; Rockefeller wasn't calling it Standard Oil philanthropy. It was notional, not operationalized in the same way as with the Silicon Valley guys."

Henry Ford had a similarly pragmatic approach. "If you go back through Ford's papers, it was very clear that, in order for him to be successful at building his large-scale car manufacturing structures, he needed to sustain the entire city of Detroit because, when the city wasn't functional, his workers weren't functional, the cars weren't made, and he couldn't make a profit," says Danah Boyd. "You hear these classic tropes that he wanted to make it so his workers could afford a Ford, and that was one of the shticks. A lot of it, however, was what we would look at now as a double bottom line, because he was so committed to making certain that Detroit was stable while he was alive, even at the expense of short-term profits, that he did all of this work on education and communities. It was necessary for his capitalist infrastructure."

Where America in the early twentieth century was a blank canvas in need of many public services (such as libraries), now poor developing markets from Africa to Myanmar—struggling with scant infrastructure, disease, and access to technology, or being hit hard by natural disasters—are luring Silicon Valley titans. Here they're moving in with promises to eradicate disease, improve education, provide internet access, and more.

"There's definitely a strong element of self-interest and of imperialism in those kinds of efforts," says Aaron Dorfman, executive director of the National Committee for Responsive Philanthropy. "Will those projects help people and make their lives better? Absolutely. Will those projects help enrich the very people who have been funding the projects? Absolutely. It's a troubling paradox. When we concentrate so much wealth in the hands of so few, they are able to pull so many more levers to try and influence how the world works. I think that can be a real danger for democracy."

Bill Gates is famously a big fan of "The Gospel of Wealth." "The difference is the economy he's operating in," says Dorfman. "Carnegie took on education with libraries, Rockefeller looked at health in the South. They could do so with an empty playing field as federal government was nonexistent in that space. They were able to assume roles to engage institutions in a way that hasn't been done before, except in the developing world, which is why some are now attracted to health and education there."

As befits Silicon Valley in general, they are not shy about their donations. All are highly public in their nature. William Hewlett and David Packard, who cofounded Hewlett-Packard in 1939, were both very active in philanthropy but lower-key about their gifts. Similarly, the two largest donations in 2016, of $500 million each, came from Nike cofounder Phil Knight and his wife, Penny, and investor Nicolas Berggruen. Knight made his donation to the University of Oregon for a center for scientific research (unusually, this did not make the headlines). Billionaire Nicolas Berggruen, a fellow in the tech community, donated to his own public policy think tank, the Berggruen Institute. Yet barely an iota was mentioned in the press.

One thing that defines tech's new philanthropic focus is its entrepreneurial approach to solving problems in a nimble, impactful, and sustainable way. Charities are encouraged to be like businesses. Hence, much of the terminology around social-good initiatives includes references to funds, ventures, and business opportunities, with an emphasis on solving problems rather than simply alleviating them.

"Silicon Valley is rejecting traditional forms of philanthropy," agrees Dorfman. "Both the Chan Zuckerberg Initiative and Laurene Powell Jobs have chosen limited liability companies (LLCs), rather than private foundations. This is a trend that is going to continue, and I think they're doing it for a number of reasons. One is a strategic reason as it gives them more flexibility for what kinds of things they can invest in. It allows them to invest in for-profits and give grants to nonprofits."

In response to Donald Trump's denials of climate change, Silicon Valley is once again taking the lead in a time of government stasis. Bill Gates announced the launch of Breakthrough Energy Ventures, a $1 billion clean-energy fund, with backers including Jack Ma and Jeff Bezos. The fund aims to invest in the next generation of energy technologies. Rise, a new $2 billion social-impact fund, is another example. It was launched in 2016 by William E. McGlashan Jr., a partner at private equity firm TPG Growth, which invested in Uber and Airbnb. Board members and investors include Bono, Jeff Skoll (the first full-time employee of eBay), Laurene Powell Jobs, Richard Branson, and Reid Hoffman.

There is the continuous thread, and comfort, of profitability and philanthropy. In fact, more than compatible, they're seen as beneficial. "What you're seeing is a concept with blurred boundaries," says Soskis.

This is also seen in Gates's grander philanthropic style, which has been termed "philanthrocapitalism"—using economies of scale and entrepreneurialism to bring resources to people in Africa, and make a profit, while also (critics say) throwing your weight around.

Bridge International Academies, a startup supported by Bill Gates and Mark Zuckerberg, is a good example of this approach in action. It provides cheap, internet-based mass education in Africa. Tech and market forces demonetize the offer and make it accessible, but the scheme also makes money because of its scale. There are now 400 Bridge International Academies in Kenya and more are coming. The company aims to educate 10 million children in Africa and Asia whose families earn less than two dollars a day, and it will make money with a standardized, internet-based education model. It uses tablets to deliver lesson plans to teachers. Economies of scale mean it charges just six dollars per month, per pupil. Its founders have estimated it could be worth $500 million in ten years, and Zuckerberg has invested $10 million in the company.

But there's a reemergence happening of late, too, in response to discomfort—ironically—about the Wild West gig economy, where benevolence blurs with simply being a fair employer. Cooperative rideshare app Juno, for example, set out to rival Uber by charging a lower commission and offering drivers equity. It touted itself as the driver-friendly car app. (This has taken a different turn of late. After the company was sold in 2017, according to Bloomberg, drivers were told their stock was void.) The principle of the original Juno is interesting to note though, and surely has potential to become a growing trend as consumer awareness evolves about the gig economy and its predication on cheap labor.

In fact, many of these big philanthropic endeavors could be read as somewhat ironic when one considers the much-documented socioeconomic divide in the area surrounding Silicon Valley and downtown San Francisco.

People have been quick to zero in on the fact that Silicon Valley's philanthropic launches have largely been categorized as LLCs, thus not requiring them to disclose their grants or any information to the public, and preventing the public from examining, questioning, or challenging their acts. LLCs allow them to take a more entrepreneurial approach, they say.

LLCs are even less transparent than the philanthropic foundations whose lack of accountability has been so criticized. "It's much worse because it's a private company," says Megan Tompkins-Stange, pointing to familiar issues with dark money and nonprofits in the United States and with Super PACs (independent expenditure-only committees permitted to raise unlimited sums and distribute these sums as they choose). "Foundations at least publish their 990 forms, their tax forms, and that sort of thing. In a way, foundations are kind of Boy Scouts compared to the LLCs and the impact investors in terms of their transparency." This also gives them the ability to weigh in on policy without accountability: "It enables them to do more lobbying and more investing outside of nonprofit grant-making," she says.

Silicon Valley focuses on measurable impact and solutions. "It's very clear that when it comes to philanthropy, this group is not interested in institutions but ideas. They go by 'problems that can be solved,' which are research based. They try to find problems that are amenable to tech solutions," says Soskis.

The young age of the current entrepreneur crop has also affected the way Silicon Valley embraces philanthropy. "There's a tighter connection between the way they make money and the way they give it away," Soskis explains. "That's the defining characteristic, and it is embodied in the Chan Zuckerberg Initiative. There's no difference between nonprofit and for-profit. It also closely aligns entrepreneurship to performance with the idea of making money and giving it away at same time."

The idea of cause is evolving in Silicon Valley's approach to philanthropy on a broader scale, beyond help for the poor and elderly. Education—not as a commercial opportunity, but a cause to fix—is being addressed, as we saw earlier. They are now looking at sustainability; connectivity and the belief that the internet is a human right that unlocks economies; and getting more women and ethnic minorities into STEM subjects. Google.org's Girls Who Code initiative is a prime example of the latter. All this, however, along with sustainable technology, can be seen as simply more business opportunities. Many also go hand in hand with endeavors such as Internet.org that blend social good with commercial ends—that being, to bring many in developing markets to the world of Facebook.

The Industrialists of the nineteenth and twentieth centuries built infrastructure to facilitate their businesses, which wound up having a wider positive impact for people, and in many instances were nationalized. They were engaged in philanthropy. The difference is that these were approached separately, in silos, not presented as one and the same as profit-making. Institutions sat on one side. Businesses, the other.

There's also a key difference in the way wealth is created now. Carnegie might have built libraries, but they were later nationalized and did not become ongoing wealth generators in the form of consumer behavioral data. On that basis, anything in this era can be a revenue stream. So while ultimately doing good, Silicon Valley's altruism is—and will continue to be for a long time—firmly symbiotic with its self-interest. Technology is always wrapped into the solution. "Silicon Valley has taken on philanthropy but from a different orientation," says Soskis. "It's engineering and tech driven. Carnegie and Rockefeller understood engineering, but they weren't engineers. Most of the folks in Silicon Valley have expertise in engineering, and you can tease that out in how you approach problems."

They are using tech in some novel ways, too. Jack Ma has started employing blockchain technology—the decentralized, instantly updated software platform—to monitor charitable donations made by Alipay users, tracking their donations with the Ant Love charity platform in response to a murky charity market.

Artificial intelligence (AI) and sensors are also seen as tools to effect change with better systems. No doubt more blockchain charity solutions are to follow. Virtual reality devices have been employed by charities and described as "empathy machines" for their transformative, immersive properties. The Clinton Foundation launched a VR experience that transported people directly to the African villages it was helping. Similarly, Charity: Water founder Scott Harrison delivered a keynote speech at Web Summit 2015 about VR as a transformative, empathetic engine, taking people to the heart of causes and their impacts. The charity has partnered with You-

Tube celebrities as well as used GPS mapping and real-time donor updates. It is also successfully delivering remote PTSD therapy to soldiers.

This is one of the most exciting aspects of Silicon Valley philanthropy. Immersive technologies from augmented reality to virtual reality can make causes more inspiring and create new avenues for storytelling. Real-time data analysis can show progress. Meanwhile, all of Silicon Valley's arsenal for efficiency and making purchases simpler has immense potential for maximizing charitable donations, while also potentially saving those charities money. Here, tech can be a force for good.

Disrupting Charity

Does philanthropy need to be entirely disrupted?

There's no doubt traditional philanthropy has faced some scrutiny in recent years, notably an influential and critical essay by Gara LaMarche, published in the *Atlantic* in 2014. LaMarche is the president of the Democracy Alliance, a network of liberal donors who coordinate their political giving. He previously served as president and CEO of the Atlantic Philanthropies. LaMarche argues that Big Philanthropy has a disproportionate impact on government policy, while enabling tax evasion. He adds that there is little emphasis on impact and accountability. He cited the outcry over an Obama administration proposal to cap the deductible income tax for charitable contributions at 28 percent (which would only affect the wealthiest donors) in order to fund the Affordable Care Act. The health-care bill, which needed to be cost-neutral, was necessarily funded by making cuts elsewhere and, he says, "the leadership of American philanthropy jeopardized health-care reform in order to let rich people shield their money from taxation.

"What that situation made plain to me was not just that philanthropy is quite capable of acting like agribusiness, oil, banks, or any other special-interest leader when it thinks its interests are jeopardized. It helped me to see that however many well-intentioned and high-minded impulses animate philanthropy, the favorable tax treatment that supports it is a form of privatization," he writes. "Money that would otherwise be available for tax revenue that could be democratically directed is shielded from public control for private use."

LaMarche argues that the original intent behind tax breaks for philanthropy was to enable the kind of risk-taking that the public sector and government weren't able to take on, and also to take a long view on issues made possible by lack of shareholder scrutiny. In most aspects, he says, it is failing. He also takes aim at the lack of diversity and distortion of focus as a result. Big Philanthropy faces too little scrutiny.

The Bill & Melinda Gates Foundation, a crossover between traditional and hacker philanthropy, was included in his critique. In 2014 it was four times bigger than any other philanthropic organization. "Not only does it make a difference to others in the fields it engages in—it can virtually define the fields and set the policy agenda for government as well as philanthropy," LaMarche says on the subject of its scale. Gates has argued that size gives more impact.

LaMarche further points out that such criticism is not new: "When the titans of their day, Andrew Carnegie and John D. Rockefeller, sought to set up trusts to spend some of their vast wealth for charitable purposes, Frank P. Walsh, a progressive lawyer who chaired a congressional inquiry into industrial relations, called the new Rockefeller Foundation and Carnegie Corporation 'a menace to the future political and economic welfare of the nation.' In that period, one hundred years ago, the foundations' endowments surpassed what the federal government, in the pre–New Deal era, spent on education and public health. Walsh called for the 'democratization of private benevolence' through more progressive taxation."

Tompkins-Stange's recent book, *Policy Patrons: Philanthropy, Education Reform, and the Politics of Influence*, looks at four major U.S. foundations that invest in education, their influence on public policy, and the effects of this on local communities and their relationships. The book's unique approach is that it features lengthy, highly candid thoughts and observations given anonymously by foundation insiders, further reinforcing the lack of transparency in big philanthropic foundations, the most pertinent being the Bill & Melinda Gates Foundation. "I don't think anyone would have talked to me and said anything of value if they were on the record," she says. "It was really striking how different the reflections were, how candid they were, when people were given that mask."

And the biggest revelations? "Someone talked about the rickety evidence around strategic philanthropy and how people don't necessarily have the most rigorous evidence-based processes around some of the projects they fund," says Tompkins-Stange. "That led me to really want to know more about how research is marshaled toward providing empirical justification for certain policy interest or certain ways of framing policies that foundations are interested in and funding . . . I had never had someone in an elite foundation really admit that."

Tompkins-Stange also found that many major foundations are not simply funding education but trying to influence policy. They are, she explains, "not just funding certain things that they hoped would have an impact on policy, but actually very intentionally and strategically undertaking agendas to set the course of policy according to their preferred models of social order or social change." Though, she adds, the Gates Foundation has started responding to such critiques of late.

Silicon Valley's solution-oriented approach to philanthropy in general is problematic. After all, what of life's most complex challenges have had absolute "fixes" that worked? "The Sean Parker–Silicon Valley mindset is very indicative of what I call technical framing, or the technical mindset. It's like, 'OK, we've put a certain amount of capital toward a problem and we will get a solution,'" she says.

Taking a moment to read LaMarche's comments and his criticisms of big traditional philanthropy is quite revealing, especially when one considers Sean Parker's characterization of Silicon Valley's shinier version.

Many problems LaMarche raises are eerily similar to Silicon Valley's practice of philanthropy. LaMarche critiques Big Philanthropy for not being diverse, for not always addressing the right issues, and for distorting the problems that are solved as a result. He says foundations wield too much power over government while not being transparent, not facing enough criticism, and trying to influence policy. In many ways the problems of Silicon Valley's version, like the scale of its donations, is Big Philanthropy x 100.

"There is a real risk as more and more philanthropically minded wealthy people seek to make the world better by using the power of markets," warns Dorfman. "The risk is that the causes that can't be helped through markets will be short-changed and get left behind, and that there will be a lack of investment available for them. Traditionally, nonprofits are doing things that meet a societal need that governments and the private sector are not meeting. I am a fan of using investment capital to make the world better as well, and we encourage foundations to devote some of their resources and their investment capital to that approach, but there is no substitute for grants to nonprofits doing good work. I worry that some of the newer donors may be overlooking that."

Indeed. Silicon Valley's empathy gap was pointed out in a widely circulated essay for *The New Yorker* written by True Ventures and GigaOM founder Om Malik in the wake of the 2016 presidential election, examining Silicon Valley's collective shock at the election of Donald Trump. "Silicon Valley's biggest failing is not poor marketing of its products, or follow-through on promises, but, rather, the distinct lack of empathy for those whose lives are disturbed by its technological wizardry," he writes. "Perhaps it is time for those of us who populate the technology sphere to ask ourselves some really hard questions . . . My hope is that we in the technology industry will look up from our smartphones and try to understand the impact of whiplashing change on a generation of our fellow citizens who feel hopeless and left behind."

"I worry about the Silicon Valley approach," reflects Tompkins-Stange. "It's very much a white, wealthy, twenty-five-year-old man's approach, with a real blind spot toward issues of race and gender, which I guess makes sense given that's the average person working in Silicon Valley." Problems that are easily solvable are not necessarily the deep structural ones, "and that's what I mean about race, class, and gender," she says. "I think if you're not surrounded by other people who are different from you, people who maybe have grown up in poverty or who are a member of a nonwhite identity group or population demographic, of course you're going to have a blind spot . . ."

She also critiques tech's "savior mentality." "It's a very classical entrepreneurial mindset: 'We're going to come in and we're going to break things and we're going to disrupt and we're going to change the world!' But that's again a white male engineer, it's not a black queer female community worker . . .

It's very much geared toward someone who by definition comes from privilege, as opposed to someone who maybe is more excluded from these social institutions that have a lot of capital traditionally."

Tompkins-Stange concludes: "There are some really promising innovations, but I think they're not thinking holistically and systematically enough about including the communities that they are trying to fix problems for. Long-term, I don't think that's going to be sustainable."

Sustainability is an interesting word, and important, when it comes to Silicon Valley having a bigger civic role. Social good and purpose are great, but when led by a private company they rely on continued, long-term participation, and as we've seen from Silicon Valley leaders, they have short attention spans. There's a danger in having social-good commerce baked in to marketing, as it requires problems themselves being aspirational—if it's not hashtaggable, it is infinitely less attractive. The impetus to solve, and solve quickly, not only skews problems—it puts Silicon Valley leaders in the cultural role as our rescuers. They will rescue us, but only as long as it suits them.

Conclusion

The Future, Maybe

The year is 2016. The sense of an unfolding existential crisis was almost palpable. Tech enthusiasts from all over the world gathered early in Lisbon at the Web Summit (relocated from Dublin) on Wednesday, November 9, having woken to the news of Donald Trump's election victory. In search of catharsis, or perhaps some live commentary on events from Silicon Valley's cognoscenti, they filled the cavernous Center Stage event space. What was intended to be a packed line-up of panels, debates, and keynotes delivered by venture capitalists, entrepreneurs, and execs about the future of tech turned into something else: group therapy.

The audience, composed of young technology and marketing professionals from Europe and around the world, were collectively astonished.

After days of swooning over robots and AI, a rare moment of visible introspection and humility settled among the leaders onstage. There was a creeping, nagging sense of unease. Had they played a role in the shocking election result? Many fingers in the media were already pointing in Silicon Valley's direction as pundits globally started talking about a populist movement caused by unemployment due to automation, the rapid growth of the technology sector, and globalization, in addition to the filter bubble and fake news that infused social media channels and woefully distorted the political discourse.

Many of the Silicon Valley speakers had stayed up all night to watch the results come in. They looked hungover. And, as one after another took to the stage, they visibly squirmed as they came to the realization that technology—in playing a profound role in creating the societal forces that created Trump—was partly responsible for his success.

Silicon Valley doesn't like to think badly of itself. And it certainly doesn't think of itself as aligned with Trump. The election results clashed jarringly with its projected "value system"—broadly likeable, progressive, and neoliberal. This is a carefully honed image, closely intertwined with Silicon Valley's brands and marketing, but it is increasingly at odds with the hard business interests and the polarizing economic effects of the companies they run (these platforms and algorithms and automation technologies are profitable, and are driving economic disparity through job loss, after all). With the exception of Peter Thiel, many Silicon Valley individuals were vocal (and financial) supporters of Hillary Clinton. The election result had caught them off guard.

But as the day progressed, and one white male executive after another appeared onstage clad in varying ensembles of luxury sportswear and six-figure statement watches, their shock manifested in the form of live self-reflection.

It was a poignant moment thinking back to Peter Thiel's statements at Web Summit 2014 in Dublin, encouraging tech companies in their divine wisdom to push forward and innovate even if it meant breaking a few rules and seeking forgiveness later. They'd done this. They'd innovated, and in so doing had changed our world irreversibly. Would we forgive them for this? Some, of course, had not sought forgiveness at all. Many a fortune had been made from disrupting various sectors (Uber's rise occurred in this very time period). Many had pushed their companies into new segments, directly flouting regulation but managing to stay in business. More companies had followed by example. This tactic had become the new model to effect change. It became evident that government was simply outmoded and needed to be forcibly overturned. We needed new laws to deal with the pace of innovation. And for almost everyone in the room, the results had been great.

As the day wore on, reactions onstage ran from muted to outraged. This was best personified by Dave McClure, former founder of 500 Startups, who couldn't even bear to stick to the line of questioning for his morning panel (McClure has since stepped down amid allegations of sexual harassment; in this moment, however, he was in the throes of pure, outspoken moral outrage). "This whole fucking election was a goddamn travesty," he fumed. "And we should not sit up here and act like nothing just fucking happened ... We were robbed, raped, we were lied to, and we were stolen from."

CNN's Laurie Segall, moderating the panel, frantically tried to steer McClure back to the subject at hand. The other panelists were twitching in discomfort as the vast Lisbon indoor stadium, filled with revelers, looked on. After several attempts to interrupt, placate, and take control, she yelped: "What role does the tech industry have to increase civil engagement?"

"Technology has a role in that we provide communication platforms for the rest of the fucking country," railed McClure. "And we're allowing shit to happen just like the cable news networks, just like talk radio. It's a propaganda medium, and if people aren't aware of the shit they're being told; if they're being told a story of fear, and a story of other; if they're not understanding that people are trying to use them to get to fucking office, then yes, assholes like Trump are going to take office." McClure said the tech industry had a responsibility to help avoid such outcomes and called on the audience to stand up in protest. "This shit will not stand! You've got to stand up for your rights. Stand up!" Cue audience cheers. The video footage was widely shared and tweeted that day. Several candid YouTube videos have since been posted online. The rant even made it onto *SIC Notícias* Portuguese cable news.

Others were more reflective. "It's very possible to just see news that you want to see," said Justin Kan, partner at Y Combinator. "As technologists we need to figure out a way to bring people together ... We disrupt industries. Uber might be a great example. Self-driving cars are coming. That's going to create a lot of job displacement. What are those people going to do? Are they going to become supporters of the next Donald Trump?"

McClure added: "We judge the leaders of countries and hold them up to certain value systems, morals, and ethics. But the people who run some of the largest companies probably have larger populations of users than many countries. I don't think we're holding those folks up to the same level of standards. Maybe that's something we need to start looking at."

Has this happened? It remains to be seen. But what's clear is that the 2016 U.S. election and Brexit decision set in motion a collective wake-up call about technology's growing civic, societal, and economic impact. It's one that is already a global and unstoppable tidal wave. One that is being driven by consumerism. And one that, in many ways, caught governments sleeping.

The balance of power between governments and digital behemoths has shifted. Netflix already operates on a global basis, creating original entertainment that moves beyond the antiquated system of regional IP. An elaborate system of loopholes ensures that these companies pay taxes in countries where the rates are most advantageous—but in essence they exist everywhere.

A global "post-border" life would put tech companies even more firmly in the driver's seat. Maybe this will inform new systems of governance. As Nick Denton comments: "It doesn't matter where in the world, we already have a whole bunch of common information, common culture. It's politics, but by another means . . . People are so fragmented; they no longer have geographical affiliations, but they do have cultural affiliations . . . Maybe you should let people vote on that basis?"

As we have seen, Peter Thiel and Mark Zuckerberg both supposedly have their eyes on traditional politics. But elsewhere Silicon Valley is reimagining governance totally. "I think that the future of cities and communities is going to be tied to much more communal forms of living and working together," says Shervin Pishevar. "I'm not talking about socialism or communism or anything like that—I'm talking about the natural course and evolution of capitalism as a living, breathing thing," he explains, defining capitalism as a market form of self-governance. Consumer constituencies, in other words. Which Uber, Amazon, and Apple effectively already are. "The invisible hand becomes much more visible, and the way it becomes visible is that the movers of our economies, which are really the collective power of the people, become the owners of that future."

In a climate where people feel disempowered by democracy and disillusioned by politicians, but able to cause change by signing off from Uber in response to its CEO's behavior (as many did when he aligned with Donald Trump), it's easy to see how this could become appealing.

That's on the assumption that consumers continue to have control, and that brands need to appease them to retain their patronage. But what happens when tech companies get so big there are no other alternatives? Consumer power of this nature, buying as voting, is predicated on competition and the chance that you might leave one brand for another. It also relies on journalism and media to highlight instances of bad behavior, forcing brands to lose popularity and respond accordingly to retain their appeal. Both of these things are changing quickly with Silicon Valley's rapid growth—not least because they are the media now. The consumer may be king at Amazon today, but when Amazon is, effectively, everything, Amazon can set the rules.

All sense of consumer power is in many ways fictional. Renowned futurist Bruce Sterling paints a dystopian picture of a future in which tech brands become societal organisms. In his paper "The Epic Struggle of the Internet of Things," for example, he describes a fully fledged feudal system where we humans are all the workers for a constant data farm, being spied on relentlessly by the tech overlords. He describes the vision and magic presented by companies around the Internet of Things as a "fairy tale." He writes, "Politically speaking, the relationship of the reader to the Internet of Things is not democratic. It's not even capitalistic. It's a new thing. It's digital feudalism. People in the Internet of Things are like the woolly livestock of a feudal demesne, grazing under the watchful eye of barons in their hilltop Cloud Castles."

And is it really so far away? Already the newest development, along with the Internet of Things (everyday objects connected to the internet), is being superseded by the Internet of Eyes and Ears. These objects have become common lifestyle accessories for the home. Taken together, the Internet of Eyes and Ears is Sterling's vision on steroids.

Voice technology, as it continues to advance and understand rare dialects and different voices, will bring yet more people onto the internet. Literacy in far-flung rural regions will not be a problem, Echo will understand. No one will need to type any personal details into anything, to enter their credit card details or ham-fistedly tap to call an Uber wearing gloves on a snowy day. The internet will know and be constantly learning, adapting, and anticipating us. We'll instruct our car to switch itself on. The internet will be like the air around us. And therefore, so will Silicon Valley technologies. But that could create a psychological shift. Technology in the home until recently has been visible, a braggable status symbol, tangible, and when we interact with it we're more engaged with our actions. We turn the TV on. We press "send." When the internet is an invisible mist around us, it will quickly become like the stars of reality TV show *Big Brother* who forget the cameras are rolling. We are the reality TV show, but it won't just be our indiscretions in the hot tub that are documented. It will be everything.

Perhaps it's unfair to cast Silicon Valley companies in such a Machiavellian light. Their founders probably didn't even register the collective impact their technologies would have on society as their uses skyrocketed, just the dollars they were making.

There are the more far-out civic ideas coming from Silicon Valley culture. Seasteading was back in the headlines after the U.S. election, first popularized by the libertarian-minded Silicon Valley–ites. It came to prominence after Peter Thiel invested in the Seasteading Institute, founded by Wayne Gramlich and Patri Friedman in 2008, an organization formed to facilitate the establishment of "autonomous, mobile communities on seaborne platforms" operating in international waters. Friedman, a libertarian activist, is the grandson of Nobel Prize–winning economist Milton Friedman and economist Rose Friedman.

Joe Quirk, coauthor with Friedman of *Seasteading: How Ocean Cities Will Change the World*, offers an interesting glimpse of what an independent Silicon Valley nation could look like. "We have the technology to solve two of the biggest problems in the world, sea-level change threatening coastal communities and island nations, and the lack of innovation in governance," says Quirk. "That technology is our floating island project, the prototype of which already floats in the Netherlands in the form of the floating pavilion. The Dutch engineers who partnered with us, DeltaSync/Blue21, designed and built the ecologically sustainable floating pavilion in Rotterdam." He adds that another project is being developed in French Polynesia. "Native Polynesians are initiating the aquatic age. I am excited by seaweed-based food and algae-based fuel, ventures spearheaded by committed Seasteaders. I am very excited by untethered fish cages that float on the deep ocean with no measurable environmental impact, producing fish that are healthier than wild fish."

Quirk believes government as we know it is broken. "Imagine if a monopoly on ice cream offered us two choices every year. You could vote for chocolate or you could vote for vanilla. If 51 percent of people voted for vanilla, everybody got vanilla for four years. Nobody could even imagine pralines and cream. What we have right now is a monopoly on governance for hundreds of millions of people. The way to discover better flavors is to allow innovation to suit individual tastes. The more startup nano-nations we can create on the sea, the faster we will discover better flavors of governance suited to the diversity of human values."

Americans, he says, "agree on almost nothing except the fact that the current system doesn't work. It's a perfect time to demonstrate that seasteading allows people to stop arguing and start creating alternatives. Seasteading has never been more appealing since monopoly governments have become increasingly inept at rising to the challenges of the twenty-first century—like sea-level change and elections that are as expensive in money as they are in emotional energy. Everybody knows you don't create mobile phones by working inside Hewlett-Packard, but by breaking away and starting Apple, which is what Steve Wozniak did."

But will this benefit us? It depends whether you believe these technology giants have benefited us overall. And whether you believe these rich white guys—who don't like criticism, are not transparent, and don't like paying taxes—are all that different from the lot we have now.

"During the dot-com boom there was tremendous optimism that the internet and the technologies of the late nineties were going to deliver a big dividend in terms of growth. Technologists and macroeconomists were quite well aligned, and so were policy makers," says Ian Stewart, chief economist and partner at Deloitte. "Policy makers generally thought we were heading to a world of stronger, more stable growth. The reverse is the case now. If you talk to policy makers or economists, everyone is worried that we are entering 'secular stagnation.' So there's a real disconnect." (Secular stagnation is defined by the *Financial Times* as "A condition of negligible or no economic growth in a market-based economy.")

In other words, while tech companies framed their activities as an industrial boom that would create long-term growth for everyone, and government supported this, there has been no resulting economic growth. And it looks unlikely there will be any. The material gains are owned by a very small group of people.

There are those who argue GDP is a flawed measure. And that the sharing economy has made some things free. Airbnb argues it's created new demand for travel. Uber, new demand for transport. But the macro effects seem undeniable.

Tech does, of course, employ people. Lots of people. The difference is the structure and the type of employees, and geography is key, explains Stewart: "Companies like Facebook, Apple, or Google are quite big employers, but one general concern is that technology is significantly increasing the rewards for very high levels of skills and education. Technology itself exacerbates the inequality and this opportunity divide . . ."

As many jobs in the next few decades look set to become automated by technologies being built in Silicon Valley and other innovation hubs around the world, focus is shifting to what work will look like and what jobs there will be. "We have been trying to think about what jobs are automatable in ten or twenty years," says Thor Berger. "To come up with a further understanding of the limits to human adaptation because, in the end, once there are robots being able to do what humans can do, at some point we will not really need humans to perform work."

Fears about the impact of artificial intelligence are interestingly coming from Silicon Valley, too. Mark Zuckerberg and Elon Musk have entered a public spat about the impact of artificial intelligence. Musk called it the "biggest risk we face as a civilization." Speaking at a National Governors Association meeting in July 2017, he said: "Until people see robots going down the street killing people, they don't know how to react because it seems so ethereal. AI is a rare case where I think we need to be proactive in regulation instead of reactive. Because I think by the time we are reactive in AI regulation, it's too late." Meanwhile, Zuckerberg dubbed his comments "irresponsible." AI has been a key focus of investment at Facebook. But it also famously had to shut down an artificial-intelligence engine in summer 2017 after developers realized that two chatbots had created their own unique language that humans couldn't understand. Zuckerberg now believes AI will be the silver bullet to eradicate fake news and ghost profiles.

The response among Silicon Valley venture capitalists to concern about future employment is that work is "boring." And that driving should not be done by humans—we aren't safe—just as planes are now, for the most part, flown by machines. They also talk about the notion of universal basic income being a solution. (A basic income is a form of social security in which all citizens or residents of a country regularly receive an unconditional set sum of money from the government. They are not required to seek work. And this is separate to any income they might generate. This has already been tested in Finland.) In some more fantastical situations, they have charged Hollywood with imagining a nicer-looking, less-scary future, with no work, so it looks more inspiring. If everyone gets on board with the idea, presumably, the apocalyptic baying mob constructing military bunkers for when society collapses will not form.

"There are so many other values and psychological benefits that come from having a job. [For] someone that's not in economics, that's like, 'Duh.' It's obvious. We should have realized this fifty years ago, but I think economists have never really thought about the sort of more societal effects of unemployment or displacement," says Berger.

Amid reports of jobless miners, truck drivers, and retail workers, many pundits, including Trump, have talked about bringing manufacturing jobs back to the U.S., and prioritizing U.S. citizens (over immigrants) for jobs in successful companies based here, not least at Big Tech companies who rely on H-1B visas to employ high-skilled workers from India and China. But it's not that simple, says Stewart, who recently published a paper called "Who Benefits from Apple?"

"Apple has kept high-value functions from product design to marketing and software development in the U.S. Despite the fact that its products and components are manufactured offshore, Apple pays more wages in America than it does overseas," writes Stewart. "The labor for assembling Apple products comes mainly from China. Yet the assembly takes place in factories owned by a Taiwanese firm, Foxconn. China benefits in terms of wages but not profits. China's share of the iPhone's price, at 2 percent, is less than one-fifth the share of Japanese, South Korean, and Taiwanese companies.

"The main beneficiaries of Apple's success are Apple itself and its predominantly American shareholders and employees. Apple demonstrates that the real value in electronics lies in design, development, and marketing, not in assembly," he continues. "In the wake of the global financial crisis, manufacturing is once again in vogue with policymakers. They would do well to heed the conclusions of the PCIC report on Apple: 'The best . . . companies will continue to create tremendous value and high-wage jobs by mobilizing the best resources, wherever in the world they may be.'"

Even coding itself looks set to be automated, becoming the equivalent of sewing in a textile factory. Governments will have to come up with some kind of solution, training, or new industry, quick, to create new work.

The pace of innovation—the emergence of everything from our phone to our home being a portal to the internet, and the continuing crossover between digital behemoths and governments—means that the future poses a plethora of issues in many directions, not least privacy. It's one that Sherif Elsayed-Ali, head of technology and human rights at Amnesty International, has had to come to grips with quickly, especially in the wake of extensive government surveillance of citizens across the world. The challenge with Silicon Valley companies is that they are developing technology that's essentially taking governments and policymakers by surprise, he says: "That means you can drive whatever agenda you have in the absence of public understanding, in the absence of regulation, in the absence of frameworks. There is this vacuum, and the companies are taking over some of this vacuum just by the fact that there's no one else there."

Part of the problem, Elsayed-Ali agrees, is government's cyclical nature, which distracts from long-term thinking: "If you're in the democratic system, you're always looking at the next four or five years. That's your planning timeframe, because you're looking at the next election. There are things that could not be anticipated, things like Uber coming up and disrupting the taxi market, or Airbnb, all of these examples. But there are other things that you could potentially anticipate." He cites a study by the chief economist of the Bank of England on jobs being disrupted by automation. "It doesn't seem to me that it's being followed up by anything concrete in the government. We know there are ongoing trends, but going from there to actually affecting policy and affecting practice, that's not happening."

In the expanded digital landscape, Amnesty International's focus is largely on privacy and censorship. "We very quickly started looking at the human rights impact [of technological change]. It is difficult to protect privacy because of the way business models have developed over time. Everything that's coming up, from better artificial intelligence to automation to genetic engineering, even things like disruptions in the energy market, may have a big effect on geopolitics. We need to be ahead of the game, we need to be much better at understanding the possible risks." On the horizon, among other issues, says Elsayed-Ali, are online violence against women and predictive policing. "The debates on the ethics of artificial intelligence that are happening now are integrated with human rights principles."

AI is a big one, says Elsayed-Ali, especially in this new public/private era. "One of the issues with AI which can be quite worrying, especially if it is used in policing, as has already started happening in the UK and the U.S. at least [in the form of image recognition algorithms used to search bodycam footage], is the opaqueness of the processes by which decisions are taken, the lack of scrutiny, the lack of transparency. At the same time, it's the issue of who has the responsibility to make sure that something is operating via principles that respect human rights." In the policing example, does responsibility lie with the police force, the AI operator, or the company providing the software?

It's a dangerous path, says Elsayed-Ali. "It's not going to be long before you start having autonomous weapons used by private security companies. But generally with AI, whether it's deciding on whether you're getting a loan or who is going to get bombed, the thread that runs through is who has responsibility for the decisions that are taken, and the transparency of those decisions."

Silicon Valley companies have varying approaches to data privacy, with Apple being pro-privacy and others such as Yahoo willing to share with governments. According to Elsayed-Ali, not sharing with the American government is in part a protective policy, setting a precedent not to share with international governments: "It means you don't have to give data to Russia, or China, or wherever else you're operating." How are Silicon Valley platforms already affecting governance? "In sub-Saharan Africa, governments are copying each other. Whenever you have an election, social media gets shut down, it gets blocked."

Unfortunately, consumer apathy is a universal issue in not driving discourse and further scrutiny, both among themselves and in prompting it by their governments. "People know that data is being used in different ways, for marketing purposes, for selling ads, being spied on by governments, but they don't know necessarily what to do about it or they feel powerless. There's a fundamentally problematic issue there. We have no real control over our data whatsoever." Yes, we all sometimes consent to conditions, but, as Elsayed-Ali points out, few people attempt to read them and they aren't very comprehensible to anyone who is not a legal expert.

Dominic Campbell, founder of FutureGov, a UK- and Australia-based consultancy aimed at helping governments navigate the digital age, agrees there is little public understanding of data or technology issues as they relate to privacy, which has potentially worrying implications as Silicon Valley expands into health care, finance, and every segment in between.

The problem is also that governments are more often reactive than proactive, says Campbell. Changes tend to come out of "failure, rather than, 'How do we think about technology on the policy basis?' or 'What does that mean for us as an organization in government? What levels of control do we have? What do we have no control over? How do we influence?' There are very few decent technologists helping governments in any country that can enable that kind of conversation," he says.

"I see things that worry me both inside government and outside government. People in power are often totally unaware of technology and have no literacy around it at all, and things are getting passed under the radar. There's an awful lot of surveillance data and sharing data sets." Already, continues Campbell, the sharing of personal financial data and personal data with governments poses conflicts, and these are not isolated to the UK.

But to hand it all over to private corporations is not the answer. For all that government systems are slow, the accelerated pace of innovation also causes problems. "Every time I defend government, I find myself in meetings with people that make me want to jump out the window," says Campbell. "Politicians and senior leaders in government have no clue about technology. But at the same time, there is a reason why that is the way it is. You can read it in different ways, and I tend to read it positively. There are meant to be checks and balances. There is something about the way government culture works, the way that it governs, that plays a stabilizing role in our society.

"Our motto is 'you've got to disrupt yourself,'" Campbell explains. "You've got to make your services attractive so that you're competitive in the modern world. This safeguards a good side of government, which is democratic diplomacy, contestability, the ability to actually challenge and hold to account the services you receive." By self-disruption, he means total disruption rather than incremental change. He means employing the tactics of Silicon Valley to reimagine sectors and industry. Break it, pretend you are a competitor, scenario-plan for the future, but be quick. Government, he says, cannot assume immunity to external disruption just because it is government—not any longer at least. But by working with governments, Campbell is witnessing firsthand the privatization of more digital aspects of governance. Large segments, and data pools, are being shared with and run by private entities.

Debra Cleaver has a similar take. Governments and democracy need to adapt with the times to remain accessible and relevant for people to engage with them. They need to understand and use technology. And they need to market themselves to new generations who have become disengaged. "We used to teach this in high school, the importance of civics, and now we don't . . . You need to be taught why government matters," she says. "Everyone knows why money matters. With Elon Musk, it's never 'Oh, he's so smart.' It's 'He's so rich.' In the U.S. we definitely equate being rich with being smart. If you have money, your opinions matter more. Elon Musk actually is very intelligent, but there's plenty of people we're paying attention to that we shouldn't."

One of Cleaver's missions at Vote.org is to market democracy. "It's so funny. To me it's common sense, but no one's out there marketing voting. They're all marketing an individual candidate. When you try to use candidates to increase turnout, you're counting on candidate charisma. That's not going to work. Especially for local elections." So Vote.org's campaigns are focused purely on the act of voting itself, not policies or individuals. "We're marketing voting like a product. How does Apple get you to buy a phone? They don't go door to door to get you to buy the phone. They run these massive marketing campaigns. That's the sort of stuff we were using last year. The way that technology was involved was we use one startup to buy billboards, we use another startup to send mail. We used technology to scale cheaply."

Cleaver pours scorn on the trope that young people don't vote. The systems are outmoded, she thinks. "Young voters aren't apathetic . . . It's just so hard for them to actually cast ballots because everything about our voting system was set up decades ago. It's this really antiquated paper-based system. Take something like voter registration. If you don't have a driver's license, you need to register on paper. You need to print and mail a form. But we don't have as many post offices as we used to have. We don't even have the boxes on the street. And no one knows where to buy stamps. And no one owns a printer. Legitimately home printer ownership is down to something like 4 percent. It's not that young people don't want to register, it just doesn't fit life anymore."

She adds: "I have no doubt that if voting was more convenient, more people would vote."

Cleaver believes millennials will transform the political landscape in the next decade. "We're already at the point that if millennials voted at the same rate as baby boomers, they would have more votes. I think things are going to get really interesting because these negative policies are going to affect the millennials for decades. The boomers are going to die. They made some bad decisions years past and they screwed us all over and the younger people are going to start taking action. It's interesting though, about millennials. They have access to this information and yet I think it takes them a little longer [to get engaged]. It takes them till after college when they start paying off student loans or when they have to think about health insurance to become politically aware. But I think they are a lot more progressive than older voters and they're really not tolerant. A young voter is like, 'Of course climate change is real. What is the government doing about climate change?'"

For now, government, conceptually, stands at a crossroads.

Digital Revolutionaries

A garage-rock band opens the scene in the music video, as three teenage girls get ready to leave their house, clad in vintage T-shirts emblazoned in feminist slogans, tattoos, and messy hair, in bedrooms surrounded by books, records, and magazines. Over the thumping music, spoken-word poetry begins—read so dramatically all that's missing is clicking fingers and a coffee house (the dynamic drums take their place).

Today, the movement of my body is simply one body in a movement. A movement where pink blush kisses skyline.

Charcoal pencil sculpts future. And notebooks breathe, themselves living organisms . . .

So reads the poem, a call to arms of creativity for personal politics. These aren't your normal teens.

The poem, entitled "Do Your Part"—or, in teen speak, #DoYourPart—is a promotional video for creative platform School of Platform, itself exemplary of the attitudinal uniqueness of Generation Z, a digital hub with multiple contributors, covering subjects including politics, feminism, craft and entrepreneurialism, and the environment.

Born from the mid-1990s to the early 2000s, Generation Z members are the first true digital natives. They grew up with social media fully in place and have used cellphones and digital platforms from a young age. On this front, they're beyond millennial. But to pass them off as millennials is to do them a discredit. They are the most politically engaged and conscientious generation to emerge in decades, already taking an active role in demonstrations, elections (where they can), and activism. The most potent example in 2018 is the protest and outspoken criticism of the government led by teens in the wake of the Florida school shooting that saw seventeen young students killed. Unafraid and enraged, students took to social media to criticize the negligent government for not protecting them and for the close connection between Washington, DC and NRA donations. A protest March for Our Lives was promptly organized mostly by young people, and backed by George Clooney, Oprah Winfrey, and other celebrities. The uproar saw the rise of a budding political figure in Emma Gonzalez, whose impassioned speech at a rally the weekend after the shooting hit the headlines for its eloquence and its pointedness, calling "B.S." to all the previous excuses for not enforcing greater gun control.

Digital platforms for these digital natives are key to making change as well as building businesses, charities, and of course their personal brands. They count themselves to be feminists, creators, and entrepreneurs. They are progressive. Having grown up when it was normal to have a black president and when gay marriage was taken for granted, they accept these as cultural norms that we cannot climb back from. They care deeply about the environment (to them, climate change is also a given, not a myth). They are also, as evidenced by the poetry, perhaps the most precocious teens to date.

Within the next two election cycles, they will nearly all become first-time voters.

This, along with millennials reaching professional maturity (and age of candidacy), means there's some hope governments will get a shake-up, rescuing them from irrelevance. It also means there's hope for the intersection of humility, diversity, social conscience, and digital platforms and technology. Futuristic tech with a soul.

Generation Z, as an electorate, will be the most ethnically diverse to date. According to a 2017 Nielsen study, Generation Z and millennials are more multicultural in their overall racial and ethnic composition than previous generations. Generation Z holds the largest percentage of Hispanics and non-Hispanic blacks, at 22 percent and 15 percent, respectively. "Compare that to the Greatest Generation (those aged seventy-one and up), whose makeup is overwhelmingly non-Hispanic white at 78 percent, with 9 percent of its population non-Hispanic black and 8 percent Hispanic," says Nielsen.

Their agenda is radically progressive. We spotted this early at J. Walter Thompson. In 2015 we ran a nationally representative survey and the majority said they didn't care about sexual orientation, and 67 percent had a friend of a different sexual orientation. Eighty-eight percent said that people were exploring their sexuality more than in the past. Eighty-one percent agreed that gender doesn't define a person as much as it used to. And race was also thought of differently, with 77 percent agreeing: "I view race differently than my parents' generation." Since then, we've continued to dig into it. In 2016 we ran a survey looking specifically at gender identity and sexuality. We found 56 percent of U.S. Gen Z-ers know someone who uses gender-neutral pronouns. Today Gen Z is regarded as one of the most progressive generations to be coming of age, with media zeroing in on its paradigm-shifting attitudes toward gender. *Time* magazine has run a 2017 cover feature, "Beyond He or She: How a New Generation Is Redefining the Meaning of Gender." *National Geographic* also published a special issue: *Gender Revolution*. Condé Nast has created an entirely new media platform, "them," aimed at teens but through an LGBTQ community lens.

It can even be seen in their heroes, all of whom have a progressive agenda. Willow Smith raises awareness about mental health. Amandla Stenberg is an activist with the No Kid Hungry organization. British Gen Z columnist for the UK's *Sunday Times Style* magazine, Scarlett Curtis, threw her support behind a nationwide movement raising awareness of period poverty (lack of access to tampons and feminine care).

The activist thread goes beyond this, though. A subtle distinction between millennials and Generation Z is that while they share superficially similar values—the environment, feminism, social good—the difference in commitment is radical. Millennials have switched their faces to rainbows on Facebook. Shared feelings of dismay at Paris shootings on Instagram by posting visual memes. Generation Z by contrast is more inclined to do something. Malala Yousafzai is most iconic of this, but many Generation Z influencers focus on real action.

And Gen Z is more likely to get out the vote. An early sign came in 2014, when the voting age for the Scottish referendum was reduced, allowing sixteen- and seventeen-year-olds to take part. Around 100,000 people under eighteen registered to vote, 80 percent of those who were eligible. About 64 percent of registered voters aged 18–24 voted in the 2016 EU referendum.

In an era of fake news, and the filter bubble, these young people are also more likely to be able to push through the noise. This generation has grown up in a highly scaled marketing landscape bombarded by constant messaging, with mature social networks and smartphones part of their everyday lives. Not only are they able to consume more information than any group before, they have become accustomed to cutting through it. They are perhaps the most brand-critical, bullshit-repellent, questioning group around and will call out any behavior they dislike on social media. (Little wonder brands are quaking in their boots.) For evidence of this, one need only survey the recent viral shaming of fashion designer Marc Jacobs for cultural appropriation in his use of dreadlocks on white models in a fashion show. It was led by teens. Similarly, a political thread runs through all of *Teen Vogue*'s coverage, from fashion brand inclusivity to representation in marketing.

The internet has rendered most news and news outlets (seemingly) equal, hard to distinguish between fact and fiction. At least, to older generations. What would have been a scrawled political flyer handed out on a street corner and quickly discarded as propaganda is given new reverence in the internet world. Generation Z, natives of this universe, already have the tools to navigate it.

Millennials were late to engage in politics, and some would say they have only done so in the U.S. and UK in the wake of Brexit and the presidential election. But they are engaging as the reality of decades ahead in the shadow of baby boomer policies, and their impact on their adult lives, become more real. Influencers like Mark Zuckerberg are more actively involved. As the older ones reach age thirty-five (Zuckerberg is thirty-three), they may yet jump in to replace the combed-over, fusty, suited boomers who currently reside in office.

What will Millennial Washington look like? Will they do a better job? Will they combine business with social good as they are doing in their work and consumption habits? Will social-good commerce be applied within the state? Can the state and private sector find new ways to work together?

The cliché goes that this generation does not handle criticism well, and is narcissistic and self-involved, but they'll be held to account by a very vocal Gen Z. Millennials have also had to endure some hard knocks: Student debt. The reality of a stagnant job market after the global economic crisis. Like Zuckerberg, they are motivated by solving problems and seek meaning in their work. Though, unlike Zuckerberg, they are living the reality of not out-achieving their parents. In cities like London and New York, they are not buying properties and are not seeing the same financial security or prosperity. They will most likely be working until they're ninety. It's a slightly grim future, potentially, so it's surprising that until now millennials have been so politically apathetic in trying to shape it.

The United States of GAFA

The way Silicon Valley leaders would tell it, unlike any industry, any institution, or government—dare it be said—they have cracked the code to the future. They're skimming Yuval Noah Harari's *Homo Deus: A Brief History of Tomorrow*. They are still reading *The Innovator's Dilemma* by Clayton Christensen. They are attending Burning Man for spiritual refreshment (chemically induced or not); clad as extras from *Mad Max*, they are stumbling inadvertently onto the next big idea. They are turning to *The Black Swan: The Impact of the Highly Improbable* by philosopher and scholar Nassim Nicholas Taleb, about anomalies of history and how to spot these in the future (and either circumnavigate them or take advantage of them) by obsessing about what you don't know, not what you do. (All history, Taleb argues, is retrospective logic applied to random events.)

The Black Swan is one of Jeff Bezos's favorite books. He is also obsessive about long-term thinking as a means to future-proof yourself—a future where Amazon owns every potential purchase one might make. This means making counterintuitive moves, such as forgoing immediate profit and being radically consumer-centric, the idea being that this will eventually pay off as Amazon becomes a 360-degree personal commerce and entertainment ecosystem. To borrow a perfect line from *New York Times* journalist David Streitfeld: "Amazon wants to be so deeply embedded in a customer's life that buying happens as naturally as breathing, and nearly as often."

The methods espoused by Silicon Valley leaders have had far-reaching influence on the entire theory of work and remaining relevant in the future. We all seek to live in Beta: "Move fast and break things." "Iterate." "Pivot." "Done is better than perfect."

Entire industries are trying to replicate Silicon Valley's behavior—the behavior of a group of businesses that, if it hasn't already eaten into their territory, may well do so very soon.

Yet again, strategic genius can be retrofitted. "We all talk about Facebook, but we don't talk about Myspace," says Ian Stewart. "On average, if you've bought the entire tech index you've done pretty well in the last ten years. But there's a survivorship bias because all the companies that fail just come out of the index."

But might Silicon Valley's hype itself become obsolete? Can it really predict the future?

"They might be forced to align if they all got nationalized," futurist Bruce Sterling predicts to me. Like the United States of GAFA. Or, he says, they could all get obliterated by cheaper and more effective Asian platforms.

"I don't think that they're really that important in the span of things," says Kevin Kelly. "They're all susceptible to being displaced, and I don't think they're going to be around in ten years. I don't think they represent anything different than thousands and thousands of others who form the second tier. They are celebrity companies in the same sense as Kim Kardashian, where everybody's focused on what they do."

"How durable is the lead that any technology company has enjoyed in the last seventy years?" asks Stewart. "What proportion of the dominant tech companies in the United States that exist now, existed twenty years ago? I suppose Apple's one, but a high proportion of them didn't . . . My view would be that the tech sector is very creative but it's also a big destroyer of capital, so it is pretty Darwinistic." So what does this mean if they take over public services? If Uber eats all public transport and eradicates all the profitable taxi companies, becoming our dominant mode of transport, but continues not to turn a profit, and eventually runs out of backers, will it eventually need to be nationalized?

So far acquisitions, expensive ones, have kept many Silicon Valley giants in business. Facebook acquired WhatsApp for $22 billion in 2014. It bought Instagram for $1 billion in 2012—though thank god it did. According to iStrategyLabs, eleven million teens left Facebook between 2011 and 2014, though Instagram continues to post double-digit growth year after year.

More recently, each has begun cannibalizing and copying each other. Fighting over driverless cars, smartphones, home speaker hubs, deliveries, business messaging, and payments, each attempting to become dominant, self-contained ecosystems. Amazon and Google are each trying to own home hubs, search, shipping, and shopping; Google and Uber, driverless cars; Uber and Amazon, urban deliveries. The list goes on.

Many are investing in augmented reality (AR), virtual reality (VR), mixed reality, and beyond (augmented reality is layering digital imagery over real-life spaces). Shipments of AR and VR headsets will grow at a compound annual growth rate of 108 percent from 2015 to 2020, reaching 76 million units, predicts IDC, a technology consultancy. Facebook, Samsung, Google, Apple, Amazon, and Alibaba are investing heavily in VR—and making the technology more social is a logical way forward.

While much attention was given to VR initially, AR seems to be the tech that has really gone viral. The Pokémon GO phenomenon was perhaps a precursor, but today Silicon Valley brands and many retailers are rushing to put AR in the pockets of millions. Alibaba created its own AR character and mobile shopping game for its annual Singles' Day shopping bonanza in late 2016. In 2017 augmented reality officially went from niche technology to must-have function, setting tech giants in a battle to own the space, introducing a host of tools that incorporate the function into mobile devices. Apple unveiled ARKit, a toolkit that lets software developers build AR experiences for the iPhone. Google launched its own ARCore, the competitor version for Android. "I don't think there is any sector or industry that will be untouched by AR," Apple CEO Tim Cook told *Vogue* in October 2017. This could have considerable runway. The possibilities with AR are endless for retail, entertainment, and ad revenue. People walking the street can call up a digital layer of information about bars, or hover it over a supermarket shelf to see the nutritional content of a chocolate bar. They can virtually see sofas in their home, the images layered over reality, before buying them. Expect more to come.

"The thing about virtual reality currently is that it is not very social and limited to gaming. That, ultimately, will stop it from reaching mass adoption. Until you make it social, it won't have as big an impact," says Rowland Manthorpe, then associate editor at *Wired UK*, betting that social VR will be the way it reaches bigger audiences. Mark Zuckerberg clearly thinks so too. At its much-vaunted 2017 V8 conference, Facebook unveiled a "spaces" feature in which users can create 3-D avatars for video calls on Facebook and on its VR headset in far-off locations.

Gaming companies such as The Void have sought to socialize it with interactive multiplayer games. But this is just the beginning. Companies such as High Fidelity, founded by Philip Rosedale, who also founded virtual world Second Life, are experimenting with VR to create limitless 3-D social landscapes. There are even VR theme parks emerging. VR World now entertains Manhattan revelers and tourists from its location just south of Times Square. (It's able to occupy a fraction of the size of an actual theme park because its wild mystical worlds are virtual.)

Hype, albeit waning, has been nothing short of breathless about the potential of virtual reality. "It's an empathy machine!" is a tagline often used, describing VR's immersive properties, which lend it special emotional powers. "It's a great soundbite to grab on to. But even if it puts you in someone else's shoes for twenty minutes, empathy has to have a lasting effect," says VR artist and pioneer Jacquelyn Ford Morie. "It's not 'I had empathy for five minutes! Oh boy!' It's not that. Empathy is something that changes you internally."

For all the hype attached to virtual reality, it's also difficult to imagine how such a chronically isolating device will become a mainstream staple in the home. Recall the now-defunct Google Glass, which layered information and imagery onto the environment, and it was still a dud. In fact, think back to pretty much any consumer technology becoming mainstream that has involved wearing a device to consume entertainment, and you'll struggle. Even glasses themselves have, in many instances, been replaced with contact lenses (save for the Brooklynites clad in Warby Parker frames). Maybe that's next.

But still. A vision of that future is not one that many consumers might desire when confronted with it. One where augmented reality ads spontaneously pop up in their vision as they navigate the streetscape, prompting them to "like" or "check in" wherever they go. A smartphone, at least, can be put inside a pocket. The inescapable human fact is that, when it comes to our environments, people don't want them to be mediated by a glass screen.

Specialist applications of VR are more compelling. It's been used as a therapeutic tool for soldiers suffering post traumatic stress disorder. Björk has created spectacular, immersive, artistic music videos. Jon Favreau has made a cognitive, nonlinear, gamified magical virtual reality movie *Gnomes and Goblins*, in which participants have to earn the trust of miniature animals by feeding them snacks amid a glowing mythic forest by night. Experiencing VR is still incredibly intense, not casual like television or movies. Experts such as Ford Morie have also expressed health concerns about using such immersive technology for long periods of time.

When technology can shape not only your life and actions but your sense of self and even memories, there's little else left to disrupt.

The Deflating Balloon?

But the tide has certainly turned for Silicon Valley. The decline in private-market valuations suggests a peak in the boom passed in 2014–2015. Valuations for the hot tech companies are down by about 40 percent. Uber continues to grow, but endures staggering losses.

For how long? Is there going to be a bubble?

The soaring heights of many Silicon Valley companies, where scale is prized over profit in valuations, suggests that there might be. "The last time we had a bubble, the fundamentals were very different," says Margit Wennmachers. "When Netscape went public, there were about fifty million people on the internet, and they were on dial-up connections. Now you have two and a half or three billion permanently on the internet. It walks with them wherever they go, so the market size has grown in a way that's hard to grasp. Ideas that didn't work out, like Webvan, were not bad ideas."

The culture of high valuations even if you don't make a profit also continues. "It's almost discouraged," says Amber Atherton.

The current climate is worse than the dot-com boom, says Debra Cleaver. "Myspace was expected to actually generate profit, so we made all of these decisions that would increase ad revenue. So many startups now are never profitable. They run entirely on venture capital. In today's funding climate it's possible Myspace would still exist," she says. "The other thing which everyone forgets is that when Myspace was huge in 2006, the government was threatening to shut it down to make the internet safe for children. Myspace had to spend millions of dollars to comply with these requirements that the government imposed on us, which was a big part of driving Myspace out of business. Total free-for-all."

So far many Silicon Valley business models are predicated on algorithms for scale—exponential growth without bodies on the factory floor—to achieve their outsized status and profit. But recently there's been pressure on them to take a greater, more grown-up responsibility for their impact and the abuses therein. Through Jigsaw, Google parent company Alphabet is using Conversation Artificial Intelligence to attempt to filter abusive speech. "I want to use the best technology we have at our disposal to begin to take on trolling and other nefarious tactics that give hostile voices disproportionate weight," Jigsaw founder and president Jared Cohen told *Wired*. But there are still flaws. Tensions will continue to mount as Silicon Valley supplants traditional industries such as media companies and hospitality but seeks to avoid responsibility.

The cultural cache of this group seems to be slipping. Beyond the dystopias that are flowing thick and fast about surveillance culture, the things that made this group novel have become so outsized they're at best corporate, and today—at least a decade old—normalized. The shouts about diversity are getting louder. The treatment of women becoming more contentious—ditto the pay grades.

More recently there has been greater emphasis on female founders and investors, not just female leadership in Silicon Valley. And, as the market expands for women-centric consumer tech products, there may be more to come. As the crueler side of the gig economy and the Wild West landscape of low-income contractors become more widely reported, we may see more pressure on companies like Uber.

Still, many of Silicon Valley's larger players' scale seems unlikely to change. And there's plenty of new rope, for now, as they swoop up new markets. Even if they don't remain the rock stars. Perhaps their fate is to be like Microsoft, then. To remain, stay omnipresent, and stay powerful. Like Word. Excel. We'll still use Facebook every day, but the magazine covers and celebrity rhetoric will move on. They'll become giant corporate institutions, then supplanted by sexier new things. No longer the stardust but the trusty furniture, albeit all-seeing, and all-knowing. And they may ultimately, and collectively, become seen as evil or demonized for this circular role in our lives. But they'll be so institutionalized we'll be powerless to change things.

You know, a bit like the government.

The Unglamorous Safety Net

People tend to overlook much of the positive work government does, and the myriad ways government-funded science and research have made possible the technological marvels we use today. Government spending funds space travel by giving contracts to Elon Musk, even if Musk gets all the glory when sending a Tesla into space. The U.S. government played a crucial role in the creation of Siri, and the internet. Government-built and -maintained roads carry tech workers to their jobs. And crucially, it may still take responsibility for the last-mile services that no company would. (Royal Mail will deliver packages to remote Scottish islands with a single resident; Amazon would not.)

In spite of this list of achievements, we are still down on the government. We still see it as slow, boring, and irrelevant.

Results of a nationally representative consumer poll of 1,000 people, conducted with J. Walter Thompson for this book, are illustrative. The purpose of the poll was to explore in a quantitative way people's attitudes to governance, the media, and technology, and some of the issues raised in this book. In 2017, in the wake of the U.S. election, 67 percent said they don't believe the current system of governance "will ever be able to create the change that Americans are currently looking for." Seventy-six percent agreed there should be better systems in elections. Only 33 percent of our respondents agreed strongly that "government officials truly have my best interests at heart." Additionally, 68 percent agreed that "government officials tend to only be liars and cheats."

But there was confusion about whether Silicon Valley should step in. Overwhelmingly, consumers felt the internet should be a public entity, but most were torn on whether it should be regulated in a similar way as, say, water or electricity or road-building. The poll asked who, between government and Silicon Valley, was best equipped to run various sectors, and 71 percent believed that government should control immigration, 59 percent our roads and bridges, 55 percent health care, 52 percent school education, 49 percent transportation, and 44 percent banking.

How would they feel if Silicon Valley took over civic sectors? A third of respondents (33 percent) said they would be "nervous" if Silicon Valley took over health insurance. There was the same response from 33 percent on health care, 37 percent on policing, 33 percent on surveillance, 41 percent on warfare, 25 percent on education, and 24 percent on urban development.

Yet half of consumers (50 percent) viewed the U.S. government as old-fashioned. Google and Facebook measured significantly higher for innovation, intelligence, and confidence compared to the government.

In other words, while we're not that satisfied with the government, total control by Silicon Valley with the important stuff in people's lives is also a scary prospect—even if this group does seem more dynamic and interesting. What's clear is that, amid dwindling resources, pressured health and education systems, and loss of faith in government, there's a renewed desire to redefine the public/private approach to problem solving.

Where did it all go wrong for government? During World War II, government leaders were our beacons of hope, our rocks and thought leaders. After WWII, citizens in Europe and America placed an unprecedented amount of faith in the government to control their lives. But since then social investment has been continually dismantled in many markets, and along with it, our sense of collective responsibility for the weak and old in society. (In the U.S. between 1949 and 2009, growth on government spending on infrastructure and social services went from 77 percent to −6 percent, according to an EPI analysis of Bureau of Economic Analysis data.) By the 1970s and '80s, leaders like Margaret Thatcher and Ronald Reagan were denigrating government as "big," "bloated," "expensive," "interfering." Meanwhile social services and the welfare state became an unnecessary drain. With the rise of neoliberalism in the Clinton and Blair era, the idea of a third way has become prominent, one in which it's possible to be efficient, commercially friendly, but kind. But the left's move to the center has only served to weaken the working class and leave the poorest in society with few protections. Hence, the rise of figures like Bernie Sanders, reinvigorating the purer leftist stance, or populist right-wing presidents like Donald Trump, appealing to the same socioeconomic group with promises of manufacturing, renewed national pride, and new jobs (though this time with a strong whiff, alas, of fascism and racism).

There are bigger cultural forces at play, too. Optically the government isn't leading in innovation—even if it may quietly be investing in high-tech inventions, usually for war. For affluent urban millennials, the biggest consumer group, it's also partly that nations are so globalized that believing in something as dorky as a common cause like their state is beyond them. They're too busy taking selfies in Cuba, Instagrams of vegan cuisine, buying Lululemon, and growing moustaches. It could also be that they're too postmodern and "meta" now to believe in something so traditional. This is the era where Hulu is producing high-concept "dramadies" set within fake reality dating shows, after all. We're more fragmented than ever, too—which means buying into a common cause feels impossible. It could simply be because all we spend our money on is tech, through digital platforms, this sector is the only one with enough resources to do anything anymore.

Sometimes it's helpful to think of this in brand terms. Part of the issue lies in government and politics not remaining relevant to young people, and therefore creating a vacuum of influence. Silicon Valley companies think like brands. Perhaps government should do the same thing, making its work and role in life seem compelling and valuable, and elections a compulsory part of citizenship. Or a politician's work appear more trustworthy. This is an era when every consumer brand is tripping over itself to seem authentic and transparent. If politicians were brands, most millennials and teenagers would not buy them.

There is also the generational divide to consider in the wake of 2016 and 2017's tumultuous political events. Overwhelmingly, young people would have voted for Hillary Clinton to be elected president, not Donald Trump. And, overwhelmingly, young people in the UK would have voted to remain in the EU. Trust and faith in democracy among young people has only been eroded, leaving many considering alternatives.

In the wake of the U.S. election and the 2017 travel ban for Muslim countries that followed, as Silicon Valley figures began vocally and publicly criticizing the American government, some people might have started to feel a curious sensation: comfort. Comfort that there was an alternate power source to the government and one that might actually have the ability to do something, or failing that, stand up to a government that they felt did not represent their positions. In this era of massive political fractiousness, volatility, and inward-looking near-fascism, Silicon Valley started not to look so bad. Which speaks volumes of how dramatic the shift has been between Barack Obama's stability and Donald Trump's administration.

A self-confessed progressive, coastal, educated, affluent urban millennial (and hypocritical Uber-addict, Amazon-shopping, Whatsapp user), I have viewed the political landscape with dismay. Edicts like the Muslim ban and the rolling back of protections to national parks were appearing left, right, and center. In the UK, the slashing of services such as free school meals and further cuts to the police seemed to be in the headlines daily. It appeared like a mounting whirlwind of horror that I was powerless to do anything about.

Yet, the events of 2017 have also been interesting from the point of view of government's power. As Trump's edicts have rung out, private companies have stepped forward to flout him, or openly challenge him; government has looked small, in mind and in influence.

Is Silicon Valley the right replacement? And should they win by default?

What they offer is undoubtedly seductive by virtue of being the most powerful and dynamic. Right now, they are dominant due to consumer buy-in and approval. But how long that will actually be necessary is an important thing to consider. Because then there will be little control over what they do.

Such is this group's reach that stepping out of their systems is increasingly impossible if anyone wishes to function in work or society. For many it would be difficult to last even a week, living and working, without using any of the following: Facebook, Google, Amazon, Uber, Microsoft, Instagram, Apple, YouTube, or Whatsapp. These are immersive brands powered by consumerism, but as they move into health care, education, transportation, and finance, as highly networked monoliths, the brand ecosystems they've created will become inescapable fortresses. And the consumer's power to effect change within them will vanish.

The magnitude of this growing power is difficult to comprehend fully. Most people know about it. Some may even put a sticker over the camera on their laptops, but few take active steps to do anything beyond that. Because the enormity of the idea, and their reach, is too big. But it's something we need to get a grip on quickly. Or more so, our governments do. Until government gets reinvigorated by millennials, or failing that, the dynamic, hyper-connected, and conscientious Gen Z, it is rapidly becoming obsolete. Meanwhile the bells, whistles, and promises of Silicon Valley (in the absence of competitors) may offer a dangerously reassuring alternative. Or, at least, better than the current greying bunch burning down the planet.

The convenience offered by Google, Apple, Facebook, Uber, Amazon, and more has already persuaded people to (willingly) hand over reams of data in order to save time, have personalized goods, and devote countless hours of their day to interact with these companies, despite anxiety about privacy. Rising critique of this group in media and in governments isn't stopping our use. And maybe they will build something better and faster—so long as it's, you know, tech-based and involves David Bowie soundtracks and saving the world. Who needs the government anyway? Jeff Bezos is rescuing Puerto

Rico and the health-care system. Uber's getting us cheap taxis. We'll all be fine! The point is most people reading this book aren't the ones who most need the government. It's the people who can't afford an Uber, or the emergency room, those who don't own Macbooks. And they may soon be reliant on the generosity of a group of white, male-dominated, private companies to maintain their livelihoods and the marketability of their problems for a new "social enterprise mission" to survive. Allowing current services and systems to be reinvented is great but it should end up with something different, and better. More inclusive, not less. Representative of everyone, not just a few. Tech's vision of the future, architected almost singularly by privileged white men, may have a futuristic veneer, but its implications remain the same, or even worse. Less inclusive. Better only for a small percentage of society.

The #MeToo movement has set in motion a tidal wave exposing abuses of power, and today's power structure disproportionately favors men over women and minorities. And wealth over poverty. It's highlighted the complex layers of what constitutes abuse and the experiences of women, and some men, of all ethnicities. From here to #TimesUp, there's been a resounding cry that this system's days are numbered. Never again. And yet, we're dangerously close to giving perhaps the most patriarchal white industry around the most powerful job of all.

ACKNOWLEDGMENTS

'd like to thank Guy Murphy, chief strategy officer at J. Walter Thompson, and Laura Agostini, chief talent officer, for their support and encouragement in taking on this book. And of course, JWT's global CEO Tamara Ingram, OBE.

I'd also like to thank Mark Truss, worldwide director of brand intelligence and leader of Sonar, J. Walter Thompson's research insights unit, for assisting in the original consumer survey data included in, and specially commissioned for, this book. I'd also like to thank my team, in particular Emma Chiu, our excellent creative innovation director, my deputy, and my friend who—among other friends and family—has tolerated me during this process.

A number of trusted, long-term collaborators assisted me with researching and finessing this book. I am forever and ever indebted to Hester Lacey for her expertise, positive spirit, and generosity. I'd also like to thank Anna Melville James and Paul Rodgers for their assistance and good humor. Also, thanks to Nayantara Dutta, Nina Jones, Julie Cotterill, and Jaime Eisenbraun.

Martin Raymond, cofounder and owner of the Future Laboratory, hired me years ago as a futurist at his company. I still consider him a mentor, friend, and person I revisit when (nearly) shying away from saying what I actually think. Thanks, Martin.

Thanks to my literary agent, Robin Straus, and Katelyn Hales. And to Dan Smetanka and his excellent team at Counterpoint Press.

Lastly, but importantly, thank you to the people who gave their time and insight to this book. I spoke to as many authoritative minds as possible. Fortunately, I was able to summon some of the best. Not all of them are quoted. Some of them offered me important introductions, some informal advice. All contributed to the bigger picture, which I hope is nuanced and thoughtful—even if you disagree.

In no particular order:

Jane K. Winn, the Charles I. Stone professor and director of the Center for Advanced Study & Research on Innovation Policy at the University of Washington, Seattle, Washington.

Andrew Blauvelt, director of the Cranbrook Art Museum in Bloomfield Hills, Michigan.

James Wallman, futurist and author of *Stuffocation: Living More with Less*.

Alexandra Lange, architecture and design critic and author of *The Dot-Com City: Silicon Valley Urbanism*, among other titles.

Puneet Kaur Ahira, cofounder & COO at Shared Magic. Formerly a special advisor to Megan J. Smith, a U.S. CTO during the Obama administration.

Dominic Campbell, founder and CEO at FutureGov.

Adam Thierer, senior research fellow with the Technology Policy Program at the Mercatus Center at George Mason University.

Benjamin Soskis, research associate at the Center on Nonprofits and Philanthropy at the Urban Institute, George Mason University.

Ben Nelson, founder, chairman, and CEO of Minerva.

Bob Safian, founder of the Flux Group. Formerly an editor at *Fast Company*.

Christopher Kirchoff, visiting technologist at the Institute of Politics at the Harvard Kennedy School, formerly a partner at DIUx at the Pentagon's Silicon Valley office.

Clair Brown, professor of economics and director of the Center for Work, Technology, and Society at the University of California, Berkeley.

Dale J. Stephens, founder of UnCollege.

Dan Pallotta, speaker, author, reformer, founder, and president of the Charity Defense Council and president and CEO of Advertising for Humanity.

Daniel Stevens, executive director at Campaign for Accountability.

Marian Goodell, CEO of Burning Man Project.

Robert Scott, lawyer, founder of Further Future.

David Callahan, founder and editor of *Inside Philanthropy*.

David Golumbia, associate professor in the Department of English/ MATX PhD Program, Virginia Commonwealth University. Author of *The Politics of Bitcoin: Software as Right-Wing Extremism*.

Nick Denton, founder of Gawker Media.

Delaney Ruston, MD, president of MyDoc Productions and creator of the documentary *Screenagers*.

Dr. Molly Maloof, a San Francisco–based physician, technologist, and wellness expert.

George Berkowski, entrepreneur and founder of Hailo. Author of *How to Build a Billion Dollar App*.

Bruce Sterling, futurist and cyberpunk author.

Tiffany St. James, digital transformation strategist and speaker, executive director of BIMA. Former UK government head of social media.

Jimmy Leach, founder of Zinzan Digital. Former head of digital engagement for the Foreign and Commonwealth Office, UK.

James Russell, architecture critic.

Joe McNamee, executive director of European Digital Rights.

Aaron Dorfman, president and CEO of the National Committee for Responsive Philanthropy.

Keith A. Spencer, cultural critic and manager of the sci/tech vertical at *Salon*.

Kevin Kelly, founding executive editor of *Wired* magazine and a former editor/publisher of the *Whole Earth Review*.

Joe Quirk, coauthor with Patri Friedman of *Seasteading: How Ocean Cities Will Change the World*.

Kosta Grammatis, engineer, scientist, entrepreneur, and presenter. Formerly with Space X and MIT, and the founder of A Human Right.

Steve Blanks, adjunct professor of entrepreneurship at Stanford University and author of *The Startup Owner's Manual*.

Tom Bedecarre, cofounder and CEO of AKQA.

Yves Behar, founder and CEO of Fuseproject.

Richard Hill, independent consultant in Geneva. Formerly a senior staff member at the UN International Telecommunication Union.

Robert J. Gordon, economist. Author of *The Rise and Fall of American Growth: The U.S. Standard of Living since the Civil War.*

Ravi Mattu, technology, media, and telecoms news editor at *Financial Times.*

Rowland Manthorpe, tech correspondant, SkyNews. Formerly associate editor at *Wired UK.*

Ryan Mullenix, partner at NBBJ architectural practice.

Shernaz Daver, partner at GV. Formerly CMO at Udacity and executive advisor at Google Ventures.

Eva Goicochea, founder of Maude.

Sherif Elsayed-Ali, director of global issues at Amnesty International.

Sylvia Allegretto, labor economist and cochair of the Center on Wage and Employment Dynamics at the University of California, Berkeley.

Thor Berger, postdoctoral fellow at the Department of Economic History, Lund University, and associate fellow at the Oxford Martin Programme on Technology and Employment, University of Oxford.

Sheila Krumholz, executive director of the Center for Responsive Politics.

Martin Husovec, assistant professor, Tilburg Institute for Law, Technology, and Society.

Michael Hawley, educator, artist, and researcher in the field of digital media. Formerly the Alexander W. Dreyfoos Jr. professor at MIT.

Leslie Berlin, project historian for the Silicon Valley Archives at Stanford University. Author of *Troublemakers: Silicon Valley's Coming of Age.*

Naveen Jain, entrepreneur, venture capitalist, philanthropist, and investor in Viome and Moon Express.

Macon Phillips, chief digital officer for CARE. Former White House director of new media.

Amber Atherton, founder of Zyper.

Edward Alden, the Bernard L. Schwartz senior fellow at the Council on Foreign Relations. Alden specializes in U.S. economic competitiveness, trade policy, and visa and immigration policy.

Dongsheng Zang, associate professor of law and director of the Asian Law Center & Visiting Scholars Program, University of Washington.

Leslie Lenkowsky, professor emeritus in public affairs and philanthropy at the School of Public and Environmental Affairs, Indiana University, Bloomington.

Max Ventilla, founder and CEO of AltSchool.

Dr. Eric Haseltine, neuroscientist and futurist. Formerly executive vice president of imagineering and head of R&D for the Disney Corporation and director of research at the National Security Agency.

Dr. Julia Powles, researcher at the University of Cambridge working on interdisciplinary projects between the Faculty of Law and the Computer Laboratory. Former contributing editor and policy fellow at *The Guardian*.

Ian Stewart, partner and chief UK economist at Deloitte.

Dr. Jacqueline Ford Morie, founder and chief scientist at All These Worlds LLC.

Margit Wennmachers, partner at the venture capital firm Andreessen Horowitz.

Louise A. Mozingo, professor and chair of landscape architecture and environmental planning at the University of California, Berkeley.

Megan Tompkins-Stange, assistant professor at the Gerald R. Ford School of Public Policy at the University of Michigan. Author of *Policy Patrons: Philanthropy, Education Reform, and the Politics of Influence*.

Roby Lloyd, CEO of Virgin Hyperloop One.

Shervin Pishevar, venture capitalist. Formerly managing director of Sherpa Capital and executive chairman of Hyperloop One.

William McQuillan, partner at Frontline Ventures.

Debra Cleaver, founder and CEO of Vote.org.

Baroness Susan Greenfield, CBE, FRCP, CEO, and founder of Neuro-Bio. Writer, broadcaster, and member of the House of Lords.

Danah Boyd, principal researcher at Microsoft Research, founder and president of Data & Society Research Institute, and a visiting professor at New York University.

Naomi Kelman, president and CEO of Willow.

Author photograph by Jason Leiva

LUCIE GREENE is the worldwide director of the Innovation Group, J. Walter Thompson's in-house futures and innovation think tank. The Innovation Group's work is frequently cited in publications including *The New York Times*, *Bloomberg Businessweek*, *The Guardian*, *WWD*, *USA Today*, and *The Times* (London). She is a thought leadership columnist for *Campaign*, has written op-eds for the *Financial Times*, *The Guardian*, and *The New York Daily News* about the future. She has spoken at conferences including TNW, WWD Digital Forum, SXSW, Web Summit, Cosmoprof, and Ad Week, discussing future trends across multiple lifestyle sectors. She has appeared on BBC, Fox News, and Bloomberg TV as an expert on the future.